Free Will as an Open Scientific Problem

Free Will as an Open Scientific Problem

Mark Balaguer

A Bradford Book
The MIT Press
Cambridge, Massachusetts
London, England

© 2010 Massachusetts Institute of Technology

All rights reserved. No part of this book may be reproduced in any form by any electronic or mechanical means (including photocopying, recording, or information storage and retrieval) without permission in writing from the publisher.

MIT Press books may be purchased at special quantity discounts for business or sales promotional use. For information, please email special_sales@mitpress.mit.edu or write to Special Sales Department, The MIT Press, 55 Hayward Street, Cambridge, MA 02142.

This book was set in Stone Sans and Stone Serif by the MIT Press. Printed and bound in the United States of America.

Library of Congress Cataloging-in-Publication Data

Balaguer, Mark.
Free will as an open scientific problem / Mark Balaguer.
   p. cm.
"A Bradford book."
Includes bibliographical references and index.
ISBN 978-0-262-01354-3 (hardcover : alk. paper)
1. Free will and determinism. I. Title.
BJ1461.B25   2010
123'.5—dc22

                                                                 2009012426

10 9 8 7 6 5 4 3 2 1

For my daughters, Emily and Drew

Contents

Acknowledgments ix

1 Introduction 1

1.1 Formulating the Problem of Free Will 1
1.2 Some Remarks on Libertarianism 15
1.3 Synopsis of the Book 18

2 Why the Compatibilism Issue and the Conceptual-Analysis Issue Are Metaphysically Irrelevant 25

2.1 Introduction 25
2.2 What Determines Whether an Answer to the What-Is-Free-Will Question Is Correct? 28
2.3 Why the What-Is-Free-Will Question Is Irrelevant to the Do-We-Have-Free-Will Question, Assuming the OL View Is Correct 30
2.4 Why the What-Is-Free-Will Question Is Irrelevant to the Do-We-Have-Free-Will Question, Even if the OL View *Isn't* Correct 35
2.5 Why the Compatibilism Question Reduces to the What-Is-Free-Will Question 45
2.6 Where We Stand and Where We're Going Next 53
2.7 An Aside: Some Remarks on the What-Is-Free-Will Question, the Compatibilism Question, and the Moral Responsibility Question 55

3 Why the Libertarian Question Reduces to the Issue of Indeterminacy 65

3.1 Introduction 65
3.2 Preliminaries 71
3.3 The Argument 83
3.4 Non-torn Decisions 120
3.5 Where We Stand 130

4 Why There Are No Good Arguments for or against Determinism (or Any Other Thesis That Would Establish or Refute Libertarianism)   131

4.1   Introduction   131
4.2   An A Priori Argument for Determinism (and, Hence, against TDW-Indeterminism)?   135
4.3   An A Priori Argument for Libertarianism (and, Hence, in Favor of TDW-Indeterminism)?   137
4.4   Empirical Arguments?   141
4.5   Where We Stand   165

Notes   171
References   185
Index   195

Acknowledgments

I would like to thank Robert Kane, Timothy O'Connor, and Carl Ginet for reading the entire manuscript and offering some very helpful feedback. In addition, I would also like to thank the following people for reading portions of the manuscript, or earlier versions of it, and offering helpful comments: John Martin Fischer, Terry Horgan, Manyul Im, Robert Jones, Neil Levy, Storrs McCall, Dave MacCallum, Michael Nelson, David Pitt, Kadri Vihvelin, Adam Vinueza, Michael Weisberg, and David Widerker. Also, versions of chapter 3 were read at the University of Sydney, California State University, Los Angeles, and the University of California, Riverside; versions of chapter 2 were read at the University of Oakland and at a conference at the University of California, Riverside; and a version of chapter 4 was read at a conference in Bled, Slovenia. I would like to thank the members of all of those audiences for some extremely helpful feedback. In addition, I would like to thank the following people for some helpful correspondence on issues relating to neuroscience and physics: Peter Dayan, Stuart Hameroff, Christof Koch, Sebastian Seung, Henry Stapp, and Max Tegmark.

The writing of this book was funded by a year-long fellowship from the National Endowment for the Humanities and a quarter-long grant from California State University, Los Angeles; I would like to thank both of these institutions. Finally, chapter 3 is an expanded and significantly altered version of a paper that appeared earlier in *Noûs*; chapter 2 is an expanded and altered version of a paper that appeared earlier in the *Southern Journal of Philosophy*; and chapter 4 is an expanded and altered version of a paper that appeared earlier in *Synthese*. I would like to thank all three of these journals, and, in connection with *Synthese*, I would like to thank Springer Science and Business Media, for their kind permission.

1 Introduction

I will argue in this book for a novel view of free will. Most centrally, I will argue that the metaphysically interesting issue in the problem of free will and determinism boils down to a straightforward (and wide open) empirical question about the causal histories of certain neural events. But it will take a long time to get to this conclusion, and along the way, I will argue for several other controversial theses about free will and determinism.

In the present chapter, I will do three things. First, in section 1.1, I will formulate the problem of free will (I begin by giving a traditional formulation of the problem, and then I provide a new and improved formulation). Second, in section 1.2, I provide a few brief remarks about libertarianism. And finally, in section 1.3, I give a quick synopsis of the rest of the book, listing the most important theses that I will be arguing for.

1.1 Formulating the Problem of Free Will

The best way to bring out the problem of free will and determinism is to begin with an old formulation of the problem. I will do this in section 1.1.1, and then in sections 1.1.3–1.1.4, I will explain how and why we have to alter this old formulation of the problem. In between, in section 1.1.2, I will say a bit about compatibilism.

1.1.1 The Old Formulation of the Problem of Free Will

Prior to the emergence of quantum mechanics (or QM) in the early part of the twentieth century, it was extremely easy to bring out the problem of free will and determinism. The problem—or the *traditional* problem, as we can call it—was generated by the fact that people had (or thought they had) prima facie reasons to believe three theses that form an inconsistent set, namely, the following:

(1) Determinism is true (i.e., every event is causally necessitated by prior events together with causal laws);

(2) Human beings have free will; and

(3) Free will is incompatible with determinism.

The prima facie reason for believing (2) was (and is) based on introspection: We have all had the experience of freely choosing from among a number of possible options. The prima facie reason for believing (3), on the other hand, can be put like this:

> If it's really true that all events are causally determined by prior events, then all of my so-called "decisions" and "actions" are determined by prior events, because they are just special kinds of events; indeed, if determinism is true, then it was already determined before I was born that I was going to make all of the decisions I have made during my life; for example, I couldn't have avoided choosing to sit down and write today, because it was already determined before I was born that I *would* choose to sit down and write today. But this is clearly not compatible with free will; we cannot say that I chose to sit down and write of my own free will if it was already determined before I was born that I was going to do this.

Finally, the prima facie case for (1) probably seemed just as obvious to pre-QM philosophers. One might have mounted an argument here in something like the following way:

> Suppose that we strike two billiard balls, A and B, and that A rolls 12 inches before stopping, whereas B rolls 12.1 inches before stopping. Prima facie, it seems that there must be some reason *why* B went farther. Perhaps it was struck a bit harder; or perhaps there was a bit less friction on the part of the table it rolled over; or whatever. We might not know the cause, but it seems that there must have been some cause, because experience tells us that things don't just happen. Prima facie, it seems that everything that happens in the physical world has a cause and, hence, that determinism is true. And this applies to human decisions as well as to any other kind of event. Suppose that I have to choose between two options, A and B, and that I choose A; and suppose that the next day, I am presented with the same choice, and I choose B. It seems that something must have been different about my mental state in the two cases. Perhaps my desire for A decreased in the interim; or perhaps my desire for B increased; or perhaps I just wanted some variety and so I chose B because I remembered choosing A the day before. Or whatever. We might not be able to figure out how my mental state changed, but prima facie, it seems that something about my mental state *must* have changed, because it seems that if I were in the exact same mental state—that is, if I had the same beliefs, desires, fears,

and so on, all of the same strengths—then I would have made the same choice. This is because our decisions flow out of our mental states, that is, our beliefs and desires and fears and so on. In other words, it seems that our decisions are determined by our mental states. And so it seems that our decisions are every bit as determined as other kinds of events are.

It is worth noting that this prima facie argument for (1) does not assume materialism about the mind–brain. If our decisions are determined by our mental states in the way suggested by the above argument, then the decisions of Cartesian souls are every bit as determined as the decisions of materialistic minds, that is, minds that supervene on brains. Note, however, that for those pre-QM philosophers who endorsed both mind–brain materialism and causal determinism about the physical, there was a very obvious argument for the thesis that our *decisions* are determined. One might have put the argument like this: "All physical objects move around according to strictly deterministic laws of motion, like little billiard balls; but human brains are just made up of little physical objects, and human decisions are just physical events, in particular, brain events; therefore, our decisions are wholly determined by the past together with the laws of physics. Thus, given the initial state of the physical world billions of years ago, and given the laws of motion, it was already determined billions of years ago that I was going to choose to write today."

This, then, was the traditional problem of free will and determinism: We had prima facie reasons to believe three theses that, together, form an inconsistent set. Accordingly, there were three possible solutions to the problem: One could reject either (1), (2), or (3). Traditionally, those who rejected (1) usually endorsed (2) and (3) and maintained that human beings possess an indeterministic sort of free will; such philosophers were called *libertarians*. Likewise, those who rejected (2) usually endorsed (1) and (3) and maintained that human beings do not have free will because their actions and decisions are fully determined; such philosophers were called *hard determinists*. And lastly, those who rejected (3) usually endorsed (1) and (2) and maintained that human beings possess free will despite the fact that they are deterministic creatures; such philosophers where called *soft determinists*. (Another term that has sometimes been used interchangeably with 'soft determinism' is 'compatibilism'. Today, however, it is worth keeping these terms separate; compatibilism is the view that (3) is false, whereas soft determinism is the view that (3) is false *and that (1) is true*. Advocates of both views almost always hold that (2) is true, but as we'll see below, many contemporary compatibilists would not want to commit to the truth of (1)—i.e., to the truth of determinism—and so it would be unwise to use 'compatibilism' and 'soft determinism' interchangeably.)

In sections 1.1.3 and 1.1.4, I will explain how and why the traditional formulation of the problem of free will needs to be altered, and in doing this, I will have a good deal to say about the libertarian view that begins by rejecting thesis (1). Before I get into this, however, I want to say a few words about the compatibilist view that (3) is false.

1.1.2 Compatibilism and the Rejection of (3)

Compatibilism can be defined as the view that free will is compatible with determinism—that is, as the claim that (3) is false. Compatibilist views go back at least to Hobbes, and they have been endorsed by many people since then.[1] Probably the most famous statement of compatibilism was given by Hume. He argued that free will is compatible with determinism by providing an analysis of the notion of free will that, unlike libertarian analyses, doesn't involve indeterminism. Hume's analysis is very commonsensical; in a nutshell, and somewhat roughly, he takes free will to be the capacity to *do what you want*. Hume put it like this (1748, 104):

> By liberty, then, we can only mean *a power of acting or not acting according to the determinations of the will*; that is, if we choose to remain at rest, we may; if we choose to move, we also may.

Putting this into contemporary lingo—and altering it somewhat—we arrive at the following definition:

> A person S has *Humean freedom* iff S is capable of acting in accordance with his or her choices, and of choosing in accordance with his or her desires; that is, iff it is the case that *if* he or she chooses to do something then he or she does it, and if (all things considered) he or she wants to make some choice then he or she does make that choice.

Hume's argument for compatibilism is that (a) Humean freedom captures the ordinary notion of free will (that is, Humean freedom *is* free will), and therefore (b) free will is compatible with determinism. The only controversial claim here is (a). The inference from (a) to (b) is entirely trivial, because Humean freedom is clearly compatible with determinism. Humean freedom requires only that our actions flow out of our decisions and our decisions flow out of our desires; but this could be the case even if all of our desires and decisions and actions are causally determined. Suppose that (i) Ralph is in some mental state M, including some particular ensemble of desires; and (ii) Ralph's being in M was causally determined by prior events (indeed, by events that occurred before Ralph's birth); and (iii) Ralph's being in *M* deterministically causes him to make some decision *D*, and this in turn deterministically causes him to perform some action *A*. Then *D* counts as a Humean free decision and *A* counts as a Humean free action (because Ralph is acting here in accordance with his decision and deciding in accordance with his desires); but, of course, *D* and *A* are also causally determined by prior events. Therefore, the claim that human beings are Humean free is perfectly compatible with the thesis that determinism is true, and so again, the only controversial part of Hume's argument is the thesis that free will is in fact Humean freedom, that is, the thesis that the notion of Humean freedom captures the ordinary notion of free will.

Humean freedom is not the only compatibilist notion of freedom in the literature; various other philosophers—P. F. Strawson (1962), Frankfurt (1971), Watson (1975), Dworkin (1988), Wolf (1990), Double (1991), Fischer (1994), Fischer and Ravizza (1998), Wallace (1994), Mele (1995), and Bok (1998), to name just a few[2]—have offered alternative compatibilist definitions of free will (and/or moral responsibility). It is important to note, however, that like Humean freedom, all of these other compatibilist notions of freedom (or at any rate, all the ones that I'm aware of) are not just compatible with determinism, but *obviously* so. For instance, to say just a few words about one of these cases, *Frankfurtian freedom* can be defined (very briefly) as the ability to control, with second-order attitudes, which of your first-order desires will affect your behavior; but given this, it seems that Frankfurtian freedom is clearly compatible with determinism, because one could be causally determined to have (and be governed by) a second-order desire *d* for some first-order desire *e* to control one's behavior (i.e., to take precedence over any conflicting first-order desire *f*). The same point can be made in connection with all of the other compatibilist notions of freedom in the literature, but I won't argue this here, because in each case the point is just as obvious and uncontroversial as it is in connection with Humean freedom and Frankfurtian freedom. In other words, in connection with each of these different kinds of freedom, the controversial question is not whether it is indeed compatible with determinism, but whether it provides a correct analysis of the notion of free will—that is, whether it *is* free will.

It perhaps goes without saying that a similar point can be made about compatibilism in general: Compatibilism is a controversial view because many people think that the correct analysis of free will is given by the notion of libertarian freedom, which, as we'll see, requires indeterminism in a completely transparent way. I will have much more to say about libertarian freedom below, in sections 1.1.3, 1.1.4, and 1.2.

It is also worth noting here that just as it's obvious that the various compatibilist kinds of freedom are in fact compatible with determinism, it is also obvious (in at least most of these cases) that human beings do in fact possess these kinds of freedom. For instance, it's obvious that we are Humean free, because we are clearly capable of acting in accordance with our decisions and deciding in accordance with our desires. Likewise, it's equally obvious that we possess Frankfurtian freedom, because we clearly have the ability to want certain first-order desires to affect our behavior, and at least sometimes, we have the ability to act on these second-order wants. The same point can be made in connection with just about all of the compatibilist varieties of freedom in the literature. I won't say that this point is *completely* obvious in connection with *all* of these kinds of freedom, because one might think there are a few problematic issues here. For instance, some compatibilist kinds of freedom require something like reasons responsiveness (see, e.g., Fischer and Ravizza 1998), and as we'll see in chapter 4, one might think that various psychological studies suggest that our actions are less responsive to our reasons than we might have thought. But in the end, it still seems pretty clear that at least sometimes, and probably very often, our actions are responsive to our reasons in obvious and important ways.

Finally, it's worth noting that in the past (before the emergence of quantum mechanics), most compatibilists endorsed determinism. Again, such philosophers were known as soft determinists. Some of these philosophers (Hobart for sure and arguably Hobbes and Hume as well) also held that freedom *requires* determinism. But today, very few compatibilists would want to commit to either of these claims. Most compatibilists would likely say that they have no idea whether determinism is true (this, they might say, is a question for physicists) but that as far as the issue of free will is concerned, it just doesn't matter whether it's true, because free will doesn't require determinism or indeterminism.

1.1.3 An Intermediate Formulation of the Problem of Free Will
The emergence of QM undermined the traditional way of understanding the problem of free will by undermining our prima facie reasons for believing determinism and, indeed, by revealing that determinism is not the sort of doctrine that can be motivated by prima facie, pretheoretic, armchair arguments. Rather, it is a controversial empirical thesis about the workings of the physical world; in short, it is a question for scientists, most notably physicists. Today, many (perhaps even most) physicists and philosophers of physics reject determinism and endorse indeterminism. And just about everyone would agree that the question is controversial—

that at present, we do not have decisive evidence for either determinism or indeterminism. (In chapter 4, I will argue for a much stronger claim; I will argue that, in fact, we have no good reason whatsoever for endorsing determinism or indeterminism.)

So, given that it no longer seems correct to claim that we have prima facie reasons to believe determinism, we can no longer formulate the philosophical problem of free will in the traditional way. But it turns out that the problem of free will can be separated from its traditional formulation; essentially the same problem (or at least a very similar problem) can be motivated without claiming that we have reason to believe determinism. In short, what we have to do here is replace the appeal to determinism, in the traditional formulation of the problem, with another thesis, one that (a) still gives rise to a traditional sort of worry about free will (just as determinism does), but (b) unlike determinism, has some prima facie support, or plausibility.

How can we come up with such a thesis? Well, we can start by noticing that the traditional worry about free will is really a worry about the existence of an *indeterministic* sort of free will—or, more precisely, a *libertarian* sort of free will—and by reflecting on what libertarianism is supposed to involve. In particular, the point I want to bring out here is that any interesting variety of libertarian free will is going to involve more than just indeterminism. At the very least, it is also going to involve some sort of *appropriate nonrandomness*.

The notion of appropriate nonrandomness is going to be crucially important in what follows. Different people might give different accounts of what this sort of nonrandomness consists in, but the basic idea is that in order for a decision to count as appropriately nonrandom (and hence free), the agent in question has to be centrally involved in the decision. Probably the most standard thing to say here—and I will go along with this—is that appropriate nonrandomness consists most importantly (but perhaps not entirely) in the given agent *authoring and controlling* the decision; that is, it has to be *her* decision, and she has to control which option is chosen. I will discuss this in more detail in chapter 3; I will also discuss some other possible requirements for appropriate nonrandomness, most notably, rationality and what Kane (1996) has called *plural* authorship, control, and rationality; but for now, these brief remarks are good enough.

It's easy to see why any interesting variety of libertarian free will is going to require not just indeterminism, but some sort of appropriate nonrandomness as well. To appreciate this point, imagine that Martians have implanted a chip in someone's head (say, Sylvia) and are controlling her choices and actions via remote control; but imagine that, sometimes, environmental noise garbles the signal from the remote control and that when the signal reaches Sylvia's head, it causes her to choose not as the Martians wanted her to choose, but in a different way; and finally, imagine that a specific signal arrives at Sylvia's head, that it's partially garbled, and that it causes Sylvia to choose as the Martians wanted her to choose but that this result was not causally determined, i.e., that the partially garbled signal might just as well have caused her to choose differently. In this scenario, it seems pretty clear that Sylvia's decision was not free because it wasn't *her* making the decision—or if you'd rather, because she didn't author or control the decision. One might put the point here by claiming that in this scenario, it seems more accurate to say that the decision *happened* to Sylvia, or was inflicted on her, than that she chose of her own free will.

It seems to follow from these considerations that some sort of appropriate nonrandomness is required for genuine free will. The ordinary notion of free will may or may not require indeterminism—that is a controversial question. But regardless of what we say about this, it seems clear that the ordinary notion does require some sort of agent-involving nonrandomness; this is why we have the intuition that in the above scenario, Sylvia's decision is not free. And this should hardly be surprising. After all, the sort of nonrandomness that we're talking about here is really just a sort of *agent-involvedness*, and it should be pretty clear that we cannot say that a person chose of her own free will if she was not relevantly involved in the given decision—that is, if the decision wasn't *hers*, or she didn't control which option was chosen, or some such thing. This just seems obvious.

Finally, given that some sort of appropriate nonrandomness is required for ordinary free will, it seems to follow that any interesting variety of libertarian freedom will require appropriate nonrandomness as well. Indeed, I think we can say that if libertarian freedom didn't require some sort of agent-involving nonrandomness, then it would be a pretty silly, uninteresting variety of freedom. But if libertarian freedom requires indeterminacy *and* appropriate nonrandomness, then it's easy to formulate a hypothesis that (a) is weaker than determinism but (b) still generates a worry about the existence of libertarian free will. The thesis I have in mind is simply this:

Determined-or-Randomism (D-or-R-ism): None of our decisions is both undetermined and appropriately nonrandom; that is, all of our decisions are either (i) causally determined by prior events or (ii) random in the sense that they're not appropriately nonrandom.

One idea, then, would be to replace the appeal to determinism, in the traditional formulation of the problem of free will, with an appeal to D-or-R-ism. If we did this, then the resulting problem of free will would be that we have prima facie reasons to believe the following three (jointly inconsistent) theses:

(1') D-or-R-ism is true;

(2) Human beings have free will; and

(3') Free will is incompatible with D-or-R-ism.

The prima facie reason to believe (2) is the same as it was before. Moreover, the prima facie reason to believe (3') has really already been given as well. For I just argued that free will requires appropriate nonrandomness, and if we combine this with the above prima facie reason to believe (3)—that is, the prima facie reason to believe that free will is incompatible with determinism—then we arrive at the result that free will is incompatible with both determinism and randomism and, hence, that it's incompatible with D-or-R-ism. (It is worth noting here that since it is more or less uncontroversial that free will requires some sort of appropriate nonrandomness, the only really controversial part of (3') is the claim that free will is incompatible with determinism. Thus, one might think that in formulating this new version of the problem of free will, we should just stick with a modified version of (3), claiming that we have prima facie reason to believe the following:

(3) Free will is incompatible with determinism [and hence also with D-or-R-ism].)

Finally, there are also prima facie reasons—or at least one such reason—to believe (1'). The main argument here has been advanced by a few different philosophers, including Hobbes (1651), Hume (1748), and Hobart (1934). We can put the argument like this:

> Indeterminism seems to entail a kind of randomness. It seems that if an event is undetermined, then it's uncaused and, hence, accidental. In other words, it *just happens*, or it happens randomly. Therefore, prima facie, it seems that if our decisions are undetermined, then they are random, and so they couldn't possibly be "appropriately nonrandom." Or to put the point the other way around, if our decisions are appropriately nonrandom, then *we* author and control them, or something along these lines, and this, it seems, can only mean that *we determine what we choose and don't choose*, presumably for rational reasons; thus, it seems that if our decisions are appropriately nonrandom, then they couldn't possibly be undetermined. Therefore, prima facie, it seems impossible for a decision to

be undetermined and appropriately nonrandom at the same time, and so it seems that D-or-R-ism is true; that is, it seems that all of our decisions are either determined or random in the sense of being not appropriately nonrandom.

(Notice that while this argument involves the claim that indeterminacy *entails* a lack of appropriate nonrandomness, D-or-R-ism itself does *not* involve this claim. D-or-R-ism just says that, in fact, all of our decisions *are* either determined or random.)

In any event, given the above remarks, it seems that there are at least prima facie reasons to believe (1'), (2), and (3'). Thus, this gives us an alternative formulation of the problem of free will.

1.1.4 The Final (or "New and Improved") Formulation of the Problem of Free Will

But this isn't yet the best way to formulate the problem of free will. The trouble is that D-or-R-ism is still too strong. It is of course weaker than determinism, and so we've made some progress here, but we can do better. In other words, it's possible to generate a traditional sort of worry about indeterministic, libertarian free will by appealing to a hypothesis that's even weaker than D-or-R-ism. And as we'll presently see, when we do this, we arrive at a much better formulation of the problem.

We can locate the hypothesis I have in mind by noticing that we haven't yet captured everything that's required for libertarian free will. In order for a decision to be genuinely free in the libertarian sense, it's not enough for it to be undetermined and appropriately nonrandom. It also needs to be the case that the indeterminacy is *relevant* to the nonrandomness. Thus, I want to define libertarianism as follows:

> *Libertarianism* is the view that human beings are L-free, where a person is *L-free* if and only if she makes at least some decisions that are such that (a) they are both undetermined and appropriately nonrandom, and (b) the indeterminacy is relevant to the appropriate nonrandomness in the sense that it *generates* the nonrandomness, or *procures* it, or *enhances* it, or *increases* it, or something along these lines.[3]

(One might want to add another thesis to libertarianism, namely, the thesis that the notion of L-freedom provides an adequate definition of the ordinary notion of free will. If we did this, then libertarianism would entail (i) that human beings have free will and (ii) that free will is incompatible with determinism. This is probably the "standard" way to define libertarianism, but I don't want to set things up this way. I will explain why in section 1.2, but for now, I just want to ignore this issue.)

It's easy to see why clause (b) is needed in the definition of libertarianism. Without this, some decidedly nonlibertarian views would count as versions of libertarianism. Consider, for instance, the following view:

> ($) Hume was essentially right about what free will is; in particular, free will consists essentially in the ability to act and choose in accordance with your desires. Moreover, we humans do in fact have free will: we are capable of choosing in accordance with our desires because most of our choices are in fact *caused by* our desires. But some aspects of Hume's view are *not* right. In particular, it turns out that our decisions are not determined, because there are various kinds of quantum indeterminacies in our decision-making processes. But our decisions are still, so to speak, "for-all-practical-purposes determined." More specifically, they are probabilistically caused—by our desires—with a high degree of certainty. For instance, suppose that some agent (say, Smith) has to choose between two options, A and B; and suppose in addition that Smith's desires, or reasons for choosing, clearly favor option A; and finally, suppose that Smith does in fact choose A. Then according to the present view, just prior to the moment of choice, the probability of Smith choosing A was very, very high (say, .9999999), but it was not 1. So our decisions are not determined, but this doesn't really matter, because they're still for-all-practical-purposes determined by our desires. Thus, our decisions are still appropriately nonrandom and free.

If we didn't include clause (b) in the definition of libertarianism, then ($) would count as a version of libertarianism, because it entails that our decisions are both undetermined and appropriately nonrandom. But ($) clearly *isn't* a version of libertarianism; it's an essentially Humean view with an unimportant smidge of indeterminism thrown in. One way to appreciate this point is to notice that according to ($), we have free will *despite* the fact that indeterminism is true. Libertarians, on the other hand, think that we have free will *because* indeterminism is true; they think that indeterminacy is *needed* for free will—or at any rate, they think it's needed for the kind of free will that they have in mind. And this is why it has to be built into the definition of libertarianism that the indeterminacy in question *generates* the nonrandomness (or enhances it, or increases it, or some such thing).

Given that libertarianism should be defined in the above way, it follows that we can weaken the thesis that we need to appeal to in order to generate a problem for free will. We don't need to appeal to determinism or even to D-or-R-ism. All we need to appeal to here is the following thesis:

> *No Freedom-Enhancing Indeterminism (or for short, FE-determinism)*: There are no freedom-enhancing indeterminacies (i.e., no freedom-enhancing undetermined events) in any human decision-making processes. In other words—and more precisely—human beings do not possess L-freedom; that is, libertarianism is false.

It is worth noting here that FE-determinism is similar in a certain way to determinism. In particular, it's just a narrowed-down version of determinism. Determinism says that there are no undetermined events of any kind anywhere in the universe. FE-determinism, on the other hand, says that there are no undetermined events *in our decision-making processes that generate or increase appropriate nonrandomness*. So determinism and FE-determinism are similar sorts of theses. The difference is that FE-determinism is a much narrower claim that zeros in on the kinds of indeterminacies that might be relevant to the issue of free will. And the benefit of narrowing the claim down in this way, as we'll presently see, is that when we do this, we arrive at a thesis that we seem to have prima facie reasons to believe.

One might put forward a few different prima facie arguments for FE-determinism. The one I'm going to describe here is similar to the Hobbes-Hume-Hobart argument for D-or-R-ism, except that it's weaker and hence more plausible. The Hobbes-Hume-Hobart argument proceeds by claiming that indeterminacy entails a lack of appropriate nonrandomness. The argument for FE-determinism is similar, but it doesn't commit to the thesis that indeterminacy automatically destroys appropriate nonrandomness; it leaves open the possibility that there might be some indeterminacies in our decision-making processes that are completely irrelevant to the nonrandomness of our decisions and, hence, that don't diminish this nonrandomness. What the argument claims, though, is that there couldn't be any indeterminacies that *increase* appropriate nonrandomness. One might formulate the argument here in something like the following way:

> It's hard to see how the introduction of an undetermined event into a decision-making process could *increase* the authorship or control that the agent in question has over the decision. It seems (prima facie) that at best, an undetermined event could be irrelevant to the agent's authorship and control. Authorship, control, and nonrandomness have to do with it being the case that it was the *agent* who made the decision, or who determined which option was chosen. But given this, it's hard to see how the insertion of an undetermined event could help. It seems that if we insert an unde-

termined event into a decision-making process, this would be to insert an element of randomness; so it seems that this would either (a) undermine the appropriate nonrandomness of the decision or, at best, (b) leave the level of appropriate nonrandomness alone. How could the insertion of a *random* element increase appropriate *non*randomness? How could this make it the case that it was the *agent* who performed the given action, or made the given decision? It's hard to see how it could.

(It's important to note that this is just one way to formulate a prima facie argument for FE-determinism—or, equivalently, against libertarianism. When we get to chapter 3, we will encounter some more detailed objections to libertarian views, e.g., the luck objection and the objection that libertarianism leads to an unacceptable regress. For now, though, the above prima facie argument is good enough.)

Given all of this, we can replace the appeal to determinism, in the traditional formulation of the problem of free will, with an appeal to FE-determinism. If we do this, we arrive at a new and improved version of the problem of free will, one that's generated by pointing out that we have—or seem to have—prima facie reasons to believe the following three (mutually inconsistent) theses:

(1") FE-determinism is true (i.e., libertarianism is false).

(2) Human beings have free will.

(3) Free will is incompatible with determinism (and, hence, with FE-determinism).

Now, it might seem that thesis (3) should be replaced, in the new and improved version of the problem, with the following:

(3") Free will is incompatible with FE-determinism.

But I want to argue that free will is incompatible with FE-determinism if and only if it's incompatible with determinism. (If this is right, then the question of whether (3") is true reduces to the question of whether free will is compatible with determinism; and given this, it makes sense to favor (3) over (3") for the simple reason that it enables us to preserve some traditional lingo, couching the important issue in terms of the question of whether compatibilism is true, i.e., the question of whether free will is compatible with *determinism*.) What, then, is the argument for the claim that free will is incompatible with FE-determinism if and only if it's incompatible with determinism? Since this is a biconditional, we can justify it by arguing for two conditional claims, namely, (a) if free will is incompatible with determinism, then it's incompatible with FE-determinism, and (b) if free will is incompatible with FE-determinism, then it's incompatible with determinism—or equivalently, if free will is compatible with determinism, then it's compatible with FE-determinism. Both of these conditionals are easy to justify.

Let's start with (b). Suppose free will is compatible with determinism. Then it's obviously compatible with FE-determinism—that is, with the claim that there are no freedom-enhancing indeterminacies in any of our decision-making processes—for the simple reason that it's compatible with the claim that there are no indeterminacies (i.e., no undetermined events[4]) of any kind anywhere in the universe.

Let's move on now to claim (a). Suppose that free will is incompatible with determinism. Then free will requires indeterminism. But it seems clear that if indeterminacies are required for free will, it's because they're required for appropriate nonrandomness. (I can't imagine why else indeterminism would be needed here; the whole worry about free will and determinism is that if our decisions are causally determined by prior events, then they aren't made by *us*, i.e., they aren't authored or controlled by us and, hence, aren't appropriately nonrandom.) But if indeterminism is required for appropriate nonrandomness, then it seems to follow that free will requires a variety of indeterminism that procures or increases appropriate nonrandomness—that is, it requires a freedom-enhancing indeterminism of precisely the kind that's ruled out by FE-determinism. But, of course, this is just to say that free will is incompatible with FE-determinism, that is, with the claim that there are no freedom-enhancing indeterminacies in any of our decision-making processes. And so it follows that claim (a) is true: if free will is incompatible with determinism, then it's also incompatible with FE-determinism.

(A second, perhaps ultimately equivalent, way to motivate thesis (a) is to point out that the libertarian notion of free will is really the only reasonable incompatibilist notion of free will out there [at any rate, I can't see how incompatibilists have any other reasonable options]. Given this, it seems very plausible to suppose that if free will is incompatible with determinism, it's because free will is what libertarians say it is—which is just to say that free will is incompatible with the falsity of libertarianism, or equivalently, with the truth of FE-determinism.)

Given (a) and (b), it follows that (3") is essentially equivalent to (3). Thus, for the sake of preserving some traditional lingo, I want to formulate the problem of free will in terms of thesis (3) and the issue of the incompatibility of free will and *determinism*.

Introduction

So, again, the (new and improved) problem of free will and determinism is that we have prima facie reasons to believe the following three (mutually inconsistent) theses:

(1") FE-determinism is true (i.e., libertarianism is false).

(2) Human beings have free will.

(3) Free will is incompatible with determinism (and, hence, with FE-determinism).

As with the traditional problem, there are three possible solutions to this new and improved version of the problem. In particular, we can reject either (1"), (2), or (3). Again, those who reject (3) are called *compatibilists*; usually these philosophers will also endorse (1") and (2); we can call these people *soft FE-determinists*. Likewise, those who respond to the problem by rejecting (2) will usually endorse (1") and (3)—this, of course, is why they reject (2); we can call these people *hard FE-determinists*.[5] And, of course, those who reject (1") are called *libertarians*. Before going on, I want to say a bit more about this view.

1.2 Some Remarks on Libertarianism

I defined libertarianism above as the negation of (1"). To repeat, in my lingo,

> *Libertarianism* is the view that human beings are L-free, where a person is *L-free* if and only if she makes at least some decisions that are such that (a) they are both undetermined and appropriately nonrandom in the sense discussed above, and (b) the indeterminacy is *relevant* to the appropriate nonrandomness in the sense that it generates it, or procures it, or increases it, or some such thing.

I should note here that other philosophers might define libertarian freedom slightly differently. For instance, Kane (1996, chapters 3 and 5) defines it in terms of an agent having ultimate responsibility for, or "sole authorship" of, his or her decisions. But as far as I know, the various definitions of libertarian freedom (Kane's included) all require indeterminism, and they all require the indeterminism to be an important factor in procuring some sort of appropriate nonrandomness, where this involves (at the very least) something like authorship and control.

Nonetheless, despite this similarity that runs through all versions of libertarianism, it should be noted that there are many varieties of libertarianism, because the thesis that we humans are L-free can be developed in a number of different ways. For instance, whereas many early libertarians endorsed mind–brain dualism, many contemporary libertarians are mind–brain materialists. And whereas some libertarians endorse the idea that there is such a thing as irreducible agent causation, others reject this idea and maintain that all causation reduces to event causation. Moreover, among those libertarians who reject irreducible agent causation, there is a distinction to be drawn between event-causal libertarians (who hold that our L-free decisions are probabilistically caused by agent-involving events) and noncausal libertarians (who hold that our L-free decisions are uncaused). And finally, some libertarian views are Valerian (i.e., they place the important indeterminacy prior to the moment of choice) and others are non-Valerian (i.e., they place the important indeterminacy *at* the moment of choice). I will say more about these different versions of libertarianism in chapter 3.

The point I want to bring out now, though, is that my definition of libertarianism is a bit nonstandard in a certain way. I have defined libertarianism as the view that human beings are L-free, but I think it is fair to say that many people have used 'libertarianism' to denote the view that human beings are L-free *and that the notion of L-freedom provides a correct analysis of the ordinary notion of free will*. I do not want to define libertarianism in this way for two reasons. First, this definition seems unpleasing to me, because it leaves out a view that I think is best thought of as a version of libertarianism. Suppose someone held that (a) human beings do possess L-freedom (and that this is an important fact about the nature of human decision making) but (b) ordinary-language utterances of 'free will' refer not to L-freedom but to some compatibilist sort of freedom (say, Humean freedom). It seems to me that this view is best thought of as a variety of libertarianism, and so I do not want to include in the definition of libertarianism the claim that L-freedom captures the ordinary notion of free will. (By the way, I would not say that the traditional definition of libertarianism is *wrong* in this respect, because 'libertarianism' is a theoretical term of art and so it is defined by stipulation; definitions of ordinary-language terms can be wrong because they can fly in the face of ordinary usage and intentions [and perhaps for other reasons as well—see chapter 2 for more on this]; but this doesn't seem to be the case with definitions of words like 'libertarianism'.)

My second reason for favoring my definition of libertarianism over the more traditional one is that it clarifies things by keeping the metaphysical thesis that human beings are L-free separate from the (entirely independent) semantic thesis that the ordinary notion of free will is accurately defined by the notion of L-freedom. Now, I suppose we could achieve even more clarity here by introducing two different terms; for example, we could define *metaphysical libertarianism* as the view that human beings are L-free and *semantic libertarianism* as the view that the notion of L-freedom provides a correct definition of 'free will'. But there is no need for me to use these terms here, because I am not going to be very concerned with semantic libertarianism; for the most part, I will be concerned only with metaphysical libertarianism—or as I will be calling it, *libertarianism*.

So those are my reasons for leaving the above semantic thesis out of the definition of libertarianism. But, of course, nothing important is going to turn on this terminological point.

Now, given that libertarianism (as I'm defining it here) does not involve the claim that free will is L-freedom, it follows that libertarianism is consistent with compatibilism. There is no inconsistency in claiming that (a) human beings possess L-freedom, but (b) L-freedom does not provide a good analysis of the ordinary notion of free will and, in fact, that notion is best analyzed in some compatibilistic way. Now, this might seem like an odd result—that libertarianism and compatibilism are consistent—but of course it's just a trivial result of the fact that I've defined libertarianism in a somewhat nonstandard way. Nonetheless, while there is nothing particularly interesting about the fact that claims (a) and (b) are consistent, there is another point lurking in the background here that I think is more interesting and important. The point I have in mind is that very few people have simultaneously endorsed these two views. This strikes me as a bit odd. Indeed, it seems more than odd; it seems *fishy*. Many people think that human beings are L-free, and many think that the ordinary notion of free will is compatible with determinism; these two theses are perfectly consistent with one another, and indeed, they are entirely independent of each other—one of them is about human decision-making processes and the other is about the meaning of a certain ordinary-language expression. So why don't more people endorse these two theses together? The answer, I think, is that philosophers have let their views on these two issues influence each other in irrational ways (for instance, I think that many people have endorsed compatibilism more or less *because* they think human beings aren't L-free, and I think that many people have endorsed libertarianism *because* they endorse incompatibilism). I will not return to this point in the present book, but in chapter 2, I will provide more reason for thinking that the two issues here are entirely independent of one another, and it will follow from this that there is simply no good reason to think that we shouldn't simultaneously endorse libertarianism (as I'm defining it here) and compatibilism.

(Indeed, as I pointed out above, this is one of my reasons for favoring my definition of libertarianism—because it helps us to keep separate two theses that are in fact completely independent of one another.)

In any event, even if libertarianism (as I've defined it here) is compatible with compatibilism, it is worth noting that almost all compatibilists reject libertarianism (as I define it), and vice versa. And again, we can call those compatibilists who reject libertarianism *soft FE-determinists*. And if we like we can call libertarians who reject compatibilism *metaphysical and semantic libertarians*—or perhaps *incompatibilistic libertarians*. Finally, it's worth noting that virtually all the proponents of both of these views endorse thesis (2)—that is, the thesis that human beings have free will. Most libertarians endorse (2) because they think that humans are L-free and that this is free will. And most compatibilists endorse (2), because, as we saw above, human beings pretty obviously possess just about all of the standard varieties of compatibilist freedom.

1.3 Synopsis of the Book

As I've set things up, the (new and improved) problem of free will is generated by the fact that we have prima facie reasons to believe the following three theses:

(1") FE-determinism is true;

(2) Human beings have free will; and

(3) Free will is incompatible with determinism (and hence with FE-determinism).

But prima facie reasons are just that—prima facie reasons. The challenge is to figure out which of these three theses are really true. Thus, if we want to *solve* the problem of free will, we have to ask the following three questions:

The FE-determinism question: Is FE-determinism true?

The do-we-have-free-will question: Do human beings have free will?

The compatibilism question: Is free will compatible with determinism (and hence with FE-determinism)?

But I will argue in chapter 2 that it's possible to get more focused with these questions. In particular, I will argue that these three questions reduce to two other questions, namely,

The what-is-free-will question: What is free will? (We can take this as being equivalent to the question 'What is the correct analysis of the notion of free will?' and also to the question 'What is the correct definition of the term "free will"?' But we cannot assume without argument that these questions are solely about folk meaning, or ordinary-language usage and intentions; I will discuss this issue in chapter 2.)

and

The which-kinds-of-freedom-do-we-have question: Which kinds of freedom do humans have? That is, do they have L-freedom?; and do they have Humean freedom?; and do they have Frankfurtian freedom?; and so on. (Actually, to be more precise, we can formulate this question as asking which kinds of "freedom" humans have, since some or all of the kinds of "freedom" we're asking about here might fail to *be* free will, according to the correct answer to the what-is-free-will question.)

I will argue that if we could answer these latter two questions, then we could thereby answer the first three questions. More specifically, I will argue that (i) the compatibilism question reduces to the what-is-free-will question; and (ii) the FE-determinism question reduces to (or collapses into) the which-kinds-of-freedom-do-we-have question; and (iii) the do-we-have-free-will question collapses into the what-is-free-will question *and* the which-kinds-of-freedom-do-we-have question. In addition, I will also argue that (iv) while the what-is-free-will question is definitely relevant to the do-we-have-free-will question in a certain sort of way, it is not relevant to that question in any nontrivial or metaphysically interesting way; indeed, I will argue that the what-is-free-will question is irrelevant to *all* substantive questions about the nature of human decision-making processes, except in a trivial way. Thus, from points (i) and (iv), it follows that (v) the compatibilism question is likewise irrelevant to substantive questions about the nature of human decision-making processes (most notably, the do-we-have-free-will question), except in a trivial way. And from points (iii) and (iv), it follows that (vi) the only metaphysically interesting question that has any bearing at all on the do-we-have-free-will question is the which-kinds-of-freedom-do-we-have question. Finally, I will also argue that the which-kinds-of-freedom-do-we-have question boils down largely (though perhaps not entirely) to the libertarian question (i.e., the question of whether human beings are L-free); and when we combine this with thesis (vi), it gives us the result that (vii) the metaphysical issue inherent in the problem of free will reduces largely (though, again, perhaps not entirely) to the libertarian question.

Given the way I've set things up here, it seems to make sense to think of the problem of free will as being *constituted by* the three questions listed above—that is, the FE-determinism question, the do-we-have-free-will question, and the compatibilism question. And given the reductive conclusions mentioned in the preceding paragraph, we might go on to say that the problem of free will is, in the end, *really* constituted by the what-is-free-will question and the which-kinds-of-freedom-do-we-have question. But in fact, there's another question that's relevant to philosophical discussions of free will that *doesn't* reduce to the what-is-free-will question and/or the which-kinds-of-freedom-do-we-have question, namely,

The moral responsibility question: Which kinds of freedom (or "freedom") are required for moral responsibility?

I think that if we could answer this last question in addition to the what-is-free-will question and the which-kinds-of-freedom-do-we-have question, then we could answer just about all of the important philosophical questions in the area of free will. But I won't argue this point here. Instead, I will argue (still in chapter 2) that (viii) like the compatibilism question and the what-is-free-will question, the moral responsibility question is essentially irrelevant to substantive questions about the metaphysics of human free will.

Because I argue in chapter 2 for thesis (vi) above—that is, the thesis that the which-kinds-of-freedom-do-we-have question is the only metaphysically interesting question that's relevant to the do-we-have-free-will question—and because my central concern in this book is the metaphysics of human free will and not the semantics of the term 'free will', most of the rest of the book is concerned with the which-kinds-of-freedom-do-we-have question, and in particular, with the libertarian question, which, again, is the most important and controversial subquestion of the which-kinds-of-freedom-do-we-have question. But before moving on to the libertarian question, I say a few words, at the end of chapter 2, about how we might answer the what-is-free-will question, the compatibilism question, and the moral responsibility question.

In chapter 3, I turn to the libertarian question. It is widely believed that libertarianism (i.e., the view that human beings are L-free) could not be true. One argument for this, sketched above, is based on the idea that even if there are various kinds of causal indeterminacies in our decision-making processes, these indeterminacies could not increase or procure appropriate nonrandomness. A few libertarians—see, for example, van Inwagen 1983, Kane 1985, 1996, and Ginet 1990—have responded to worries like this by trying to explain how libertarianism *could* be true, that is, by trying to show that libertarianism is at least possible. In chapter 3, I will argue for a much stronger conclusion. I will argue that there's a certain category of our decisions (I will call them *torn decisions*, and I'll characterize them in chapter 3) for which the following is true: If they're undetermined in the appropriate way (and I'll be very clear about the sort of indeterminacy that's required here), then they're L-free—that is, (a) they're not just undetermined but also appropriately nonrandom, and (b) the indeterminacy in question increases or procures the appropriate nonrandomness. Notice that my claim here is not simply that if our torn decisions are appropriately undetermined, then they *could* be L-free; I'm going to argue that if they're appropriately undetermined, then they *are* L-free. If I'm right about this (and about a couple of other minor points that I will argue in chapter 3), then the question of whether libertarianism is true—that is, of whether human beings are L-free—just reduces to the question of whether some of our torn decisions are undetermined in the appropriate way.

(It might seem that my thesis here—that if our torn decisions are undetermined in the right way, then they're also appropriately nonrandom and L-free—is inconsistent with something I said in section 1.1.3, when I was discussing the case of Sylvia. Sylvia's decision was undetermined but *not* appropriately nonrandom [and hence not L-free]. But in fact, there is no inconsistency here, because (a) Sylvia's decision was not a *torn* decision, and (b) it wasn't undetermined *in the right way* [and again, I'll characterize torn decisions and the required sort of indeterminacy in chapter 3].)

In developing my arguments in chapter 3, I will also be constructing a novel version of libertarianism. The view will be non-Valerian (i.e., it will place the important indeterminacy at the moment of choice), and it will be entirely naturalistic and event-causal; that is, it will not involve any sort of mind–brain dualism or irreducible agent causation. Thus, combining this with my conclusion that the libertarian question reduces to the question of whether some of our (torn) decisions are (appropriately) undetermined at the moment of choice, we obtain the result that the libertarian question reduces to a straightforward empirical question about the physical world. More specifically, it reduces to a question about the causal histories of the neural events that are our (torn) decisions. In particular, it's just the question of whether any of these neural events are causally undetermined in the appropriate way.

Finally, in chapter 4, I will argue that there are no good arguments on either side of the question of whether some of our torn decisions are undetermined in the appropriate way, that is, the way that's required for L-freedom. Since this is an empirical question, there is, I argue, no real hope that any a priori argument could succeed here. Nonetheless, I begin by saying what's wrong with a few a priori arguments (or allegedly a priori arguments) that one might attempt here; most notably, I say a few words about what's wrong with the Kant-inspired argument that human beings must be L-free because they're morally responsible for their actions. Then I turn to empirical arguments. I examine the existing evidence in physics and neuroscience and argue that we have no good empirical reason to endorse or reject the thesis that some of our torn decisions are undetermined in the relevant way. I spend most of my time arguing that we have no good empirical reason to *reject* this thesis, because I think it's more or less obvious and uncontroversial that we have no good empirical reason to *endorse* it. Finally, if I'm right that there are no good arguments for or against the relevant sort of indeterminism, then it follows that there are no good arguments for or against libertarianism.

The arguments and conclusions of this book can be seen as fitting into a certain kind of antimetaphysical view. If my arguments here are cogent, then the main philosophical questions about free will reduce to the following three questions:

The which-kinds-of-freedom-do-we-have question: Which kinds of freedom (or "freedom") do humans have? That is, do they have L-freedom?; and do they have Humean freedom?; and do they have Frankfurtian freedom?; and so on.

The what-is-free-will question: What is free will?

The moral responsibility question: Which kinds of freedom (or "freedom") are required for moral responsibility?

In addition, if my arguments are correct, we get the following results: (a) the metaphysically interesting issue inherent in the problem of free will reduces to the which-kinds-of-freedom-do-we-have question; and (b) the which-kinds-of-freedom-do-we-have question reduces largely to the libertarian question; and (c) the libertarian question reduces to a wide open empirical question about whether our torn decisions are (appropriately) undetermined at the moment of choice. Moreover, in connection with the use of the word 'largely' in point (b), I think it can also be argued—though I won't really argue it here—that if there are any other controversial subquestions of the which-kinds-of-freedom-do-we-have question, aside from the libertarian question, then they too boil down to empirical questions about human decision-making processes. And if this is right, then it follows that the metaphysically interesting issue inherent in the problem of free will reduces to straightforwardly empirical questions about us and our decision-making processes.

What about the what-is-free-will question and the moral responsibility question? Well, if my arguments are correct, then we know that these two questions aren't relevant (in any nontrivial way) to metaphysical questions about the nature of human beings, for example, the do-we-have-free-will question. But what *are* they relevant to? What are these two questions *about*? Well, as we'll see in chapter 2, there are multiple views one might endorse here. One view is that the what-is-free-will question and the moral responsibility question are straightforward empirical questions about the ordinary-language meanings of 'free will' and 'morally responsible'—that is, about the usage and intentions associated with these two expressions among ordinary folk. But one might doubt this view; one might think that when philosophers are trying to figure out what free will and moral responsibility are, they're not just trying to capture ordinary-language meaning. One might think they're also trying to improve upon ordinary usage. But if we ask ourselves what sorts of facts might be relevant here—that is, might be relevant to determining which answers to the what-is-free-will question and the moral responsibility question are correct—there aren't very many plausible candidates. Now, there are certainly a few things one might reasonably say here; for example, one might appeal to facts about the coherence of the various notions of free will and moral responsibility, or perhaps to facts about how well these notions "carve nature at the joints." But I think it can be argued—though, again, I won't argue this point here—that all of the different kinds of facts that one might plausibly appeal to here are either empirical facts or logical facts.

If this is right, and if the various points that I'm going to argue in this book are also right, then it would seem to be a confusion to think of the problem of free will and determinism as a *metaphysical* problem at all—unless by 'metaphysical problem' you simply mean a problem about the nature of reality. If that's all a metaphysical problem is, then the problem of free will is indeed a metaphysical problem, but of course, so are the problems of empirical science. If, however, a metaphysical problem is supposed to be somehow different from the problems that we address in the empirical and logico-mathematical sciences (and if the arguments of this book are cogent), then the problem of free will is not a metaphysical problem, because it reduces to straightforwardly empirical questions and possibly some logical questions.

Now, I actually think the conclusion of the last paragraph can be generalized; I think it can be argued that *all* so-called metaphysical problems reduce to questions that are either empirical (and about the nature of the physical world), or logical, or factually empty in the sense that there are no facts of the matter about their answers. But again, I will not try to argue for this sweeping conclusion here.

So perhaps the two central aims of this book are to provide (a) a defense of libertarianism and (b) an attack (or at any rate, *part* of an attack) on metaphysics. These two aims might seem like strange bedfellows, because it might seem that libertarianism is the most "metaphysically loaded" view in the free will literature. But by now it should be clear that it is also an aim of this book to "demetaphysicalize" the libertarian view. Once we see (in chapter 3) that libertarianism follows from the relevant kind of indeterminism, we will also see that there is nothing "metaphysically loaded" about libertarianism at all. It's just a straightforward empirical hypothesis about the neural events that are our (torn) decisions. Moreover, if the arguments of chapter 4 are correct, then the question of whether the libertarian hypothesis is true is a *wide open* question. Again, I am going to argue that, at present, we don't have any good reason for taking sides on this question. Thus, I am not going to argue in this book that libertarianism is true. I'm going to defend it against various objections, and I'm going to argue that we do not currently have any good reason to reject it. But I will not argue in its favor, because I also think that we don't have any good reason to endorse it. Again, I think the question of whether libertarianism is true is an open empirical question.

2 Why the Compatibilism Issue and the Conceptual-Analysis Issue Are Metaphysically Irrelevant

[Compatibilism] is a wretched subterfuge with which some persons still let themselves be put off, and so think they have solved, with a petty word-jugglery, [the problem of free will].
—Immanuel Kant (1788, 95–96)

[Compatibilism] is a quagmire of evasion under which the real issue of fact has been entirely smothered. . . . No matter what the soft determinist mean by ['freedom'], . . . there is a problem, an issue of fact and not of words.
—William James (1884, 149)

2.1 Introduction

The recent literature on the problem of free will has been dominated by the debate about whether compatibilism is true. I think this is unfortunate, because I think the question of whether compatibilism is true is essentially irrelevant to metaphysical questions about human free will—that is, about the existence or nature of the freedom inherent in human decision-making processes. This view of the compatibilism debate is *metaphysically* similar to the views of Kant and James, but I should say here that I would not go along with the dismissiveness of their remarks. I think the question of whether compatibilism is true is interesting in its own right, and as will become clear below, I think it may be worth caring about for reasons that go beyond our purely theoretical interests. Moreover, I think there has been a lot of good philosophical work on this question that is both interesting and important. But I also think that on reflection, it turns out that this question—the question of whether compatibilism is true—is independent of metaphysical questions about the nature of human decision-making processes, except in a trivial way. This is what I want to argue here. Moreover, as we'll see, my argument points to a more general result, namely, that conceptual analysis is essentially irrelevant to metaphysics.

Before getting into the issues of this chapter, I want to rehearse a few definitions from chapter 1, beginning with the notion of *appropriate nonrandomness*. I will discuss this notion in more detail in chapter 3; for now, it is enough to say that in order for a decision to count as appropriately nonrandom, the agent in question has to be appropriately involved in the decision. This is going to consist at least in the agent having something like *authorship* and *control* over the decision; that is, it has to be *her* decision, and she has to control which option is chosen. (In chapter 3, we will see that there might be other requirements for appropriate nonrandomness, but for now, this is good enough.) Given this, we can define *libertarianism* as the view that human beings possess libertarian free will, or *L-freedom*, where a person is *L-free* if and only if she makes at least some decisions that are such that (a) they are both undetermined (i.e., not determined by prior events together with physical laws) and appropriately nonrandom, and (b) the indeterminacy here is relevant to the appropriate nonrandomness in the sense that it *generates* the nonrandomness, or *procures* it, or *enhances* it, or *increases* it, or something along these lines.[1] Finally, *FE-determinism* is the view that there are no freedom-enhancing indeterminacies—that is, no undetermined events that increase or procure appropriate nonrandomness—in any of our decision-making processes. Thus, FE-determinism is just the view that libertarianism is false.

We saw in chapter 1 that in order to solve the problem of free will, we need to answer the following three questions:

The FE-determinism question: Is FE-determinism true?

The do-we-have-free-will question: Do human beings have free will?

The compatibilism question: Is free will compatible with determinism (and hence with FE-determinism[2])?

But we can get more focused than this. If we ask ourselves what we really don't know here—that is, if we ask what the fundamental questions are here that are such that (a) we cannot currently answer them, and (b) if we could answer them, then we could answer the three questions listed above—then we come up with just two questions. In particular, I think it can be argued that these three questions (i.e., the FE-determinism question, the do-we-have-free-will question, and the compatibilism question) reduce to the following two questions, which can be thought of as more fundamental:

The what-is-free-will question: What is free will? (We can take this to be equivalent to the question 'What is the correct analysis of the notion of free will?' and also to the question 'What is the correct definition of the term "free will"?' But we cannot assume without argument that these questions are solely about folk meaning, or ordinary-language usage and intentions; I will discuss this issue below.)

The which-kinds-of-freedom-do-we-have question: Which kinds of freedom do humans have? That is, do they have L-freedom?; and do they have Humean freedom?; and do they have Frankfurtian freedom?; and so on.³ (Actually, to be more precise, we can formulate this question as asking which kinds of "freedom" humans have, since some or all of the kinds of "freedom" we're asking about here might fail to *be* free will, according to the correct answer to the what-is-free-will question.)

If we could answer these two questions, then (I will argue) we could answer all three of the above questions. In particular, I will argue that (i) the compatibilism question reduces to the what-is-free-will question; (ii) the FE-determinism question reduces to (or collapses into) the which-kinds-of-freedom-do-we-have question; and (iii) the do-we-have-free-will question collapses into the what-is-free-will question *and* the which-kinds-of-freedom-do-we-have question.

I will argue point (i) below, in section 2.5, but (ii) and (iii) are more or less obvious and can be motivated right here in just a few words. In connection with (ii), all we need to say is this: Since FE-determinism is just the negation of libertarianism, it follows that the FE-determinism question is essentially equivalent to the libertarian question (i.e., 'Are humans L-free?'). But the libertarian question clearly collapses into the which-kinds-of-freedom-do-we-have question—after all, the former is just a sub-question of the latter—and so it follows that the FE-determinism question also collapses into the which-kinds-of-freedom-do-we-have question.

Thesis (iii) is just as obvious: If we could answer the what-is-free-will question and the which-kinds-of-freedom-do-we-have question, then we could also answer the do-we-have-free-will question, because we would know what free will is and whether we have it. Of course, we would also know more than this—in particular, we would know whether we possess various kinds of pseudo-freedom—but this doesn't undermine the claim that the do-we-have-free-will question is subsumed by the what-is-free-will question and the which-kinds-of-freedom-do-we-have question.

But the main thing I want to argue in the present chapter is this:

(iv) While the what-is-free-will question is clearly relevant to the do-we-have-free-will question in a certain way, it is not relevant to that question in any nontrivial or metaphysically interesting way; indeed, the what-is-free-will question is not relevant to *any* substantive question about the nature of human decision-making processes, except in a trivial way.

I will argue this point in sections 2.3 and 2.4. And if we combine thesis (iv) with thesis (i)—which, again, I'll argue for in section 2.5—we obtain the result that the compatibilism question is also essentially irrelevant to substantive questions about the nature of human decision-making processes, e.g., the do-we-have-free-will question.

If my arguments are correct, then what we might think of as the *semantic* component of the problem of free will (namely, the what-is-free-will question) is essentially irrelevant to the *metaphysical* component of the problem (e.g., the do-we-have-free-will question and the which-kinds-of-freedom-do-we-have question). But this isn't all there is to the problem of free will. There is also a *moral* component to the problem, for we also want to answer the following:

The moral responsibility question: Which kinds of freedom (or "freedom") are required for moral responsibility?

But I will argue in section 2.4 that however important this question is to moral issues, it is—like the compatibilism question and the what-is-free-will question—essentially irrelevant to metaphysical questions about the nature of human decision-making processes, for instance, the do-we-have-free-will question.

Finally, after briefly taking stock in section 2.6, I will say a few words in section 2.7 about how we might answer the what-is-free-will question, the compatibilism question, and the moral responsibility question. Of course, we will have found by then that these three questions are not relevant to the metaphysics of human free will. But again, I think they are interesting and important questions in their own right, and so I want to say a few words about how we might answer them.

2.2 What Determines Whether an Answer to the What-Is-Free-Will Question Is Correct?

Before I construct my main argument (in sections 2.3–2.5), I need to discuss an important question: What determines whether a given answer to the what-is-free-will question is correct? There are numerous views one might adopt here. Here's one very simple view:

The OL View: An answer to the what-is-free-will question is correct iff it captures the ordinary-language meaning(s) of the expression 'free will'—

Compatibilism and Conceptual Analysis

that is, what's picked out by the usage and intentions associated with this expression among ordinary folk. (Of course, it doesn't follow from this that ordinary usage of 'free will' picks out a unique, well-defined concept; proponents of the OL view can allow that there might be vaguenesses, inconsistencies, ambiguities, and so on built into our usage here. But they would say that if the ordinary term 'free will' is indeed vague or ambiguous, then a complete and correct answer to the what-is-free-will question would tell us about this.)

This view is at least initially plausible. One point that counts in its favor is that (a) it makes the what-is-free-will question *factual* (it is undeniable, I think, that there are facts about how ordinary folk use expressions like 'free will', 'can', 'could have done otherwise', and so on); and (b) it's not obvious that any other plausible view does this. A second point that counts in favor of the OL View is that it fits very well with the methodology that philosophers actually use when they try to answer questions like 'What is free will?', 'What is knowledge?', and so on. One of the main things philosophers do here is use ordinary-language intuitions (about the applicability of our concepts in real and imagined scenarios) to confirm and falsify theories; for instance, if a given theory of free will—that is, a given answer to the what-is-free-will question—flies in the face of our intuitions about when the concept of free will does and doesn't apply, this is seen as falsifying evidence. But it seems to me that this methodology would make little sense if we weren't at least partially engaged in trying to uncover ordinary-language meaning. For while it's plausible to suppose that our intuitions reliably track facts about ordinary-language meaning, it's not very plausible to suppose that they reliably track other kinds of facts.

(By the way, I should say that the OL view is neutral on the question of whether, in trying to answer the what-is-free-will question, we should be doing real empirical studies on folk intuitions. According to one traditional view, we don't need to do this, because we are ourselves native speakers of ordinary language, and so we can use our own intuitions. But there is another view that's growing in prominence [see, e.g., Nichols 2006 and Nahmias et. al. 2005] that holds that our answers to questions like the what-is-free-will question should be based on real empirical data about the intuitions of ordinary folk, in particular, nonphilosophers. The OL view is consistent with both of these methodological views, and the issue here will not be relevant to what I will be arguing.[4])

In any event, it seems to me that the OL view is at least initially plausible, and it might even be the right view. But on the other hand, it might not be, for there are other views one might endorse here. For instance, one might maintain that while it is important to uncover the facts about what ordinary folk mean by the term 'free will', this isn't all there is to arriving at a fully acceptable answer to the what-is-free-will question. One might think that other issues need to be considered as well, for example, issues having to do with the coherence of ordinary-language conceptions of freedom, or with the kinds of freedom that are required for moral responsibility, or with the kinds of freedom that are actually at work when human beings have the experience of acting and choosing freely.

Here's what I'm going to do: In section 2.3, I will assume that the OL view is correct, and based on that assumption, I will argue that the what-is-free-will question is essentially irrelevant to the do-we-have-free-will question. Then in section 2.4, I will argue that even if we drop the assumption that the OL view is correct, we still get the same conclusion about the metaphysical irrelevance of the what-is-free-will question. Indeed, I will argue that we get this result no matter what view we adopt of the correctness conditions of answers to the what-is-free-will question—that is, no matter what we say about what determines whether an answer to the what-is-free-will question is correct.

2.3 Why the What-Is-Free-Will Question Is Irrelevant to the Do-We-Have-Free-Will Question, Assuming the OL View Is Correct

In this section, I will assume that the OL view is correct and argue for the following thesis:

> (iv) While the what-is-free-will question is clearly relevant to the do-we-have-free-will question in a certain way, it is not relevant to that question in any nontrivial or metaphysically interesting way; indeed, the what-is-free-will question is essentially irrelevant to *all* substantive questions about the nature of human decision-making processes.

Before giving my argument, I want to say what I mean by 'metaphysically interesting'. In the present context, I'm using 'metaphysical' to mean something like *about the world*; thus, since the topic here is human decision-making processes and human freedom, 'metaphysical' is being used to mean something like *about human beings or human decision-making processes*. Thus, if I say that a question is not relevant to the do-we-have-free-will question in any metaphysically interesting way, what I mean is essentially that it's not relevant to that question in a way that's substantively relevant to the goal of discovering the nature of human beings and, in particular, human decision-making processes. And note that I'm not claiming here that this is what anyone else means by 'metaphysically interesting'. I'm just specifying what *I* mean. Thus, if someone were to respond that, on their view, conceptual analysis is a *part* of metaphysics and, hence, that it's obviously metaphysically interesting, my response would be to give them the expression 'metaphysically interesting'. I would just rephrase my thesis in terms of relevance to the goal of discovering the nature of human beings and human decision-making processes.

I want to begin my argument for (iv) by saying why someone might want to reject it. Thus, consider the following counterargument or objection to (iv):

> Until we determine what free will *is*, we can't determine whether humans have free will because we won't even know what we're talking about, or looking for. Thus, the what-is-free-will question is obviously relevant to the do-we-have-free-will question, and moreover, philosophers who are engaged in trying to answer the what-is-free-will question are *doing metaphysics* because they're doing something that's centrally important to the task of answering the do-we-have-free-will question, which is clearly a metaphysical question about the nature of human beings.

I think the central claims in this objection are essentially right; but I also think they overlook an important point, and it's for this reason that thesis (iv) contains a proviso about metaphysical interestingness. What I want to argue here is that when we take this proviso seriously, we see that thesis (iv) is importantly correct. Or more precisely, I want to argue this point on the assumption that the OL view is correct—that is, on the assumption that an answer to the what-is-free-will question is correct if and only if it captures the ordinary-language meaning(s) of 'free will'.

Let me begin here by changing the example and showing how awkward the line of thought in the above objection would be if we employed it in other settings. To this end, suppose that Carstairs and Caruthers are linguists (or sociologists or psychologists or whatever) who specialize in trying to figure out the ordinary-discourse meanings of scientific terms, as they're actually used by working scientists (and perhaps ordinary folk); and suppose in particular that Carstairs and Caruthers have competing theories of the ordinary-discourse meaning of the word 'planet'. Finally, suppose that the dispute between Carstairs and Caruthers has implications for the truth values of various astronomical sentences. For instance, suppose that astronomers have discovered an object, call it Wilma, that's orbiting the sun beyond Pluto and that counts as a planet if Carstairs's theory of the meaning of 'planet' is right but doesn't count as a planet if

Caruthers's theory is right, so that the truth value of the sentence 'There is a tenth planet in our solar system' depends on whether Carstairs or Caruthers is right (of course, if you don't think Pluto counts as a planet, then the question would be whether there's a *ninth* planet in the solar system, but let's ignore this complication). Now, if we take the style of thinking inherent in the above objection and apply it in the present case, we seem to obtain the result that when Carstairs and Caruthers are debating what the ordinary meaning of 'planet' is, they're doing *astronomy*. But, of course, they're not doing astronomy; they're doing empirical semantics. Their investigation isn't relevant in any nontrivial way to an inquiry into the nature of the solar system. If astronomers know that Wilma is there, and if they know how big Wilma is, and what it's made of, and what its orbital path is like, and so on and so forth, then their work is done. It would be a bizarre, misleading representation of the situation to claim that Carstairs and Caruthers were disputing an open astronomical question—that is, a question about the nature of the solar system—and that they were trying to settle this question by studying the ordinary usage of astronomers.

Similar remarks, it seems, can be made about free will. Philosophers involved in trying to answer the what-is-free-will question are not engaged in a genuine inquiry into the nature of human-decision making processes, and indeed, their investigations are not relevant to such inquiries in any nontrivial way. Like Carstairs and Caruthers, what these philosophers are doing is empirical semantics; they're engaged in an investigation of ordinary-language usage and intentions.

Let's change the example now. Let's suppose it's an open astronomical question whether Wilma exists. For instance, we can suppose that some astronomer has discovered some perturbations in Pluto's orbital path and hypothesized Wilma's existence to explain these perturbations but that, as of yet, no one has actually found Wilma. And let's suppose that a dispute has arisen over this issue and that people characterize this dispute by saying that there's a controversy among astronomers over the following:

> *The tenth-planet question*: Is there a tenth planet in our solar system (or a ninth planet, if you think that Pluto isn't a planet)?

Now suppose that Caruthers announces that he has discovered the answer to the tenth-planet question; he argues that Wilma may or may not exist—he has no idea about this—but that it doesn't matter because even if Wilma does exist, it is not a planet, and so the answer to the tenth-planet question is 'No'. And, finally, suppose that Carstairs argues that Caruthers is mistaken; he says that if Wilma exists then it *is* a planet, and so, he says, we have to determine whether Wilma exists in order to answer the tenth-planet question. Now, what I want to ask is this: Is the Carstairs-Caruthers debate relevant to the tenth-planet question? Well, there is obviously a sort of relevance here because Caruthers's semantic thesis (together with various theses about the solar system that we're assuming are endorsed by all the parties to the dispute) entails that the answer to the tenth-planet question is 'No'. But from an *astronomical* point of view—that is, from the point of view of the goal of discovering the nature of the solar system—this is clearly a trivial sort of relevance. When we ask the tenth-planet question, we are presumably trying to learn something about the nature of the solar system; but the Carstairs-Caruthers debate is relevant to that goal in at most a trivial way, for how the word 'planet' happens to be used in ordinary discourse doesn't tell us anything important or nontrivial about the nature of the solar system. Therefore, it seems fair to say that while the Carstairs-Caruthers debate is obviously relevant to the tenth-planet question in a certain sort of way, it is not relevant to that question—or indeed to any question about the nature of the solar system—in any nontrivial or astronomically interesting way. (This, of course, is not to say that the Carstairs-Caruthers debate is itself trivial or uninteresting; it's just to say that it's not an astronomical debate, i.e., a debate about the nature of the solar system, except in a trivial way.)

Likewise, if we ask whether the what-is-free-will question is relevant to the do-we-have-free-will question, we can say that there is obviously a sort of relevance here, because, for instance, Hume's answer to the what-is-free-will question (together with other theses that just about all of us accept) entails that the answer to the do-we-have-free-will question is 'Yes'. But from a metaphysical point of view—that is, the point of view of the goal of discovering the nature of human decision-making processes—this is clearly a trivial sort of relevance. When we ask the do-we-have-free-will question, we are presumably trying to learn something about the nature of human decision-making processes; but the what-is-free-will question is relevant to that goal in at most a trivial way, for how the expression 'free will' happens to be used in ordinary discourse doesn't tell us anything important or nontrivial about the nature of human decision-making processes. Therefore, once again, it seems fair to say that while the what-is-free-will question is obviously relevant to the do-we-have-free-will question in a certain way, it is not relevant to that question—or indeed to any question about the nature of human decision making—in any nontrivial way. And again, the point here is not that the what-is-free-will question is itself trivial or uninteresting. The point is that it is not a question about human beings, or human decision making, except in a trivial way. It is rather about the semantics of a certain expression.

There's another parallel between the planet case and the free will case that's worth commenting on. If what I'm arguing is correct, then the metaphysically interesting issue behind the do-we-have-free-will question is captured by the which-kinds-of-freedom-do-we-have question, which is entirely independent of the what-is-free-will question (indeed, this question was purposely formulated in a way that would make it independent of the ordinary-language meaning of 'free will'). If we could fully answer the which-kinds-of-freedom-do-we-have question, then we would have all the relevant facts about the nature of human decision-making processes that we might need in order to answer the do-we-have-free-will question; we still might not know the answer to the do-we-have-free-will question, but that would just be a function of our not knowing the ordinary-language meaning of the term 'free will'; it would not signify any substantive ignorance about the nature of human beings. Likewise, it seems that the astronomically interesting issue behind the tenth-planet question is captured by a question that's entirely independent of the Carstairs-Caruthers debate, namely, the question 'Is there any such thing as Wilma?' If we could answer this question, we would know all the relevant facts about the nature of the solar system; we still might not know the answer to the tenth-planet question, but that would just be a function of our not knowing what 'planet' means; it would not signify any substantive ignorance about the nature of the solar system.[5]

The point here can be generalized. Whenever you're trying to discover something about the nature of the world, you can always proceed straight to the point at hand, without having to determine the meaning of some folk expression, by simply introducing some theoretical terms and defining them by stipulation. Thus, for example, if you just want to know what the solar system is like, you can forget about folk terms like 'planet' and introduce some new terms with clearly defined meanings. And if you just want to know what human decision-making processes are like, you can simply use terms of art like 'Humean freedom' and 'L-freedom' and so on and proceed straight to the point at hand, trying to determine which of the various kinds of freedom (or "freedom") human beings actually possess without first determining the ordinary-language meaning of the folk term 'free will'. And if you're in a situation where you already know all the relevant metaphysical facts but don't know what some folk term means, then you can describe the metaphysical facts using technical terms with stipulated definitions, and so your lack of knowledge of the meaning of

Compatibilism and Conceptual Analysis   35

the folk term shouldn't be treated as a genuine ignorance of (nonsemantic) metaphysical facts. (Another way to appreciate the generality of the issue here is to note that behind *every* question about the nature of the world, there are semantic questions about the meanings of the words in the given about-the-world question, and these semantic questions are, in some sense, logically prior to the question about the nature of the world; but insofar as one is interested in discovering the nature of the *world* when one is asking the about-the-world question, and not in discovering the meanings of the words in that question, there is no need to trouble oneself with the semantic questions before addressing the issue about the nature of the world.)

Before going on, I want to draw a distinction between two different aspects of conceptual analysis and acknowledge that one of them is in fact relevant to metaphysical questions about human beings (but in a way that doesn't undermine my position here). The distinction I have in mind is between (a) the *articulation* of concepts, or conceptual analyses, and (b) arguments for and against the *correctness* of the various analyses that have been offered. The former is definitely relevant to metaphysical questions about the nature of human decision-making processes: Every time someone comes up with a new analysis of free will, it generates a new subquestion of the which-kinds-of-freedom-do-we-have question, and so this can lead to the discovery of new and interesting facts about humans. What I'm claiming is *not* relevant (in any nontrivial way) to metaphysical questions about human beings is the question of which of the many analyses of free will that people have articulated are *correct*. And this, of course, is just what the what-is-free-will question asks.

2.4 Why the What-Is-Free-Will Question Is Irrelevant to the Do-We-Have-Free-Will Question, Even if the OL View *Isn't* Correct

I just argued that the what-is-free-will question is essentially irrelevant to the do-we-have-free-will question. In arguing this point, I assumed the OL view; that is, I assumed that an answer to the what-is-free-will question is correct if and only if it captures the ordinary-language meaning(s) of 'free will'. I now want to argue that even if we reject the OL view, we still get the result that the what-is-free-will question is essentially irrelevant to the do-we-have-free-will question.

If the OL view is wrong, then we can't answer the what-is-free-will question by looking only at facts about ordinary-language meaning; we need to look at other kinds of facts as well (or instead, as the case may be). Indeed, one might think that in order to adequately answer the what-is-free-will question, we need to take a variety of different issues into account. One way to motivate this stance would be to endorse something like the following view:

> *The Hybrid View*: It's true that *part* of what we're doing in trying to answer the what-is-free-will question is trying to figure out what ordinary folk mean by 'free will'. But that's not all we're doing. We're also trying to improve upon folk usage, or supplement it, or some such thing. In doing this, we might need to consider a number of different issues. For instance, we might want to eliminate some incoherence or imprecision from the ordinary folk notion of free will. Or, second, we might want to take into account the issue of what's *worth wanting*; in other words, in order to determine what free will is, we might need to figure out which kinds of freedom are *valuable*; in particular, we might need to figure out which kinds of freedom are required for moral responsibility, or autonomy, or dignity, or other things we might value. Or, third, we might want to take into account the kinds of freedom that humans actually have; for one might think that what free will *is* is at least partially determined by the kinds of freedom that are actually at work when people have the experience of acting and choosing freely.

Regardless of whether the Hybrid view, as its stated here, is the best alternative to the OL view, it seems that the sorts of considerations mentioned in the Hybrid view—most notably, those having to do with coherence, moral responsibility, and the nature of actual human freedom—are the most plausible candidates for what might be relevant to the what-is-free-will question, if that question isn't simply about ordinary-language meaning. Thus, it seems to me that if we reject the OL view, we're going to wind up saying that questions like the following are relevant to the what-is-free-will question:

> *The which-kinds-of-freedom-do-we-have question* (see section 2.1 for a formulation).
>
> *The coherence question*: Which kinds of freedom (or "freedom") are coherent, or conceptually possible?
>
> *The moral responsibility question*: Which kinds of freedom (or "freedom") are required for moral responsibility?

Now, I think there are potential problems with the view that questions like these are relevant to the what-is-free-will question—for instance, one might argue that the OL view is the best view after all—but I don't want to pursue this issue here. Instead, I want to argue that even if we assume that questions like these *are* relevant to the what-is-free-will question, we still get the result that the what-is-free-will question is essentially irrelevant to the do-we-have-free-will question (and, indeed, to other questions about the nature of human decision-making processes). I will argue this point in connection with the three questions listed above in sections 2.4.1–2.4.3. Then in section 2.4.4, I will construct a more general argument, one that motivates the idea that no matter what we say about the kinds of facts and questions that might be relevant to the what-is-free-will question, we still get the result that that question is essentially irrelevant to the do-we-have-free-will question.

2.4.1 The Which-Kinds-of-Freedom-Do-We-Have Question

There are a few reasons one might give for thinking that the which-kinds-of-freedom-do-we-have question is relevant to the what-is-free-will question. For instance, one might think that our predicates should be interpreted in ways that enable them to "carve nature at its joints," and given this, one might argue that we ought to take 'free will' to refer to a kind of freedom that humans actually have—that is, a kind that's actually present when people have the experience of acting and choosing freely. Or alternatively, one might argue that 'free choice' is a kind term, or a paradigm-case term, and one might infer from this that 'free will' refers to the kind of freedom that's inherent in ordinary human choices, whatever that turns out to be. I have serious doubts about both of these views, and more generally, I have doubts about the claim that the which-kinds-of-freedom-do-we-have question is relevant to the what-is-free-will question. But again, I don't want to pursue this here.[6] Instead, I want to argue that even if the which-kinds-of-freedom-do-we-have question *is* relevant to the what-is-free-will question, this doesn't undermine my claim that the what-is-free-will question is essentially irrelevant to the do-we-have-free-will question. The argument for this, as we'll presently see, is very simple.

The view I've been advancing here is that (a) the do-we-have-free-will question decomposes into the which-kinds-of-freedom-do-we-have question and the what-is-free-will question, and (b) the which-kinds-of-freedom-do-we-have question contains everything that's metaphysically interesting here, so that the what-is-free-will question doesn't add anything of metaphysical interest. Now, if it turns out that the which-kinds-of-freedom-do-we-have question is relevant to the what-is-free-will question, then the latter question is obviously a metaphysically interesting question. But it's not metaphysically interesting in any *new* way. For the metaphysically interesting facts that would be relevant to the what-is-free-will question in this scenario are the very same facts that are relevant to the which-kinds-of-freedom-do-we-have question, and so they're the same facts that are *already* relevant to the do-we-have-free-will question.

In short, the point is this: Even if we assume that the which-kinds-of-freedom-do-we-have question is relevant to the what-is-free-will question, we still get the result that if we could answer the which-kinds-of-freedom-do-we-have question, we would have all the relevant metaphysically interesting information we would need in order to answer the do-we-have-free-will question—and so we still get the result that the what-is-free-will question adds nothing here that's metaphysically interesting. In other words, we still get the result that if we could already answer the which-kinds-of-freedom-do-we-have question, then by moving on and answering the what-is-free-will question, we would not be learning anything new about the nature of human beings or human decision-making processes. And so our situation here isn't changed at all by assuming that the which-kinds-of-freedom-do-we-have question is relevant to the what-is-free-will question.

Another way to put the point here is in terms of direction of relevance: If the which-kinds-of-freedom-do-we-have question were relevant to the what-is-free-will question, this wouldn't give us the result that the what-is-free-will question was relevant to metaphysical questions about human decision making; rather, it would give us the opposite result—that is, that metaphysical questions about human decision making were relevant to the what-is-free-will question. In this scenario, we could independently discover facts about humans that turned out to be relevant to determining what free will *is*; but we could not independently discover what free will is in a way that would make this relevant to figuring out which sorts of freedom human beings actually possess; for in this scenario, in order to figure out what free will is, we would first have to figure out which sorts of freedom humans actually have.

2.4.2 The Coherence Question

A very similar argument can be used in connection with the coherence question. Now, I want to admit that the coherence question is itself a metaphysically relevant question. After all, if a kind of freedom is incoherent, or conceptually impossible, then it follows that humans do not possess that kind of freedom. Thus, the coherence question is directly relevant to the which-kinds-of-freedom-do-we-have question, and so it is a metaphysically relevant question. But the coherence question is not metaphysically relevant in any way that undermines my position here. Recall my thesis: (a) If we could answer the which-kinds-of-freedom-do-we-have question, then we would have all the relevant metaphysically interesting information we would need in order to answer the do-we-have-free-will question, and (b) by going on and answering the what-is-free-will question, we wouldn't be learning anything that was both new and metaphysically interesting—that is, we wouldn't be learning anything new about the nature of human decision-making processes. But this will be true even if we assume that the coherence question is relevant to the what-is-free-will question. For, in short, the metaphysically relevant features of the coherence question are *already* relevant to the which-kinds-of-freedom-do-we-have question (and, hence, to the do-we-have-free-will question). If we could already answer the which-kinds-of-freedom-do-we-have question, and if some specific kind of freedom *F* were conceptually impossible, or incoherent, then we would *already know* that we didn't possess *F*. Thus, even if we could use this information about *F* in answering the what-is-free-will question—for example, even if we could use it to determine that free will isn't *F*—in doing this, we wouldn't be learning anything new about human beings or human decision making. For, again, we would already know all the relevant metaphysically interesting facts. Thus, again, even if we assume that the coherence question is relevant to the what-is-free-will question, we still get the result that the what-is-free-will question adds nothing of metaphysical interest to the which-kinds-of-freedom-do-we-have question.

2.4.3 The Moral Responsibility Question (and the Issue of What's Worth Wanting)

Once again, I have serious doubts about the thesis that the moral responsibility question is substantively relevant to the what-is-free-will question, but again, I don't want to pursue this here. Instead, I want to argue that even if we assume that the moral responsibility question is relevant to the what-is-free-will question, it doesn't matter (in the present context) because the moral responsibility question is itself essentially irrelevant to metaphysical questions about the nature of human decision-making processes.

One might argue that the moral responsibility question is relevant to metaphysical questions about humans by saying something like this:

> Suppose we knew which kinds of freedom (or "freedom") humans possessed but didn't know which of them were required for moral responsibility. Then we wouldn't know whether humans were morally responsible for their actions, and so by answering the moral responsibility question,

we could discover a fact *about humans*—namely, whether they were morally responsible for their actions.

I have two responses to this argument. The first is this: Even if the moral responsibility question is relevant to a question about humans (namely, the question of whether humans are morally responsible for their actions), in the present context, this isn't the right kind of metaphysical relevance. In order to undermine my position, we would need the result that the moral responsibility question is relevant to questions about the nature of human decision-making processes, and it's hard to believe that this is true. If the moral responsibility question is relevant to the what-is-free-will question, then we might get the result that the what-is-free-will question is relevant to questions about the moral status of humans. But we don't get the result that it's relevant to questions about the metaphysical nature of human decision-making processes; for, again, by answering the moral responsibility question and, hence, the what-is-free-will question, we wouldn't be learning anything new about the nature of our decision-making processes, in particular, about the kinds of freedom (or "freedom") that we actually have.

The second response to the above argument is that, perhaps surprisingly, the moral responsibility question is in fact not relevant (in any metaphysically interesting way) to the question of whether human beings are morally responsible for their actions. To argue this point, let me assume, for the sake of simplifying things, that (a) aside from the issue of the kinds of freedom that are required for moral responsibility, we know roughly what moral responsibility is, and (b) we also know that humans do satisfy all the requirements for moral responsibility except possibly for the freedom requirement. (Of course, we don't really know these things, but I won't be begging any questions by assuming them here. Indeed, it's easy to see that if humans fail to satisfy some other requirement for moral responsibility—i.e., some non-freedom requirement—then the above objection to my view completely falls apart because we would already know, independently of the free will issue, that humans aren't responsible for their actions.) In any event, given these assumptions, let's suppose that we already knew the answer to the which-kinds-of-freedom-do-we-have question but didn't know the answer to the moral responsibility question, and hence, didn't know whether we had free will or moral responsibility, because we didn't know what free will or moral responsibility were. Then we could define a series of kinds of moral responsibility (or "moral responsibility," as the case may be) corresponding to the different kinds of freedom (or "freedom"). For instance, if we had named the various kinds of freedom F_1, F_2, and so on, then R_1 would be a kind of moral responsibility that required F_1 (and no other kind of freedom); R_2 would be a kind of moral responsibility that required F_2 (and no other kind of freedom); $R_{7,12}$ would be a kind of moral responsibility that required F_7 and F_{12} (and no other kind of freedom); and so on. It follows from everything we're assuming here that in this scenario, we would already know which of these kinds of responsibility we possessed and which we didn't. We might not know the truth value of the sentence 'Humans are morally responsible for their actions,' but that wouldn't be a function of any lack of knowledge *about humans*. It would simply be because we didn't know what moral responsibility *was*, or what 'moral responsibility' meant, or some such thing. Thus, it seems to me that the moral responsibility question isn't relevant, in any metaphysically interesting way, to the question of whether humans are morally responsible for their actions—or, indeed, to any question about humans.

To give a concrete example here, my claim is this: Suppose that (a) we already knew that humans were Hume-responsible but not libertarian-responsible, but (b) we didn't know whether moral responsibility was Hume-responsibility or libertarian-responsibility (although we can assume that we had figured out that it was one of the two and not some third kind of responsibility); then we wouldn't be lacking any knowledge here about humans, in any interesting sense; we would simply be lacking knowledge of what moral responsibility is.

What sort of knowledge is this that we would be lacking? Well, one view is that it's essentially just knowledge of ordinary-language meaning. On this view, to say that moral responsibility is, for example, libertarian-responsibility is to make a claim about the ordinary concept of moral responsibility—that is, about the way that ordinary folk use the term 'moral responsibility'. If this view is right, then for all the reasons given in section 2.3, the moral responsibility question is not relevant in any metaphysically interesting way to any questions about humans.

What other sort of question might the moral responsibility question be, if not a question about ordinary-language meaning? Well, the only other plausible view, I think, is that it's partially about capturing ordinary-language meaning and partially about improving on ordinary-language meaning. One way to improve on ordinary meaning would be to eliminate incoherences, but I could presumably take the same line here that I took on this issue in section 2.4.2. Another way to improve on the ordinary usage of 'moral responsibility' would be to figure out which of the various kinds of moral responsibility are *fair* (where a kind of responsibility is fair iff it would be fair to hold someone morally responsible because he or she had that kind of responsibility). But it's hard to believe that we could make any progress here by appealing to the notion of fairness because, presumably, each kind of responsibility brings with it its own kind of fairness. For instance, if humans were Hume-responsible for their actions but not libertarian-responsible, then, presumably, it would be Hume-fair but not libertarian-fair to hold them responsible for their actions. Now, of course, one might argue that in order to answer the moral responsibility question, we would need to determine which of the various kinds of responsibility are *really fair*; but by doing this, we wouldn't be learning anything new *about humans*; we would rather be learning which of the various kinds of fairness (or "fairness," as the case may be) count as *real* kinds of fairness. That is, we would be learning what fairness is, or what 'fair' means. Thus, we still wouldn't get the result here that the moral responsibility question is relevant, in a metaphysically interesting way, to questions about the nature of human beings.

(And once again, this is not to say that the moral responsibility question is unimportant, or not worth caring about. We may have very good reasons for caring deeply about this question, as well as the question of what moral responsibility is. But this doesn't alter the fact that these questions are essentially irrelevant to questions about the nature of human decision-making processes.)

Before moving on, I want to consider an objection that one might raise against the argument of the present subsection. One might object here by taking the old Kant-inspired argument for free will—that is, the argument that we have free will, because we're morally responsible for our actions and this requires free will—and using it to argue that the moral responsibility question is in fact relevant to the which-kinds-of-freedom-do-we-have question. One might put the argument like this:

(1) Human beings are morally responsible for their actions. Therefore,

(2) Human beings possess moral-responsibility freedom, whatever that turns out to be. Therefore,

(3) By answering the moral responsibility question, we would uncover a fact that was clearly relevant to the which-kinds-of-freedom-do-we-have question and, hence, to the do-we-have-free-will question—namely, that humans possess the kind(s) of freedom that we found to be required for moral responsibility. For instance, if we found that L-freedom was required for moral responsibility, we would thereby have shown that human beings are L-free.[7]

This reasoning is pretty hard to swallow. If this argument were cogent, then from the theses that (i) humans are morally responsible for their actions and (ii) moral responsibility requires L-freedom and hence indeterminism, we could infer that (iii) indeterminism is true. But indeterminism is a substantive empirical thesis about the workings of the physical world; it just doesn't seem that it can be cogently motivated by premises like (i) and (ii). Now, of course, there's nothing wrong with the *form* of the argument in (i)–(iii); the form is just 'P; P requires Q; therefore, Q', and this is of course a valid argument form. The problem is that we've got no good reason to think that (i) and (ii) are both true. It seems to me that we are far more certain that, at present, we don't have any good reason to believe indeterminism (and that a good argument for indeterminism would have to be more centrally about the actual causal behavior of physical particles) than we are of either (i) or (ii). Now, having said this, I should also say that I don't think that either (i) or (ii), taken in isolation, is particularly implausible. But it seems to me that, given our current epistemic situation, it would be wrongheaded for us to endorse both (i) *and* (ii). For it seems to me that if (ii) is true (i.e., if moral responsibility requires L-freedom), then we do not currently have any good reason to believe that (i) is true (i.e., that we humans are morally responsible for our actions), because we don't have any good reason to believe that we are L-free, because we don't even know whether indeterminism is true. (This response to the above objection is a bit quick, but I will argue for my stance here in much more detail in chapter 4, section 4.3.)

(By the way, I don't mean to suggest here that I think we really *don't* have good reasons to believe that we're morally responsible for our actions; on the contrary, I think it might very well be that we do have good reasons for this. But it seems to me that if we do have such reasons, then (ii) is false, i.e., moral responsibility doesn't require L-freedom [and, again, I will argue for this stance in section 4.3]. Finally, it's also worth noting that there might not even be a fact of the matter as to whether (ii) is true or false—i.e., whether moral responsibility requires L-freedom. I don't need this point here, but I think it's at least somewhat plausible. I will return to this issue, very briefly, at the end of the present chapter, in section 2.7.)

The last point I want to make in this section is that what I've said here about the moral responsibility question can be generalized and said about the issue of what's worth wanting. To appreciate this, consider the following question:

> *The worth-wanting question*: Which kinds of freedom (or "freedom") are worth wanting? (This question presumably subsumes the moral responsi-

bility question, but it is more general, because there may be other things, aside from moral responsibility, e.g., autonomy or dignity, that are worth wanting and that require various kinds of freedom [or "freedom"].)

I think this question is important for a variety of reasons, but it is not relevant in any substantive way to metaphysical questions about the nature of human beings, and this point can be argued in the exact same way that I argued the analogous point about the moral responsibility question. There's the job of figuring out which kinds of freedom are worth wanting, and there's the job of figuring out which kinds of freedom we've got, and the former is not relevant to the latter.[8]

2.4.4 Generalizing the Argument

I now want to construct a general argument for thinking that no matter what we say about the kinds of facts that might be relevant to the what-is-free-will question—that is, the kinds of facts that might determine which answer to the what-is-free-will question is correct—we still get the result that the what-is-free-will question is essentially irrelevant to the do-we-have-free-will question (and, indeed, to all questions about the nature of human decision-making processes). There are two sorts of facts that one might think relevant to the what-is-free-will question, namely, (i) facts that are relevant to the which-kinds-of-freedom-do-we-have question, and (ii) facts that aren't relevant to that question, for example, facts about ordinary-language meaning. But as we saw in section 2.4.1, type-(i) facts aren't relevant in any *new* way to the do-we-have-free-will question, because we already have to answer the which-kinds-of-freedom-do-we-have question in order to answer the do-we-have-free-will question. And, second, it's hard to see how type-(ii) facts could be relevant, in any metaphysically interesting way, to the do-we-have-free-will question. For the which-kinds-of-freedom-do-we-have question seems to capture *all* the metaphysically interesting facts that might be relevant to the do-we-have-free-will question. In other words, once the which-kinds-of-freedom-do-we-have question has been answered, there are simply no facts left to discover that are both relevant to the do-we-have-free-will question and metaphysically interesting in the sense of being about the nature of human beings. Thus, the conclusion I want to draw is that no matter what we say about the kinds of facts that might be relevant to the what-is-free-will question, that question is not relevant in any metaphysically interesting way to the do-we-have-free-will question. The only really metaphysically important question here is the which-kinds-of-freedom-do-we-have question.

Finally, it's worth noting that the point I have argued here—that the what-is-free-will question is essentially irrelevant to the do-we-have-free-will question—is a special case of a more general point, namely, that conceptual analysis is essentially irrelevant to metaphysics. I will not argue this point here, but the main idea should be clear by now: We cannot make any nontrivial progress toward discovering the nature of the world (or at any rate, the nonsemantic part of the world) by analyzing a concept, that is, by figuring out what some word means or should mean. Now, of course, if we already knew what some part of the world was like but didn't know what some folk term meant, then a conceptual analysis could tell us that certain about-the-world sentences were true; but in this case, we wouldn't really be learning anything nontrivial about the nature of the (nonsemantic part of the) world.

And to repeat a point I've made several times now, this doesn't mean that conceptual analysis is unimportant. My only claim is that it's not relevant in any substantive way to metaphysical inquiries into the nature of the (nonsemantic part of the) world.

2.5 Why the Compatibilism Question Reduces to the What-Is-Free-Will Question

I have now argued that the what-is-free-will question is irrelevant to the do-we-have-free-will question in all but a trivial way. But I also want to argue that the compatibilism question is irrelevant to the do-we-have-free-will question. To establish this, I will argue in the present section that the compatibilism question reduces to the what-is-free-will question.

The argument for this is very simple. The first point to note is this: Just as we found that the do-we-have-free-will question reduces to, or is subsumed by, the what-is-free-will question and the which-kinds-of-freedom-do-we-have question, so too it seems that the compatibilism question reduces to, or is subsumed by, the what-is-free-will question and what might be called the *which-kinds-of-freedom-are-compatible-with-determinism question*. The second point to be made here is this: Prima facie, it seems that all of the subquestions of the which-kinds-of-freedom-are-compatible-with-determinism question—for example, 'Is Humean freedom compatible with determinism?', 'Is L-freedom compatible with determinism?', and so on—are trivial and obvious. In other words, it seems that all of the analyses of free will in the literature are either obviously compatible with determinism or obviously incompatible with it.

For instance, L-freedom is obviously incompatible with determinism because it is by definition indeterministic. And Humean freedom is obviously compatible with determinism because it's essentially just the ability to act and choose in accordance with your desires, and it could be that our desires are causally determined by prior events and that these desires determine our decisions, which in turn determine our actions (see section 1.1.2 for a bit more detail on why Humean freedom is compatible with determinism). And Frankfurtian freedom is obviously compatible with determinism because it's just the ability to control, with second-order attitudes, which of your first-order desires will affect your behavior, and it could be that we are causally determined to have (and act on) second-order desires of this sort. Now, of course, these aren't the only analyses of the notion of free will in the literature; there are no other significant incompatibilist analyses, aside from the libertarian analysis, but in recent years, a number of different compatibilist analyses of free will (and/or moral responsibility) have been put forward (see, e.g., the proposals of P. F. Strawson [1962], Watson [1975], Dworkin [1988], Wolf [1990], Double [1991], Fischer [1994], Fischer and Ravizza [1998], Wallace [1994], Mele [1995], and Bok [1998]). But all of these analyses—or at any rate, all of them that I'm aware of—are obviously compatible with determinism. Indeed, in each case, this point is just as obvious as it is in connection with Humean freedom and Frankfurtian freedom.

In sum, then, there don't seem to be any mainstream analyses of free will that generate substantive, nonobvious compatibility questions. Thus, prima facie, we seem to have some reason to endorse the following thesis:

> (No Controversial Subcompatibility Questions): There are no controversial or nontrivial subquestions of the which-kinds-of-freedom-are-compatible-with-determinism question.

In a moment, I will consider a few objections that one might raise against this thesis, but before I do this, let me note that if this thesis is indeed true, then it follows that the only controversial part of the compatibilism question is the what-is-free-will question—which is just to say that the compatibilism question reduces to the what-is-free-will question.

I will now consider three objections to (No Controversial Subcompatibility Questions). In each case, we will find either that the objection does not go through or that it does go through—that is, it does give us a reason to doubt (No Controversial Subcompatibility Questions)—but it does not undermine my overall stance here. The first objection can be put like this:

Compatibilism and Conceptual Analysis

Objection 1: There seem to be a number of rather obvious analyses of free will that generate nontrivial compatibility questions. Consider, for instance, the view that free will is the ability to do otherwise. This view generates the following compatibility question: 'Is the ability to do otherwise compatible with determinism?' But this question is clearly controversial and nontrivial, and so (No Controversial Subcompatibility Questions) is simply not true.

I agree that this compatibility question is controversial and nontrivial; but this is only because the analysis of free will that it's based on—that free will is the ability to do otherwise—is so thin and underdeveloped. In particular, we aren't told here what the ability to do otherwise *is*. Thus, the compatibilism question remains unsettled by the claim that free will is the ability to do otherwise for the simple reason that we still have some conceptual analysis to do, in particular, because we still need to figure out what the ability to do otherwise is. Now, the question of what the ability to do otherwise is is obviously a controversial question. But, of course, it's not a compatibility question; it's a conceptual-analysis question, and indeed, on the view that free will is the ability to do otherwise, it's part of the what-is-free-will question.

Thus, even if objection 1 provides a counterexample to (No Controversial Subcompatibility Questions), it doesn't provide a good objection to my overall stance here because it doesn't undermine my claim that the compatibilism question reduces to the what-is-free-will question. In order to do that, objection 1 would need to be combined with the thesis that there are some (at least initially plausible) analyses of the ability to do otherwise that generate nonobvious compatibility questions. But as far as I know, there are no such analyses in the literature. We've got some compatibilist analyses of the ability to do otherwise, and we've got some incompatibilist analyses of that ability, and the controversial issue isn't whether the various analyses here are compatible or incompatible with determinism; it's whether they're *correct*, that is, whether they adequately capture the notion of ability to do otherwise.

So the appeal to the view that free will is the ability to do otherwise doesn't seem to generate a good objection to my claim that the compatibilism question reduces to the what-is-free-will question. Instead, it just moves everything back a step. For given this analysis—that is, given that free will is the ability to do otherwise—the compatibilism question seems to turn on the question of what the ability to do otherwise is, and again, according to the view that free will is the ability to do otherwise, this question is a *part* of the what-is-free-will question.

The second objection to (No Controversial Subcompatibility Questions) can be put in the following way:

Objection 2: Whatever we say about the analyses of free will that philosophers have come up with so far—or to piggyback on objection 1, about the analyses that philosophers have come up with for related notions like the ability to do otherwise—it seems that in the future someone could come up with a new kind of freedom that (a) was precisely defined, but (b) still generated a pure compatibility question that was nontrivial and controversial. This would presumably be a purely logical question; it would be of the form 'Is the concept of X-freedom compatible with determinism?'

I think this is right, but it doesn't undermine my stance here, because we can just relativize my conclusion to the current state of the debate. In other words, all I want to claim here is that as of right now—relative to the current state of the debate—the compatibilism question reduces to the what-is-free-will question and, hence, isn't relevant in any metaphysically interesting way to substantive questions about the nature of human decision-making processes. It may be that in the future someone will come up with a nontrivial question about the compatibility of determinism and some precisely defined and hitherto-unthought-of kind of freedom (or "freedom"); but this is simply not relevant to the point I'm making here.

The third and final objection to (No Controversial Subcompatibility Questions) can be put like this:

Objection 3: Consider the view that 'free will' is a kind term that denotes human-being freedom, whatever that turns out to be. This analysis generates the following compatibility question: 'Is human-being freedom compatible with determinism?' But this question is clearly nontrivial; we don't know whether human-being freedom is compatible with determinism, because we don't know whether it involves L-freedom.

There are three problems with this objection. First, the above kind-term analysis of 'free will' is in fact implausible. I said a few words to motivate this point in note 6 of the present chapter; I won't say any more about it here.

Second, objection 3 confuses concept and reference. If 'free will' is a kind term that denotes human-being freedom, whatever that turns out to be, then the concept of free will (as opposed to the reference of 'free will') is clearly compatible with determinism. We can appreciate this point by noticing that we would make analogous claims about other kind terms, for instance, 'water'. The standard analysis of 'water' is that it's a kind term that denotes the stuff in our lakes and pipes and so on, whatever that stuff turns out to be; moreover, it's part of the standard view that 'water' is rigid, so that the sentence 'Water is H_2O' is metaphysically necessary (assuming it's true). But, of course, 'Water is H_2O' is not conceptually necessary, or analytic, and so the thesis that the stuff in our lakes and pipes and so on is water is conceptually compatible with the thesis that it's not H_2O. (We can put the point this way: There is a possible world in which (i) we believe for many years that 'water' denotes H_2O, and then (ii) we discover that it doesn't denote H_2O. If this happened in the actual world, it would be a discovery that water isn't H_2O; but if water is H_2O in the actual world, then it's H_2O in all worlds in which it exists, and the world described here is not a world in which water isn't H_2O; it is rather a world in which 'water' doesn't denote water. Thus, while 'Water is H_2O' is metaphysically necessary, it is not conceptually necessary.) Likewise, if we use 'free will' as a kind term to denote human-being freedom, whatever that turns out to be, then even if it turned out that 'free will' denoted an indeterministic sort of freedom (e.g., L-freedom), the sentence 'Free choices are undetermined' would not be conceptually necessary, or analytic, and so the thesis that humans have free will would be conceptually compatible with determinism. We might capture this point by saying that on this analysis of 'free will', the *concept* of free will is compatible with determinism. Or if we wanted to say that kind terms are directly referential and hence don't express concepts at all, then we could say something a bit different. For example, we might say that on this analysis of 'free will', the rules of use that one must know in order to be a competent user of 'free will' are compatible with determinism—or something along these lines.[9]

The third problem with objection 3 is that even if it were correct, in the present context, it wouldn't matter, because it wouldn't undermine my overall position here. According to the objection, we get the following nontrivial subquestion of the which-kinds-of-freedom-are-compatible-with-determinism question:

(Q) Is the existence of human-being freedom (i.e., the existence of the actual *referent* of 'human-being freedom') compatible with determinism?

But (Q) reduces to the libertarian question; for the answer to (Q) turns on whether humans possess an indeterministic kind of freedom, and this would presumably be L-freedom. Thus, if the above objection is correct, then the compatibilism question reduces to the what-is-free-will question and, possibly, the libertarian question. But even if the libertarian question were relevant to the compatibilism question, in the present context, it wouldn't matter, because it wouldn't undermine my overall thesis that the compatibilism question is essentially irrelevant to the do-we-have-free-will question. For the libertarian question is *already* relevant to the do-we-have-free-will question, because it's a straightforward subquestion of the which-kinds-of-freedom-do-we-have question. Thus, in this scenario, the compatibilism question still wouldn't add anything of metaphysical interest to the which-kinds-of-freedom-do-we-have question.

It seems to me, then, that none of the three objections succeeds in undermining my position here. Relative to the current state of the debate, the compatibilism question does seem to boil down to the what-is-free-will question, and even if it didn't—even if the author of objection 3 were right in thinking that there is a slight nonsemantic residue here—this would not undermine my overall conclusion that the compatibilism question adds nothing of metaphysical interest to the which-kinds-of-freedom-do-we-have question.

Before we move on, it is important to note that the point I'm arguing here—that the compatibilism question reduces to the what-is-free-will question—does not constitute an *objection* to any important part of the literature on the compatibilism question. Indeed, it seems to me that when we look closely at this literature, we find that it fits very nicely with my thesis. We can divide the literature on the compatibilism question into four main strands, namely, (i) the literature on the Humean conditional analysis of free will, e.g., the 'if's-and-'can's debate started by Austin;[10] (ii) the literature regarding recent compatibilist attempts to construct an acceptable analysis of the notion of free will;[11] (iii) the literature on the consequence argument for incompatibilism;[12] and (iv) the literature on the Frankfurt-case argument for compatibilism (actually, the Frankfurt-case argument is more often brought up in connection with the issue of the compatibility of determinism and moral responsibility, but all the arguments here can be reproduced in connection with the issue of the compatibility of determinism and free will—though, of course, one might doubt that the corresponding arguments always stand or fall together[13]).[14] I think it can be argued that in all four of these strands, the really controversial issues boil down to semantic questions about the meanings of various terms (not just 'free will' but related expressions like 'can', 'could have done otherwise', and so on). This is more or less obvious in connection with strands (i) and (ii).[15] It is perhaps a bit less obvious in connection with strand (iv), but not much. The issues there center around various thought experiments and intuitions, and this alone suggests that conceptual analysis is what's at issue. The question is not whether some clearly defined concept is compatible with couldn't-have-done-otherwise; rather, it's whether we should interpret the term 'moral responsibility' (or 'free will') as expressing a certain sort of concept—in particular, one that's compatible with couldn't-have-done-otherwise. Finally, the point is probably least obvious in connection with strand (iii), that is, the consequence argument, because on the surface, the issue there doesn't seem to be one of meaning or conceptual analysis. But upon reflection, it becomes clear that this is precisely what's at issue. I cannot argue this point in very much detail, but I'd like to say at least a few words about it.

The main idea here is as follows: (a) Every version of the consequence argument is couched in terms of some crucial expression like 'has a choice about'; and (b) if we interpret these expressions along incompatibilist lines, the argument is clearly sound; but (c) if we interpret them along compatibilist lines, the argument is clearly unsound; so (d) the issue boils down to a question about how these expressions ought to be interpreted.

Let me give an example of this. Let P_0 be a complete description of the world at some time in the distant past, before any humans were born; let L be a conjunction of the laws of nature; let P be a complete description of the world at some moment when someone made an ordinary decision that we would ordinarily think of as free (e.g., for specificity, let's suppose that at the relevant moment, Jay decided to order chocolate ice cream rather than vanilla); and let N be an operator such that '$N(p)$' means something like 'p is true and no one has ever had any choice about it being true' (one might want to give a slightly different reading to this operator, but the differences between the various ways of proceeding won't matter here at all). Given all of this, one very simple way to formulate the consequence argument is as follows:

(1) $N(P_0 \& L)$.

(2) If $N(P_0 \& L)$, and if determinism is true so that $(P_0 \& L)$ entails P, then $N(P)$. Therefore,

(3) If determinism is true, then $N(P)$.

This argument is obviously valid. Moreover, if the conclusion is true, then it would seem that determinism is incompatible with free will; for $N(P)$ seems to entail that Jay didn't have free will in deciding to order chocolate ice cream, and thus, since this is an ordinary case, it seems to follow that if determinism is true, then no human being ever has free will. If this is right, then the only real question here is whether (1) and (2) are true. Now, these two premises might seem immediately obvious, but the problem is that any compatibilist reading of the expressions in N—in particular, 'has a choice about'—will render (1) or (2) false (assuming that determinism is true). Suppose, for instance, that we give a standard Humean conditional analysis to 'has a choice about'; that is, suppose we take '*S had a choice about p being true*' to mean something like *if S had chosen to render p false, then she would have*. Then on the assumption that determinism is true, (2) comes out false: for on the conditional analysis, $N(P_0 \& L)$ is true (no one has ever had any choice about $(P_0 \& L)$ being true, because even if people chose to render that conjunction false, they wouldn't succeed), and N(P) is false (there was a time when someone had a choice about P being true, for if Jay had chosen to order vanilla ice cream, then he would have, and hence, he would have rendered P false).

On the other hand, if we interpret the expressions in N along standard incompatibilist lines, then (1) and (2) will pretty clearly be true. On an incompatibilist reading of 'has a choice about', it seems pretty clear that none of us has ever had any choice about the past or the laws—that is, we're not *able* (on an incompatibilist reading of 'able') to alter the past or the laws. And if a complete formulation of the past and the laws entails that Jay is going to order chocolate ice cream, then clearly (on an incompatibilist reading of 'has a choice about') he has no choice about whether he orders chocolate ice cream.

In sum, then, if we give an incompatibilist reading to the expressions in N, then (1) and (2) will come out true; and if we give a compatibilist reading to these expressions, then one of those premises will come out false. Moreover, analogous points can be made about alternative formulations of the consequence argument—they go through only if we read the relevant expressions along incompatibilist lines. And this should not be surprising. After all, we already *know* that the various compatibilist conceptions of freedom are compatible with determinism. Clearly, no good argument could show that any of those kinds of freedom (or "freedom") are incompatible with determinism. Thus, it seems to me that the real issue here is one of meaning: Since the consequence argument goes through if we read the expressions in operators like N along incompatibilist lines and doesn't go through if we read these expressions along compatibilist lines, it seems that the real question is how we should interpret these expressions—that is, expressions like 'free', 'has a choice about', 'can', 'could have done otherwise', 'able', and so on.

Finally, to return to the point that led me into a discussion of the consequence argument in the first place, it's important to note that my discussion here does not constitute an *objection* to the consequence argument.

One could grant my point that the real issue here is one of meaning and still claim that the consequence argument is cogent; for one could claim that (a) premises like (1) and (2) seem intuitively obvious to us, and (b) this is evidence that incompatibilists are right about the meanings of the relevant expressions in those premises. Indeed, this was essentially van Inwagen's stance in his original formulation of the argument (1975, 58).

2.6 Where We Stand and Where We're Going Next

In chapter 1, we found that in order to solve the problem of free will, we need to answer the following three questions:

The FE-determinism question: Is FE-determinism true?

The do-we-have-free-will question: Do human beings have free will?

The compatibilism question: Is free will compatible with determinism (and hence with FE-determinism)?

But in this chapter, we have found that these three questions reduce to two other questions, namely the following:

The what-is-free-will question: What is free will?

The which-kinds-of-freedom-do-we-have question: Which kinds of freedom (or "freedom") do humans have? That is, do they have L-freedom?; and do they have Humean freedom?; and do they have Frankfurtian freedom?; and so on.

Moreover, we have also found that the first question here has nothing much to do with the second. In other words, we have found that what might be thought of as the *semantic* component of the problem of free will has little substantive bearing on what might be thought of as the *metaphysical* component of the problem.

Now, of course, there is also a *moral* component to the problem of free will, which centers around the following:

The moral responsibility question: Which kinds of freedom (or "freedom") are required for moral responsibility?

But we have found that this question—like the what-is-free-will question and the compatibilism question—is also essentially irrelevant to metaphysical questions about the nature of human decision-making processes, most notably, the do-we-have-free-will question and the which-kinds-of-freedom-do-we-have question.

Therefore, it seems that if one is interested in the metaphysical component of the problem of free will—that is, in discovering the nature of the freedom that's inherent in human decision-making processes—one ought simply to focus on the which-kinds-of-freedom-do-we-have question.

But now notice that most of the subquestions of the which-kinds-of-freedom-do-we-have question are fairly trivial. In particular, it seems more or less obvious that we do possess most of the standard compatibilist kinds of freedom, e.g., Humean freedom, Frankfurtian freedom, and so on. There might be a few kinds of compatibilist freedom that are slightly controversial; for example, kinds of freedom that require reasons responsiveness (see, e.g., Fischer and Ravizza 1998 on this topic) might be somewhat problematic because one might think that the literature on things like situationism and confabulation suggests that we're less reasons responsive than we might have thought. But even if this is true, it seems pretty obvious that lots of our decisions are at least significantly influenced by our reasons. In any event, it seems to me that the *main* controversial subquestion of the which-kinds-of-freedom-do-we-have question is the libertarian question, that is, the question of whether we're L-free. If this is right, then the metaphysical component of the problem of free will boils down largely, though perhaps not entirely, to the libertarian question.

Now, in this book, I am more concerned with metaphysics than with semantics or ethics. Therefore, at the end of this chapter, I am going to leave behind the what-is-free-will question, the compatibilism question, and the moral responsibility question, and I am going to focus on the which-kinds-of-freedom-do-we-have question and, in particular, on the libertarian question. I will not claim that the libertarian question is the only subquestion of the which-kinds-of-freedom-do-we-have question that's at all interesting or controversial; but it seems to me to be the most interesting and controversial, and in any event, it is the question that I will concentrate on in chapters 3 and 4. In particular, I am going to explain what exactly the libertarian question turns on, and I am going to argue that as of right now, we have no good reason for believing either answer to this question—that is, for believing or disbelieving that humans are L-free.

Before I turn to the libertarian question, however, I would like to say just a few words about the what-is-free-will question, the compatibilism question, and the moral responsibility question, as a sort of aside. I will turn to this presently, in section 2.7 of the present chapter. Before I discuss these three questions, though, it is important to note that one of the main consequences of the arguments of the present chapter is that the fundamental questions that we've located here might all have very different kinds of answers. For instance, it may be that (a) in answering the which-kinds-of-freedom-do-we-have question, we find that human beings do possess L-freedom, so that libertarianism (or at any rate, metaphysical libertarianism) is true; but (b) in answering the what-is-free-will question, we find that compatibilism is true because the expression 'free will' is best interpreted as denoting some compatibilist kind of freedom and not L-freedom. There is no inconsistency between the metaphysical libertarianism mentioned in (a) and the semantic compatibilism mentioned in (b). Indeed, there's not even any tension between these two views, and so there is no good reason for thinking that we shouldn't endorse them together.

2.7 An Aside: Some Remarks on the What-Is-Free-Will Question, the Compatibilism Question, and the Moral Responsibility Question

The what-is-free-will question, the compatibilism question, and the moral responsibility question are all interesting enough in their own right to merit a short aside. Thus, even though they won't be relevant to anything else I do in this book, I would like to say a few words about them here. I will discuss the first two of these questions in section 2.7.1, and then I will discuss the moral responsibility question in section 2.7.2.

2.7.1 The What-Is-Free-Will Question and the Compatibilism Question

Since the compatibilism question reduces to the what-is-free-will question, I will speak mainly about the latter, although at the end, I will return briefly to the former. The main point I want to make about the what-is-free-will question is that as of right now, we don't seem to have any good reason for thinking that it has a unique correct answer. One obvious way in which there could fail to be a unique correct answer to the what-is-free-will question—though not the only way—is if it turned out that the ordinary-language expression 'free will' was ambiguous, or contextually sensitive, so that in some contexts it was best interpreted as referring to one kind of freedom (e.g., L-freedom) whereas in other contexts it was best interpreted as referring to other kinds of freedom (e.g., Humean freedom).

But this is not the only way in which the what-is-free-will question could fail to have a unique correct answer. Another way would be if it turned out that (a) the usage and intentions of ordinary folk concerning 'free will' were simply not precise enough to settle the question, and (b) there was no good reason for "improving" ordinary usage in one direction rather than another. It seems to me that the situation I've got in mind in (a) happens all the time. Consider, for instance, the concept of *sameness* and the Ship of Theseus story. According to this story, Theseus has a boat, and over the course of several years, he replaces various parts of the boat, one by one, until eventually, he has replaced *every* part of the boat. Is the boat that he now owns the *same boat* as the one that he used to own? Intuitively, it seems that it is. But now imagine that as Theseus replaces the parts, he dumps the old ones on the beach and that after he has replaced them all, Ralpheus picks up all of the old parts, puts them back together in their original configuration, and sets sail. Is this the same boat that Theseus sailed years earlier? Intuitively, it seems that it is. But how can this boat and Theseus's new and improved boat both be the same boat that Theseus originally owned? Intuitively, it seems that given what 'same' (or 'same boat as') means, this is impossible.

Most (or at least many) speakers of ordinary English are puzzled by this case in the sense that they have no clear intuition about what we ought to say about it. Here is one explanation of this puzzlement (I think this is the right explanation, but I won't try to argue this here): The ordinary concepts of sameness and same-boat-as are just not precise enough to settle the question. This is not to say that these concepts are useless; it's just to say that there is some imprecision in them and that in connection with certain "weird" scenarios (e.g., the Ship of Theseus scenario), the imprecision *matters*—that is, there is no clear fact of the matter as to whether the concepts apply. Thus, on this view, there is a range of possible situations in which our concepts of sameness and same-boat-as clearly apply, and there is a range of possible situations in which these concepts clearly don't apply, but there are also some possible situations in which these concepts neither clearly apply nor clearly don't apply. Now, I suppose one might wonder how a concept can be imprecise in this way. The answer to this question is obvious. Suppose, for instance, that something like the OL view (or rather, an analogue of the OL view that's about analyses of *sameness*, rather than *free will*) is correct, so that the only facts that could settle whether the concept of sameness applies in a given situation are facts about ordinary language—facts about things like ordinary-language usage and intentions. If this is right, then if our usage and intentions are too imprecise to settle the Ship of Theseus question, then there is simply no fact of the matter as to whether the ordinary concept of sameness is applicable in this case. In any event, what I am suggesting here is that the best explanation of the fact that ordinary speakers are intuitively befuddled by the Ship of Theseus case is that, in fact, the ordinary-language usage and intentions associated with 'same' and 'same boat as' *are* imprecise in the

Compatibilism and Conceptual Analysis

above way. (We can describe this situation by saying that our usage and intentions pick out a concept that's imprecise in the above way; or we can say that our usage and intentions aren't precise enough to pick out a unique precise concept, i.e., that they're consistent with multiple precise concepts that dictate different things about the Ship of Theseus case.)

Regardless of whether this is the right thing to say about the Ship of Theseus case, though, the question I want to ask is whether something like this is going on in connection with the ordinary-language expression 'free will'. I don't want to claim that it's obvious that something like this is going on, but I do want to claim that this is at least somewhat plausible. Why? Because our intuitions about free will seem to fail us in a similar sort of way. To appreciate this, consider an ordinary case in which the ordinary-language concept of free will seems clearly to apply. For instance, suppose that during a court martial hearing for an Army soldier, a prosecuting attorney points out that the soldier (let's call him "Private John Q. Public") was not ordered to act in the way that he did, and suppose that while making this point, the attorney utters the following sentence:

(C) Private Public acted of his own free will.

Intuitively, it seems plausible to suppose that the attorney did not say something whose truth is contingent upon a controversial thesis of physical theory (namely, causal indeterminism); it seems that he said something whose truth is contingent only upon whether Private Public was ordered to act as he did, or held at gunpoint, or some such thing. But if this is right, then it seems plausible and intuitive to suppose that the attorney could not have been talking about L-freedom when he used the term 'free will'—and hence that the concept of free will at work here is compatible with determinism.

Things, however, are not as simple as this. To see why, let's suppose now that somehow or other, we find out for certain that full-blown causal determinism is true, so that before Private Public was born, it was already determined how his life would proceed, including all of his actions and decisions, down to the smallest detail. Most ordinary speakers have the intuition that (C) is false in this scenario, because they have the intuition that Private Public doesn't have any free will at all in this scenario—that is, that none of his actions or decisions is free. (Anyone who has ever taught the issue of free will to a classroom full of students with no previous exposure to the problem knows how strongly ordinary speakers have this intuition.)

So our intuitions seem to go like this: When we assume that determinism *is* true, so that everything Private Public has ever done was already determined to occur thirteen billion years ago, we have a strong intuition that he does not have free will—that is, that (C) is false. But in the absence of any knowledge about whether determinism is true—that is, from our actual epistemic vantage point—it seems intuitively that when we say things like (C), the truth values of our utterances are not contingent upon the truth of indeterminism. That is, intuitively, is seems that we can evaluate ordinary claims like (C) in the absence of any knowledge about whether determinism is true.

So there is something odd about our intuitions here. What should we say about this? Well, it seems to me that there are at least five different strategies one might pursue in response to this situation. First, one might embrace the compatibilist intuition that the attorney didn't say anything whose truth is contingent upon the truth of indeterminism, and one might try to explain away the incompatibilist intuition that if we assume that determinism is true, then (C) is false. That is, one might try to tell a story about why people have this latter intuition despite the fact that they use 'free will' in a way that allows that (C) could be true, even if determinism is true. (One might try to do this by arguing that what drives our reactions to the deterministic scenario is in fact not a genuine semantic intuition, but rather an implicit, nonintuitive [and misguided] belief. More specifically, one might argue that while people in fact use 'free will' in a compatibilistic way, they, for some reason, mistakenly believe that free will is incompatible with determinism. I don't know how plausible this is.)

Second, one might embrace the incompatibilist intuition that if determinism is true then (C) is false, and one might try to explain away the compatibilist intuition that determinism is irrelevant to our present-situation evaluations of ordinary utterances of sentences like (C). (One might try to do this by arguing that the reason determinism seems not to matter in connection with our present-situation evaluations of sentences like (C) is that people just don't ordinarily think about the possibility of determinism being true. This, however, strikes me as implausible; for as long as we don't assume that determinism is definitely true, merely thinking about the possibility of it being true seems not to undermine the compatibilist intuition; for again, the compatibilist intuition is that we can evaluate the attorney's claim without knowing whether determinism is true. In other words, the intuition is that the attorney didn't say anything whose truth is contingent upon the question of whether determinism is true.)

Third, one might try to argue that the fact that we have both compatibilist and incompatibilist intuitions shows that our concept of free will is incoherent. But the mere presence of these intuitions does not force this conclusion on us, and indeed, this conclusion strikes me as pretty implausible—especially given the tenability of the view described below, that is, the view that deals with the above intuitions by taking the concept of free will to be imprecise rather than incoherent. In general, I think we should be fairly slow to conclude that the concept of free will is incoherent. The claim that 'free will' is at least reasonably well behaved seems more certain to me than any semantic analysis that we have of this expression. The term 'free will' might have a very complicated semantics, involving imprecision, ambiguity, vagueness, and so on, but this just means that we need a complicated semantic theory for it, not that there is something wrong with the term. (Of course, there are also other arguments for the incoherence of the notion of free will; for instance, some people have argued that this notion is incoherent because it's incompatible with both determinism and indeterminism. It follows from the arguments of chapter 3 below, however, that the notion of free will is perfectly compatible with indeterminism, and so this other argument for the incoherence of the notion of free will is mistaken.)

Fourth, one might endorse a sort of contextualism according to which our compatibilist and incompatibilist intuitions are both perfectly acceptable because the term 'free will' is ambiguous, or contextually sensitive, or some such thing. In particular, one might claim that when we have the intuition that the truth of determinism is irrelevant to the truth of the attorney's claim, we are using 'free will' to pick out a compatibilist sort of freedom; and when we have the intuition that if determinism is true then Private Public has no free will, we are using 'free will' to pick out something like L-freedom. This doesn't seem very plausible to me; in order to motivate this view, we would have to tell a story about how the supposition that determinism is true alters the context of utterance to such an extent that the term 'free will' takes on a different meaning but without this being apparent to ordinary speakers.

Fifth, one might maintain that the ordinary-language expression 'free will' is imprecise in the following way: The ordinary-language usage and intentions associated with the term 'free will' don't zero in on a unique, precise concept of freedom, and in particular, they are consistent with, but don't zero in on, at least one compatibilist concept and at least one incompatibilist concept, presumably something like L-freedom. Moreover, one might supplement this imprecisionist hypothesis with a story about why our intuitions go different ways in different cases, depending on what's being emphasized. I am not going to try to tell a story of this kind here, and more generally, I am not going to provide a positive argument for the hypothesis that the folk term 'free will' is imprecise in the above way. I'm just throwing it out there as a possibility. It seems to me at least initially plausible that (a) the term 'free will' is imprecise in the above way, and (b) this is part of the reason why our intuitions go the way they do (and why the compatibilism issue is befuddling to us).

In any event, if the folk term 'free will' is indeed imprecise in the above way, then the facts about ordinary language fail to settle the what-is-free-will question (and the question of whether the concept of free will is applicable in any deterministic scenarios). Now, of course, it doesn't follow from this alone that there is no unique correct answer to the what-is-free-will question (or the question of whether the concept of free will is applicable in deterministic scenarios). For one might reject the OL view; that is, one might deny that facts about ordinary language are the only facts that are relevant to the what-is-free-will question. But it's important to appreciate what we would have to say in order to maintain that there *is* a unique correct answer to the what-is-free-will question. One way to do this would be to embrace the OL view and deny that the ordinary expression 'free will' is imprecise in the above way. In other words, we could endorse the following:

(i) The facts about ordinary language are sufficient to settle the what-is-free-will question; that is, they pick out a unique kind of freedom.

On the other hand, if we didn't believe (i), or if we didn't believe that we had any good evidence for (i), we could instead say something like this:

(ii) The OL view is false; that is, there are other facts, aside from facts about folk meaning, or ordinary-language usage and intentions, that are relevant to the what-is-free-will question. Moreover, the facts in question here actually *settle* the matter. In other words, while ordinary usage and intentions do not pick out any specific kind of freedom, there is nevertheless a specific kind of freedom that *is* free will.

Or perhaps one could get by saying something more like this:

(iii) There are good reasons for thinking that we ought to "precisify" the concept of free will and, indeed, there are good reasons for favoring one specific "precisification" over the others.

Now, I suppose there are other things one might want to say here instead of (i), (ii), or (iii); but it seems to me that if we want to claim that there is a

Compatibilism and Conceptual Analysis 61

unique correct answer to the what-is-free-will question, we are going to have to say *something* controversial. In particular, we're going to have to endorse a hypothesis that's at least roughly similar to (i), (ii), or (iii). But it is not obvious to me that we have any good reason right now for endorsing any such hypothesis. And so at the very least, it seems to me controversial to claim that there is a unique correct answer to the what-is-free-will question.

I suppose one might think that we're *committed* to finding some determinate answer to the what-is-free-will question. One might argue this point by saying something like the following:

> Free will is an extremely important capacity. It seems to be required not just for moral responsibility but autonomy and dignity as well. Thus, while we might struggle to figure out what exactly free will is, we are committed to finding a determinate answer to the question of what free will is, not to mention the question of whether human beings in fact have free will. Free will is just too important a notion for there to be no determinate fact of the matter as to what it is.

But even if we're committed to *looking* for a unique answer to the what-is-free-will question, it doesn't follow that there *is* one. Even if free will is very important to us, it simply doesn't follow that there are facts out there that settle the question of what free will is, or that there are good reasons for "precisifying" the notion in some specific direction rather than other directions.

In sum, then, it doesn't seem to me that we have very good reasons right now for believing that there is a unique correct answer to the what-is-free-will question. Now, of course, I haven't given any compelling argument on the other side of this issue either, so I do not want to claim that there definitely *isn't* a unique correct answer to the what-is-free-will question. Again, I'm just suggesting an initially plausible possibility. In particular, it seems to me that for all we know, it might be that the following is true:

> *Semantic no-fact-of-the-matter-ism*: (a) ordinary usage and intentions concerning the expression 'free will' are imprecise in the above way, and (b) there are no other facts out there that are capable of settling the what-is-free-will question.

It seems to me that at the very least, we ought to take this hypothesis seriously. But again, I will not try to argue here that it's true, partly because I'm not convinced that it *is* true, but mainly because this is all an aside anyway—that is, because semantic no-fact-of-the-matter-ism is wholly irrelevant to what I will do in the rest of this book.

Finally, if we assume that semantic no-fact-of-the-matter-ism is indeed true, then what should we say about compatibilism? Is it true, or is it false, or is there no fact of the matter as to whether it's true or false? Well, I can imagine an incompatibilist saying something like this:

> If 'free will' is imprecise in the above way, then the concept of free will is not really applicable in cases in which determinism is true. So in this scenario, free will is not really compatible with determinism.

And I can imagine a compatibilist saying something like this:

> If 'free will' is imprecise in the above way, then there is nothing about indeterminism built into the concept of free will, and so there is no incompatibility between that concept and determinism.

But I'm inclined to say that if 'free will' is imprecise in the above way, then there is no fact of the matter as to whether the concept of free will is applicable in cases in which determinism is true, and so there is no right answer to the question of whether compatibilism is true. Now, I suppose we could manufacture an answer to the compatibilism question here by coming up with a precise definition of 'compatibilism' that dictated that it was true (or false) in the above 'free-will'-is-imprecise scenario. But it seems to me that any such definition would be stipulative, and so I think the best thing to say—or perhaps the least misleading thing—is that if semantic no-fact-of-the-matter-ism is true, then there is no fact of the matter as to whether compatibilism is true. In any event, it seems right to say that if semantic no-fact-of-the-matter-ism is true, then this derails the compatibilism debate in an obvious sort of way.

2.7.2 The Moral Responsibility Question

The really controversial part of the moral responsibility question is the question of whether moral responsibility requires an indeterministic sort of freedom (presumably L-freedom), and this latter question boils down to the question of whether moral responsibility is compatible with determinism. But given this, I want to say the same thing here that I said in the last section about the compatibilism question. We have a strong intuition that if determinism is true, so that before Private Public was born, it was already determined how his life would proceed, including all of his actions and decisions, then he is not morally responsible for his actions. But from our current epistemic vantage point—in particular, in the absence of any knowledge about the truth or falsity of determinism—there seem to be scenarios in which claims of moral responsibility are intuitively independent of the question of whether determinism is true. Consider, for example, the sentence, 'It was Dick Cheney and not George W. Bush who was responsible for getting the United States into the war in Iraq'. Intuitively, it seems that the truth values of ordinary responsibility claims like this are not contingent upon the question of whether determinism is true. So I think that all the same considerations arise here that arose in connection with the term 'free will'. And so I think that as of right now, there is no good reason to think that there is even a fact of the matter as to whether moral responsibility is compatible with determinism. And because of this, I think there is no good reason to think that there's a fact of the matter about the answer to the moral responsibility question.

3 Why the Libertarian Question Reduces to the Issue of Indeterminacy

But don't you see, Boris Dimitrovich, that the right kind of indeterminacy procures appropriate nonrandomness and L-freedom?
—Sonja Karenina, *War and Death*

3.1 Introduction

We saw in chapter 2 that the metaphysically interesting issue in the problem of free will boils down to the following question:

The which-kinds-of-freedom-do-we-have question: Which kinds of freedom (or "freedom") do humans have? That is, do they have L-freedom (i.e., libertarian freedom)?; and do they have Humean freedom?; and do they have Frankfurtian freedom?; and so on.

We also found, at the very end of chapter 2, that among all the subquestions of this question, the most controversial, and probably the most philosophically interesting, is the question of whether humans are L-free. I won't claim that this is the only interesting or controversial subquestion of the which-kinds-of-freedom-do-we-have question, because, for instance, one might think there are interesting and controversial questions about whether human beings possess various compatibilist kinds of freedom that require reasons responsiveness.[1] But I won't have anything to say about these other kinds of freedom here. In the remainder of this book, I am going to concentrate on the question of whether humans are L-free, that is, the question of whether libertarianism is true.

Libertarianism, as I'm defining it here, is the view that human beings possess L-freedom, where a person is *L-free* if and only if she makes at least some decisions that are such that (a) they are both undetermined and appropriately nonrandom, and (b) the indeterminacy is relevant to the appropriate nonrandomness in the sense that it *generates* the nonrandomness, or *procures* it, or *enhances* it, or *increases* it, or something along these lines. Now, in order to make this definition more precise, we need to say something about what appropriate nonrandomness amounts to. I will have a good deal to say about this below, but for now, we can just note that the central requirement that a decision needs to satisfy in order to count as appropriately nonrandom is that of having been *authored and controlled* by the agent in question; that is, it has to have been *her* decision, and she has to have controlled which option was chosen.

Many (probably most) philosophers think that libertarianism is untenable. One way to argue this point (though, I think, not the most plausible way) would be to say something like this:

> Any event that's undetermined is uncaused and, hence, accidental. That is, it *just happens*; or it happens randomly. Thus, if our decisions are undetermined, then they are random, and so they couldn't possibly be "appropriately nonrandom." Or to put the point the other way around, if our decisions are appropriately nonrandom, then they are authored and controlled by us; that is, *we determine* what we choose and don't choose, presumably for rational reasons. Thus, if our decisions are appropriately nonrandom, then they couldn't possibly be undetermined. Therefore, libertarianism is simply incoherent; it is not possible for a decision to be undetermined and appropriately nonrandom at the same time.

One might call this the Hobbes-Hume-Hobart argument.[2] However, those who are opposed to libertarianism do not need to argue in this strong way. Instead, they can say something like this:

> There might be some indeterminacies in our decision-making processes that don't utterly destroy appropriate nonrandomness, and so the Hobbes-Hume-Hobart argument is too strong. Nonetheless, it's hard to see how there could be any indeterminacies in these processes that *generated* or *enhanced* or *increased* appropriate nonrandomness. Appropriate nonrandomness has to do with the agent being in control. How could this be increased by the insertion of an undetermined event into a decision-making process? It seems that when we insert an undetermined event into such a process, we are inserting an element of *randomness*. So how could this possibly increase *non*randomness? It seems that it couldn't, and so it seems that libertarianism could not be true.

I will argue in the present chapter that this sort of reasoning—not just this argument, but any argument of this general kind—is wrongheaded. I will do this by showing that libertarianism is virtually *entailed* by the appropriate kind of indeterminacy. More specifically, I'm going to argue that there's a certain category of our decisions for which the following is true: If they're undetermined (in the appropriate way—more on this below), then (a) they are also appropriately nonrandom, and (b) the indeterminacy in question increases or procures the appropriate nonrandomness. And I should note here that in arguing this point, I will not be appealing to anything like Cartesian souls or irreducible agent causation; that is, I will assume that some form of mind–brain materialism is true and that all causation is ordinary event causation.

(Along the way, I will be responding not just to the above objection but to a number of other well-known objections to libertarianism, e.g., the widely discussed luck objection and the objection that libertarianism could not be right because it leads to an unacceptable regress.[3])

The libertarian view I will be defending against these arguments is similar in a number of ways to other libertarian views in the literature, but it is original (one might even say radical) in one crucially important way. The similarities to other views will emerge as we proceed, but for now, let me say that the view I have in mind is (i) *event-causal* (more specifically, it doesn't involve any sort of irreducible agent causation, but it does hold that undetermined L-free decisions are (ordinarily) causally influenced by—indeed, probabilistically caused by—agent-involving events, most notably events having to do with the agent having certain reasons and intentions); and (ii) *non-Valerian* (i.e., according to this view, the important indeterminacy is located at the moment of choice, rather than prior to choice, as with Valerian views[4]). This general sort of view was hinted at by Wiggins (1973) and later developed by Kane (1985, 1996, 1999), Nozick (1981), and Ekstrom (2000);[5] of these, my view is most similar to Kane's, but as we'll see, it is also importantly different from his view. My view is less similar to noncausal non-Valerian views, which take free decisions to be uncaused (see, e.g., Ginet 1990, 2002, 2007, McCann 1998, McCall 1994, and Goetz 1997), though as I point out in note 13 of the present chapter, one might maintain that there is a sort of noncausal thread in the event-causal view I develop here. Finally, my view is even less similar to Valerian views, which have been developed, though not endorsed, by Dennett (1978) and Mele (1995), and to agent-causal views, which have been developed by a number of philosophers, including Reid (1788), Chisholm (1964a), R. Taylor (1966, 1974), C. A. Campbell (1967), Thorp (1980), Rowe (1987), Donagan (1987), O'Connor (1993, 2000), and Clarke (1993, 1996, 2003).

But there is one important way in which my view differs from all of these other views. Almost everyone involved in this debate, whether libertarian or antilibertarian, believes something along the following lines:

> It may very well be that our decisions are undetermined in some sense; we have to acknowledge that this is a real possibility, because quantum mechanics contains probabilistic laws and some of the most widely accepted interpretations of quantum mechanics take these laws to capture irreducible indeterminacies that exist at the most fundamental level of nature. In short, it may be that there are causal indeterminacies all over the place, and so it may be that neural events and, in particular, decisions are indeterministic. So *half* of the libertarian thesis is a real possibility. But the other half—*indeterminacy-enhanced appropriate nonrandomness*—is the really hard part.

In short, the main worry about libertarianism is that even if we assume that lots of our decisions are undetermined, it's hard to see how this could lead to any significant gain in appropriate nonrandomness. What libertarians have generally tried to do in response to this worry is construct a model—or a possible scenario—in which humans are L-free, that is, in which there is a genuine freedom-enhancing sort of indeterminacy in our decisions. Thus, the goal has been to establish that libertarianism is a *coherent, viable option*. But I want to argue for a stronger position than this. In section 3.3, I will argue for the following claim:

> (*) There is a significant subset of our decisions (in particular, *torn* decisions, which I will characterize in section 3.2.1) for which the following is true: If they are undetermined at the moment of choice (in a certain specific way that I'll describe below), then they are L-free—that is, (a) they are not just undetermined but also appropriately nonrandom, and (b) the indeterminacy in question increases or procures the appropriate nonrandomness.

Notice that I am not just saying that if our torn decisions are undetermined, then it *could be* that (a) and (b) are also true, so that libertarianism is coherent. There would be nothing new in that; Kane (1985, 1996) and Ginet (1990) have argued points that are essentially equivalent to this, and indeed, just about every libertarian (certainly all those mentioned in the preceding paragraph) has tried at least to defend the thesis that libertarianism is coherent. But, again, I am making a stronger claim than this. I am going to offer a positive argument for the thesis that if our torn decisions are undetermined at the moment of choice, then (a) and (b) *are* true—that is, our torn decisions are appropriately nonrandom, and the indeterminacy in question does procure this result, so that libertarianism is not just coherent, but *true*. Thus, on my view, it is indeterminacy and not appropriate nonrandomness that is the really controversial thesis in libertarianism. Indeed, if I'm right about (*)—and about a few other minor points that I'll argue below—then the question of whether libertarianism is true just reduces to the question of whether some of our torn decisions are undetermined in the appropriate way.[6] This, of course, is a straightforward empirical question about the neural events that are our torn decisions. Moreover, as we'll see in chapter 4, it is also a *wide open* question; I will argue there that (as of right now) we have no good reasons for favoring either answer to this question. It may be that some of our torn decisions are undetermined and hence that libertarianism is true, and it may be that all of our torn decisions are determined and hence that libertarianism is false; but right now, we just don't have any good reason for taking sides on this question.

So this is the central point I want to argue—that the question of whether libertarianism is true reduces to a straightforward (and as we'll see in chapter 4, wide open) empirical question about the causal histories of the neural events that are our torn decisions. I will argue this point in section 3.3. Moreover, since a well-developed libertarianism should provide some account of decisions that aren't torn, I will say a few words at the end of the present chapter (in section 3.4) about how various kinds of non-torn decisions fit into the overall libertarian view that I have in mind.

I want to emphasize here that when I talk about "the libertarian view I have in mind," or even "*my* libertarian view," as I sometimes call it, I do not mean to imply that I *endorse* this view. My goal is to develop a certain libertarian view, to defend it against criticism, and to argue that there is no good reason whatsoever to disbelieve it. As we will see in chapter 4, however, I also think that there is no good reason to *believe* this libertarian view, and for this reason, I do not endorse it. Again, I think the question here is a wide open empirical question, and I think that at present, we have no good evidence either way, and so I do not want to take a stand on the issue. To me, the question of whether libertarianism is true is (epistemically) like the question, 'Does Alpha Centauri have any planets that have rings?' All we can do at the present time is shrug and say, "Who knows?"

It is worth noting, however, that while it is an open empirical question whether my version of libertarianism is true, the view is not overly speculative, as some libertarian views seem to be. Indeed, the fact that my libertarian view isn't very speculative is, to my mind, the second crucial difference between my version of libertarianism and Kane's. The first important difference is the one mentioned above: Whereas Kane has essentially argued that if any of our decisions are undetermined, then it *could be* that this indeterminacy leads to an appropriate nonrandomness, I am going to argue here that if our torn decisions are undetermined in the right way, then this indeterminacy *does* lead to an appropriate nonrandomness (and hence, we *are* L-free). The second important difference is that Kane's view might be deemed overly speculative by some. This is because his model (of how there could be freedom-enhancing indeterminacies in our decision-making processes) involves a whole network of controversial empirical hypotheses. To name just a few of these, on the model Kane constructs, undetermined free choices involve conflicting efforts of will that are realized physically by conflicting neural networks that create "indeterministic noise" for each other and that "stir up chaos" in the brain and magnify quantum-level indeterminacies. I think Kane is right that all of this might turn out to be true, but one might feel that the probability that *all* of these hypotheses are true is not very high. But my version of libertarianism is much less speculative than this. Again, if I'm right, then the whole issue reduces to a single empirical question about whether certain neural events are undetermined. And if the arguments I give in chapter 4 are correct, then we have no good reason at all, at least right now, to favor *either* answer to this question. Thus, if I'm right, then my version of libertarianism is no more speculative or empirically unlikely than antilibertarianism is.

(Having said how my version of libertarianism is different from Kane's, I should also say that my view is similar to his in important ways, most notably, I think, in the way that torn decisions play a prominent role in both theories; I will say more about this below, in section 3.2.1.)

Before going on, I should say a few words about the kind of mind–brain materialism that I will assume. In short, I want to assume only a very weak version of materialism. Once we reject mind–brain dualism, we are left with the view that decisions are physical events, presumably neural events; the weakest version of this view is the *token–token identity theory of decisions*, and this is all I will assume here. It is worth emphasizing how weak this theory is: All it says is that every particular (human) decision is a particular neural event. It does not take a stand on the type–type question, that is, the question of whether all decisions are neural events of some specific kind, and indeed, the token–token theory is consistent with—in fact, entailed by—all of the standard (noneliminativist) views in the philosophy of mind, for example, type–type identity theories, functionalist theories, nonreductive physicalist theories, and so on. Thus, I think it's safe to say that, at present, most people working in the area of the mind–brain would accept the token–token identity theory of decisions, and I think it's also safe to say that we have pretty good reasons to believe this theory. (There are two other materialistic views that one might endorse here, namely, the eliminativist view that there are no such things as decisions, and the nonspecificist view that while mental phenomena like decisions supervene on neural phenomena in general, there is no good way to correlate *specific* neural events with specific decisions. But I will ignore these two views here, because (a) they are implausible,[7] and (b) my argument could be reformulated so as to fit with them, so that in the present context, it simply wouldn't matter if eliminativism or nonspecificism turned out to be true.[8])

Finally, I should point out that I will not be concerned in this chapter with the question of whether the notion of L-freedom captures the ordinary notion of free will. This issue arises in connection with the compatibilism debate, and I discussed it at length in chapter 2; but it is not relevant at all to the questions that I'm concerned with in the present chapter, namely, the question of whether libertarianism is true—that is, whether human beings are L-free—and the question of what exactly needs to be the case in order for libertarianism to be true. (As I pointed out in chapter 1, some philosophers use 'libertarianism' to denote the view that human beings are L-free *and* that the notion of L-freedom captures the ordinary notion of free will. That's not how I'm using the term here, although, of course, this doesn't really matter—I could just as easily define my terms differently.)

3.2 Preliminaries

3.2.1 Torn Decisions

A *torn decision* is a decision in which the person in question (a) has reasons for two or more options and feels torn as to which set of reasons is strongest, that is, has no conscious belief as to which option is best, given her reasons; and (b) decides without resolving this conflict—that is, the person has the experience of "just choosing." (In such cases, subconscious reasons, and subconscious weightings of reasons, can come into play; I will discuss this issue below, in section 3.3.4, but for now, I want to ignore the complication of the subconscious. Thus, for the time being, when I speak of reasons, I mean *conscious* reasons.)

Let's look at two examples of torn decisions, one very important and the other not so important. To begin with, let's suppose that Ralph, a lifelong resident of Mayberry, North Carolina, is trying to decide whether or not to move to New York City. He has safety-and-stability-based reasons for wanting to stay in Mayberry (he's been offered a position as assistant day-shift manager at the local Der Wienerschnitzel and is clearly being groomed for the manager position, and his sweetheart, Robbi Anna, has offered him her hand in marriage); and he has fame-and-fortune based reasons for wanting to move to New York (he longs to be the first person to start at middle linebacker for the Giants while simultaneously starring on Broadway in a musical production of Sartre's *Nausea*). He deliberates for several days, considering all of his reasons for choosing, but he is unable to come to a view as to which set of reasons is stronger. He feels genuinely torn. But Robbi Anna and Der Wienerschnitzel, Inc. are waiting, and he feels he has to make a decision. (Indeed, while this isn't necessary for the example, we can suppose that he has a deadline; for instance, he may have been offered a part in *Nausea*, and he may have to accept or decline the offer by a certain time.) Finally, Ralph decides to move to New York, but not because he came to believe that his reasons for moving to New York outweighed his reasons for staying in Mayberry. He was unable to come to a view either way on that question, and in the end, he *just decided to go*. Period.

Torn decisions aren't always big life-shaping decisions like this, and indeed, it seems to me that we make torn decisions all the time, every day of our lives. To appreciate this, consider a second case, involving a decision more mundane than Ralph's. Jane is in a restaurant, deliberating about whether to order tiramisu or a fruit plate for dessert. She thinks that the former will taste better but that the latter will be better for her health. She has no clue which reason is stronger and feels genuinely torn. Suddenly, it's her turn to order; the waiter is looking at her; she has to pick; oh, God; "I'll have the tiramisu," she says. That is, she just chooses. Period.

Of course, this is just a description of how torn decisions feel to us; it *seems* that we just make them. For all we know, however, it may be that all of our torn decisions are causally determined by prior physical events in our brains that precede these decisions. Whether or not our torn decisions are in fact causally determined is an empirical question.

It is important to note that torn decisions are different from what might be called *Buridan's-ass decisions*. Buridan's-ass decisions are like torn decisions except that, with the former, the reasons for the various tied-for-best options are the *same* reasons. For instance, if Bill is waiting for an elevator and two cars arrive at the same time, he might hesitate for a moment and then consciously and purposefully choose to enter elevator 1 instead of elevator 2. In this case, Bill does have a reason for choosing to get on elevator 1—namely, to get to the seventh floor, or wherever he's going—but this is also a reason for getting on elevator 2, and he doesn't have a reason for choosing elevator 1 over elevator 2. Decisions like this do not count as torn decisions (i.e., don't satisfy the above definition of 'torn decision') because in these cases, the agent doesn't feel torn as to which option is best, or which reasons are best, and because it's not the case that the agent has no conscious belief as to which option is best; on the contrary, in ordinary Buridan's-ass cases, the agent knows perfectly well that the various live options are, from the point of view of her reasons, equally good. I think that almost everything I say in this chapter about torn decisions applies equally well to Buridan's-ass decisions, but I will not argue this point here, because Buridan's-ass decisions are just far less interesting than torn decisions. And the reason they're less interesting should be obvious: In Buridan's-ass cases, the agent just doesn't care at all which option she chooses, whereas in torn decisions, the agent usually does care which option she chooses.

(I suppose one might object here that if an agent is genuinely torn between two options, and if she has to choose now, then she ought *not* to care which option is chosen. Well, I don't know whether we *ought* to care which option is chosen; all I know is that we *do* care. People in situations like Ralph's usually care very much which option they choose. And even in situations like Jane's, which are far less important than Ralph's, we usually care which option we choose. Ordinarily, when we are feeling torn about what to order for dinner, we just don't have the experience of not caring. It is just very different from the experience of having two elevator doors open at the same time, or having a waiter bring two versions of the same entrée, one for you and one for your friend, and asking which plate you want. In cases like this, we in fact don't care. But in general, that's just not the case with torn decisions.)

The notion of a torn decision that I have defined in this section is similar to Kane's (1996) notion of a *self-forming action* (SFA). But there are four differences here that are worth noting. First, SFAs are by definition undetermined, and so it is an open question whether there actually exist any such things. Torn decisions, on the other hand, are not defined as being undetermined; they are defined in terms of their phenomenology; thus, it is clear that there do exist torn decisions—we know this by experience—but it is an open question whether any of our torn decisions are undetermined.

A second difference between torn decisions and Kanean SFAs is that the former needn't involve what Kane calls *efforts of will*. Now, this isn't to say that efforts *can't* play a role in torn decisions, and indeed, I think that some torn decisions do involve something like efforts of will (think, for instance, of someone who is trying to quit smoking and who, at some specific moment, badly wants a cigarette but is trying to resist). My point here, though, is that torn decisions don't *have* to involve efforts of will; and for whatever it's worth, it seems to me that, in fact, most of our torn decisions don't involve anything that we would ordinarily call efforts of will.

A third difference between torn decisions and Kanean SFAs is that the former needn't have much of anything to do with the *formation* of the agent, or with the agent being torn between two visions of *who she wants to become*. Now, as we've seen, *some* of our torn decisions are momentous events in our lives; they can have to do with where we will live, or who we will marry, or whether we will have children, or what careers we will pursue, or what sorts of people we will become. But on my view, we make numerous torn decisions every day, and most of these decisions are pretty insignificant and have little or nothing to do with the kinds of people we are becoming. (Note, however, that this doesn't change the fact, mentioned above, that we *care* about these decisions. Even if you know that within a couple of days, some decision of yours won't matter at all—you might just be deciding whether to stay home and work or go to dinner with a friend—at the time, you can be quite invested in what you decide to do.)

A fourth difference between SFAs and torn decisions is as follows: (a) in order for a decision to count as a torn decision, the agent in question has to be more or less neutral between her various live options; but (b) a decision can be an SFA even if the agent is "leaning toward" one or more of her live options. This difference is theoretically unimportant, because on my view, decisions involving "leanings" of this sort can still be L-free (and for roughly the same reasons that torn decisions can). The reason I restrict the notion of a torn decision to cases in which the agent is roughly neutral between her various live options is simply this: Throughout most of my argument, I am going to be concentrating on decisions that involve this sort of neutrality, and so I simply want to have a term that refers to the sorts of decisions I'm going to be discussing. But in section 3.4, I will turn to a discussion of decisions that involve "leanings" of the above kind, and we will find there that we can endorse a view of these decisions that is essentially analogous to the view of torn decisions that I develop in section 3.3. For now, though, I want to ignore decisions that involve leanings of this sort.

(I suppose one might object here that it might be that torn decisions—involving true neutrality, as opposed to leanings of the above kind—are very rare or even nonexistent in humans. But frankly, this is hard to believe. Since the notion of a torn decision is defined in terms of the phenomenology of the decision, and not in terms of the actual moment-of-choice probabilities of the various options being chosen, it seems pretty obvious that we make lots and lots of torn decisions. It just seems to be a fact about us that we often make choices while feeling genuinely torn. Think, for instance, of decisions concerning what to eat for dinner, whether to bring flowers or wine to a dinner party, whether to go to a movie on a given night or stay home and work, whether to stay on the freeway during a traffic jam or get off and take surface streets, whether to vacation in Paris or Rome, etc., etc., etc.)

Let me make one more point before going on. One might think that, at least sometimes, the formation of a judgment about the relative strengths of the reasons for two different options could count as something like a torn decision. Now, I have defined torn decisions here as decisions in which the person in question decides without consciously resolving the question of which option is best, or which set of reasons is strongest. But it's easy to imagine a slightly different kind of case. Suppose, for instance, that (i) Cindy has to decide between A and B, and she has a deadline, and right up to the last minute, she feels torn; and (ii) at the last minute, she chooses A, and the phenomenology of her choice—that is, what she experiences at the moment of choice—is not an I'll-just-choose-A phenomenology, but an I-think-A-is-better-than-B phenomenology, or an I-think-A's-reasons-are-stronger-than-B's phenomenology. Now, again, as I've set things up here, this does not count as a torn decision. But cases like this are obviously very similar to torn decisions, and I think similar sorts of things can be said about them. I will not go into this here, though. For the sake of simplicity, I will ignore decisions of this kind and stick to torn decisions as I defined them above, that is, decisions in which the person in question decides without coming to a view as to which set of reasons is strongest.

3.2.2 Indeterminacy

As I pointed out above, when I say that if a torn decision is undetermined then it's L-free, what I mean is that if it's undetermined *at the moment of choice* then it's L-free. Thus, if I say that a decision was determined, that does not mean that it was determined prior to the agent's birth, or any such thing; if an undetermined quantum event occurs in my head two seconds prior to a decision (and if the undetermined event is not *part of the decision*), and if this event (together with other circumstances) causally determines my decision, then on my usage, the decision counts as determined. So while there can be prior-to-choice indeterminacies that are relevant to the occurrence of a torn decision, such indeterminacies, as we'll see, are not needed for L-freedom, and they do not play any role in my theory. This is what makes my libertarian view non-Valerian.

A second point that needs to be made here is that an agent's reasons could causally determine that a given torn decision will occur, and could causally determine that the choice will come from a specific set of possible options, without determining which option will be chosen. For example, it could be that (a) Jane had compelling reasons for choosing *something* when it was her turn to order, and these reasons deterministically caused her to just pick; and (b) it was causally determined by Jane's reasons that she would choose either the tiramisu or the fruit plate, that is, that she wouldn't pass on dessert or order something else, like pea soup; but (c) the fact that Jane chose the tiramisu over the fruit plate was not causally determined (by her reasons or anything else). When I speak of a torn decision being undetermined at the moment of choice, what I mean is captured by clause (c): I mean that it wasn't determined which option was chosen. Whether or not it was causally determined that *some* choice would be made, or that the choice would come from some specific set of options, will not matter. (One could also make a torn decision about whether to make a given decision or remain in a state of indecision; but this is just a special case of an ordinary torn decision; in particular, it's just a case where the tied-for-best options are *choose now* and *don't choose now*.)

(Actually, I think a stronger claim can be made in connection with point (b) in the preceding paragraph. It's not just that it *could* be that, in torn decisions, our reasons cause our choices to come from among our reasons-based tied-for-best options; it seems likely that in fact our reasons do play a causal role here. For (i) it's just a fact that our torn decisions dovetail with our reasons—in particular, when we make torn decisions, we almost always end up choosing one of our reasons-based tied-for-best options—and (ii) it's hard to believe that this is a coincidence, that our reasons don't play a role in making this the case.)

A third issue that needs to be discussed here is this: Whatever actually happens in human heads leading up to torn decisions, conceptually speaking, there can be different *degrees of determinacy* here. Let me explain what I mean by this. In any torn decision, the agent feels neutral between her tied-for-best options, given all of her conscious reasons and thought. Thus, we might describe this by saying that the *reasons-based probabilities* of the various live options being chosen are all even, or at least roughly even. (I'm using 'reasons-based probability' here, and throughout this chapter, in a way that makes the previous sentence essentially *definitional*; to say that an agent made a torn decision between two options, A and B, just *is* to say that the reasons-based probabilities of A and B being chosen were roughly even.) But it could be that factors external to the agent's conscious reasons and thought (e.g., unconscious compulsions, or wholly nonmental brain events that precede the decision in the agent's head) causally influence the choice and wholly or partially determine which option is chosen. Indeed, there is a continuum of conceptually possible cases here. At one end of the spectrum, which option is chosen is *wholly undetermined* (that is, the moment-of-choice probabilities of the various reasons-based tied-for-best options being chosen match the reasons-based probabilities, so that these moment-of-choice probabilities are all roughly even, given the complete state of the world and all the laws of nature, and the choice occurs without any further causal input, i.e., without anything else being significantly causally relevant to which option is chosen). At the other end of the spectrum, which option is chosen is causally determined by prior events. And in between, there is a continuum of possible cases where the moment-of-choice probabilities of the various tied-for-best options being chosen are altered, away from the reasons-based probabilities, to a greater or lesser extent, due to some sort of causal input; in connection with these in-between cases, we can say that which option is chosen is partially determined—or, equivalently, partially undetermined.

We can make this a bit more concrete by looking at an example. If we return to Ralph's decision, we can say that there is a continuum of conceptually possible cases in which the moment-of-choice probability of Ralph choosing to move to New York (given the complete state of the world and all the laws of nature) becomes higher and higher, despite the fact that the reasons-based probability of his so choosing is still 0.5.[9] When the moment-of-choice probability is 0.5, the decision is wholly undetermined in the above sense; as the moment-of-choice probability moves farther and farther away from 0.5 (i.e., as it gets closer and closer to 0 or 1), which option is chosen becomes more and more determined; and when the moment-of-choice probability is either 0 or 1, the decision is fully causally determined (I'm assuming here that the only viable options are New York and Mayberry, so that if the probability of Ralph choosing to move to New York is 0, then the probability of his choosing to stay in Mayberry is 1).

I think libertarians should respond to this situation—that is, to the possibility of there being different degrees of determinacy in our torn decisions—by allowing that (conceptually speaking) there can be different degrees of L-freedom. Given this, we can split the thesis of the present chapter (i.e., the thesis that if our torn decisions are undetermined then they're L-free) into two different theses, one having to do with full-blown indeterminacy and L-freedom and the other having to do with degrees of partial indeterminacy and L-freedom. The first of these theses (i.e., the one having to do with full-blown L-freedom) is by far the more important of the two, and indeed, we'll see below that in the present context, there is no need even to argue for the other thesis (i.e., the one having to do with partial L-freedom). The first thesis can be put in the following way:

(A) If an ordinary human torn decision is wholly undetermined in the above sense, then it is L-free (or as we might want to say, full-blown L-free)—that is, (a) it is not just undetermined but also appropriately nonrandom (or as we might want to say, full-blown appropriately nonrandom), and (b) the indeterminacy in question increases or procures the appropriate nonrandomness.

If this thesis is correct—and I will argue at length in the present chapter that it is—then the question of whether any of our torn decisions are (full-blown) L-free reduces to the question of whether the following empirical hypothesis is true:

TDW-indeterminism: Some of our torn decisions are *wholly undetermined* at the moment of choice, where to say that a torn decision is wholly undetermined at the moment of choice is to say that the moment-of-choice probabilities of the various reasons-based tied-for-best options being chosen match the reasons-based probabilities, so that these moment-of-choice probabilities are all roughly even, given the complete state of the world and all the laws of nature, and the choice occurs without any further causal input, that is, without anything else being significantly causally relevant to which option is chosen.[10]

Again, if I'm right about (A) being true, then the question of whether any of our torn decisions are L-free reduces to the question of whether TDW-indeterminism is true. Now, this might seem wrong. For since (A) is not a biconditional—that is, since it's only a conditional—it follows that (A) is consistent with the thesis that some of our torn decisions could be (full-blown) L-free even if they aren't wholly undetermined in the manner of TDW-indeterminism. But in order to argue for (A), I need to argue that

TDW-indeterminism is a freedom-enhancing sort of indeterminism, and in order to argue this point, I am going to argue (in section 3.3.2) that if our torn decisions are *not* wholly undetermined in the manner of TDW-indeterminism, then they have less appropriate nonrandomness then they would have had if they were wholly undetermined. Thus, if my argument for (A) is cogent, then our torn decisions are full-blown L-free *if and only if* they're wholly undetermined in the manner of TDW-indeterminism. And so if (A) is true—or more precisely, if my argument for (A) is correct—then the question of whether any of our torn decisions are (full-blown) L-free does reduce to the question of whether TDW-indeterminism is true.

Given this, we can also say—with a slight caveat—that if (A) is true, then the question of whether libertarianism is true (or more precisely, whether full-blown libertarianism is true, i.e., whether human beings have full-blown L-freedom) reduces to the question of whether TDW-indeterminism is true. The reason we need a caveat here is that torn decisions are not the only decisions that can be L-free. As we'll see in section 3.4, decisions of other kinds can be L-free as well—for example, Buridan's-ass decisions and decisions involving *leanings* of the sort discussed in section 3.2.1 (i.e., decisions in which the agent isn't entirely neutral between her live options but is leaning toward one or more of these options).[11] But in the end, this is relatively unimportant; for the sort of indeterminacy that's required in connection with decisions of these other kinds is essentially analogous to the sort of indeterminacy that's required in connection with torn decisions, and it's pretty implausible, I think, to suppose that this sort of indeterminacy is present in some of our decisions of these other kinds but not in any of our torn decisions. And so it seems to me plausible to suppose that if some of our decisions of these other kinds are undetermined in the way that's required for L-freedom, then some of our torn decisions are too.[12] And given this, the question of whether (full-blown) libertarianism is true reduces to the question of whether TDW-indeterminism is true after all. In any event, from here on out, I will assume this point; that is, I will assume that if the arguments of the present chapter are cogent and (A) is true, then the question of whether libertarianism is true reduces to the question of whether TDW-indeterminism is true.

So the libertarian view I have in mind involves a commitment to both (A) and TDW-indeterminism. But I myself am not claiming that TDW-indeterminism is true; I'm claiming only that (A) is true, that is, that *if* our torn decisions are wholly undetermined in the manner of TDW-indeterminism, then they're L-free.

It's important to note that 'wholly undetermined', as I'm using it here, does not mean wholly uncaused. Taking Ralph's decision as an example, if it was wholly undetermined in the manner of TDW-indeterminism, then the fact that Ralph chose New York over Mayberry was not causally determined. But libertarians of the sort I have in mind can still say that this was *probabilistically caused*; in particular, they can (and will) maintain that it was probabilistically caused by Ralph having the reasons and intentions that he had just prior to choice. Or to put the point another way, libertarians of this sort will say that Ralph's choice flowed out of his reasons and intentions in a nondeterministically causal way. The reason they say this is simply that the scenario they've got in mind—that is, the scenario in which Ralph's decision was wholly undetermined in the manner of TDW-indeterminism—fits perfectly with what people mean by 'probabilistically caused'. In particular, the salient point here is that if Ralph's decision was wholly undetermined, then the moment-of-choice probability that he would choose to move to New York (and, likewise, the probability that he would choose to stay in Mayberry) *depended on what his reasons were* in the sense that different reasons sets would have given rise to different probabilities, holding other things fixed. For instance, it might be that if Ralph hadn't wanted to be a professional football player, then the probability of his deciding to move to New York would have been lower than 0.5. (Libertarians of this sort might also want to say that the justification for the claim that Ralph's reasons probabilistically caused his choice is that his reasons deterministically caused it to be the case that the moment-of-choice probabilities of the two live options being chosen were 0.5 each.[13])

I said above that because there can be degrees of causal determination, we can split the thesis of the present chapter (i.e., the thesis that if our torn decisions are undetermined then they're L-free) into two different theses, one having to do with full-blown L-freedom and the other having to do with degrees of partial L-freedom. The first and by far the more important of the two theses is (A). The second—the one about partial L-freedom—is difficult to formulate. As a first shot, one might try something like this:

(B) If a torn decision is partially undetermined at the moment of choice, then it is L-free to the extent that it is undetermined at the moment of choice. We can make this more precise by noting that there is a continuum of conceptually possible cases involving partial determination. For instance, in connection with Ralph's decision, there is a continuum of conceptually possible cases in which the moment-of-choice probability of Ralph choosing to move to New York (given the complete state of the world and all the laws of nature) moves farther and farther away from 0.5

Libertarianism Reduces to a Kind of Indeterminacy 81

and closer and closer to 0 or 1 (despite the fact that the reasons-based probability of his so choosing is still 0.5) and, hence, which option is chosen becomes more and more determined. Given this, the claim here is that as we move along the continuum toward the case of a torn decision that's wholly undetermined in the manner of TDW-indeterminism—that is, as the moment-of-choice probabilities of the various live options being chosen move closer to the reasons-based probabilities and, hence, which option is chosen becomes more undetermined at the moment of choice (or equivalently, less determined)—the decision becomes more L-free.

But this is an oversimplification. The problem is that there can be different kinds of causal influences—that is, different kinds of events that could partially determine a torn decision by altering the moment-of-choice probabilities of the various live options being chosen—and these different kinds of causal influences could have different effects on appropriate nonrandomness and L-freedom. For instance, it's plausible to suppose that if a torn decision were causally influenced by subconscious mental states of the agent, this would be less damaging to appropriate nonrandomness and L-freedom than if it were causally influenced by wholly nonmental factors, e.g., brutely physical, nonmental neural events in the agent's head. (Indeed, one might think that determination by subconscious mental states is consistent with full-blown appropriate nonrandomness; we will see below, however, in section 3.3.2, that at least in connection with torn decisions, this is simply false.) In any event, given that different kinds of causal influences can have different impacts on L-freedom, thesis (B) can't be the whole story; for given this, it is at least conceptually possible for there to be two partially determined torn decisions—call them D1 and D2—such that the moment-of-choice probabilities associated with D1 are, say, .6 and .4, and the moment-of-choice probabilities associated with D2 are .7 and .3, but D2 is still more L-free than D1, because the causal influence that partially determines D2 is of a kind that is not very damaging to L-freedom, whereas the causal influence that partially determines D1 is of a kind that is more damaging to L-freedom. One way to deal with this problem would be to list a few different kinds of causal influences that could partially determine a torn decision and formulate a different version of thesis (B) for each of these different kinds of causal influences. One might treat each of these different theses as subtheses and then formulate a new (overall) version of thesis (B) that was just a conjunction of all of the different subtheses. I won't bother with any of this here, though, for as we will presently see, however we formulate thesis (B), in the present context, I don't need to argue for it.

I can see why one might want to argue that, in addition to (A), something like (B) is also true; for one might want to show that even if all of our torn decisions are partially determined, as long as they're not all wholly determined, we will still have some degree of partial L-freedom. But in the present context, it is hardly necessary to argue this point. For as we've already seen, if (A) is true, then regardless of whether something like (B) is also true, we get the result that the question of whether human beings have full-blown L-freedom reduces to the straightforwardly empirical question of whether TDW-indeterminism is true; moreover, I am going to argue at length in chapter 4 that there are no good arguments for or against TDW-indeterminism. Thus, given this, if I can argue in the present chapter that (A) *is* true—and that's exactly what I will try to do—then I will have established what I want to establish, namely, that the question of whether human beings have full-blown L-freedom (i.e., the question of whether libertarianism is true) reduces to a wide-open empirical question about the causal determinacy of the neural events that are our torn decisions. Thus, given this, it doesn't matter very much (in the present context) whether something like (B) is true, and so I won't bother to argue for it. Moreover, there's also a second reason why I won't bother to argue here for thesis (B): Once I argue for (A), it will be pretty obvious how I would go on to argue for (B), or something like it, and it would be somewhat tedious, I think, to actually run through the argument, especially since it doesn't matter very much, in the present context, whether something like (B) is true.

(I should note, though, that if, in addition to (A), something like (B) *is* true, then this gives us another open question that's relevant, if not to the full-blown truth of libertarianism, then at least to the issue of whether human beings are partially L-free. But (i) this further question is just another empirical question about the causal histories of our torn decisions [in particular, it asks whether any of our torn decisions are partially determined at the moment of choice and, if they are, what sorts of events they're partially determined by and to what extent they're partially determined]; and (ii) arguments analogous to the ones I give in chapter 4 suggest that this further question is also a wide-open question [and it will be pretty obvious in chapter 4 that this is the case]. Thus, in terms of what I'm trying to argue here, it doesn't change things very much if, in addition to (A), something like (B) is also true.)

In any event, since I am going to argue for thesis (A) only and not for thesis (B), the relevant kind of indeterminacy here is the one at work in (A), that is, the one captured by the notion of a wholly undetermined decision. Thus, when I say that if our torn decisions are undetermined at the moment of choice then they're L-free, what I mean is that if they're *wholly undetermined in the manner of TDW-indeterminism*, then they're L-free.

3.2.3 Appropriate Nonrandomness

As I said above—and I am here just echoing the standard view of the matter—the heart of appropriate nonrandomness is captured by the idea that in order for a decision to be L-free, it has to be authored and controlled by the agent in question; that is, it has to be *her* decision, and she has to control which option is chosen. But while authorship and control form the heart of appropriate nonrandomness, this is not all there is to the story. At least in connection with torn decisions, appropriate nonrandomness also requires what Kane has called *plural authorship and control*,[14] which can be understood as follows: If an agent S is trying to decide between multiple options, say, A, B, and C, and if S eventually chooses A in a torn-decision sort of way, then in order for the choice to be plurally authored and controlled by S, it must be the case that (i) the choice was authored and controlled by S, and (ii) there was at least one other option, say, B, such that if S had chosen B, then this choice would also have been authored and controlled by S. Moreover, appropriate nonrandomness also seems to require some sort of *rationality* (and at least in connection with torn decisions, *plural rationality*); in section 3.3.4, I will describe a few different kinds of rationality, and I will try to determine which of them are required for appropriate nonrandomness and L-freedom.

(I suppose one might try to argue that authorship and/or control are in fact not needed for L-freedom, or for the ordinary notion of free will. But I already argued in chapter 1 [section 1.1.3] that (a) authorship and control *are* needed for the ordinary notion of free will, and because of this, (b) libertarians would be wise to maintain that they're required for L-freedom. Now, it's important to remember that since 'L-freedom' is a term of art, what's needed for L-freedom is something that libertarians can *stipulate*. Thus, *some* libertarians might want to assert that authorship and control aren't needed for the sort of L-freedom that they have in mind [though one might wonder whether the terms 'libertarian' and 'L-freedom' would really be appropriate here]. But I simply want to assert that the kind of L-freedom that I'm interested in here *does* require authorship and control.)

3.3 The Argument

In this section, I will argue for thesis (A) from section 3.2.2. Or to phrase the thesis a bit differently, I will argue for the following claim:

(**) For any ordinary human torn decision, if it is wholly undetermined in the manner of TDW-indeterminism, then it is L-free—that is, (a) it is not just undetermined but also appropriately nonrandom (i.e., it is authored and controlled by the agent in question in an appropriately rational way and in a way that satisfies the requirement for plural authorship, control, and rationality), and (b) the indeterminacy in question increases or procures the appropriate nonrandomness.

I will argue for this thesis as follows. In section 3.3.1, I will argue that if our torn decisions are wholly undetermined, then we author and control them. In section 3.3.2, I will argue that the authorship and control in question here are in fact procured by the indeterminacy in question, i.e., that this indeterminacy is *freedom-enhancing*; moreover, I will also argue in section 3.3.2 that if our torn decisions are wholly undetermined, then we have *full-blown* authorship and control over them—that is, we have as much authorship and control over them as we possibly could. In section 3.3.3, I will argue that the variety of L-freedom developed in sections 3.3.1–3.3.2—or more precisely, the variety of indeterminacy-enhanced authorship and control—are *worth wanting*, or *worth caring about*. In section 3.3.4, I will argue that if our torn decisions are wholly undetermined in the manner of TDW-indeterminism, then they are sufficiently rational, that is, rational in all the ways that might be required for appropriate nonrandomness. And finally, in section 3.3.5, I will argue that if our torn decisions are wholly undetermined, then they satisfy the requirement for plural authorship, control, and rationality. Thus, taken together, the arguments of these subsections entail that if our torn decisions are wholly undetermined, then they are L-free (and that the variety of L-freedom that's procured here is worth wanting). I should say in advance that I will spend far more time discussing authorship and control than rationality and the plurality requirements. As we'll see, this is because (a) authorship and control are the most important requirements for appropriate nonrandomness, and (b) it is authorship and control that, on my view, are enhanced or procured by TDW-indeterminism.

3.3.1 If Our Torn Decisions Are Undetermined, Then We Author and Control Them

In this subsection, I will argue that if our ordinary torn decisions are wholly undetermined in the manner of TDW-indeterminism, then we author and control them. I will begin by providing two positive arguments for this thesis (in sections 3.3.1.1 and 3.3.1.2), and then in section 3.3.1.3, I will respond to a pair of objections to the thesis.

3.3.1.1 The argument from token–token identity
My first argument is based on the token–token identity theory of decisions. This is a bit ironic, because mind–brain materialism has often led people to doubt libertarianism. People sometimes say things like this:

> If decisions are just neural events, and if in addition, they're not determined by the neural states that are our reasons (i.e., our beliefs and desires and so on), then presumably they arise out of brutely physical (i.e., wholly nonmental) neural events in our brains, and so it could not be that we author and control them.

But this is confused. This is what we would say to a materialist who claimed that our decisions are determined but not by our reasons. But that's not the picture I'm proposing at all. On the view I have in mind, our torn decisions aren't determined by anything; they're not determined by our reasons, and they're not determined by nonmental neural events in our brains. This, of course, is perfectly consistent with the token–token identity theory; all that follows from that theory is that our torn decisions are themselves neural events; it doesn't follow that they're causally determined by other neural events. Moreover—and this is the point that provides a segue into my argument—while it's true that if the token–token theory is correct, our torn decisions are physical events, they are also *mental* events. In particular, they are purposeful, intentional decisions. Ralph, for instance, decided to move to New York consciously and on purpose, fully aware of what he was doing and in full possession of his faculties. Thus, it doesn't follow from the mere fact that our torn decisions are physical events that they're unfree, or random in some appropriate sense of the term; for (a) it doesn't follow from this that our torn decisions are inappropriately caused by nonmental events, and (b) given the token–token identity theory, the physical events in question here (i.e., the neural events that are our torn decisions) are still *mental* events, and in particular, they are still conscious, intentional, purposeful, and so on.

This opens the door to an initial argument for the thesis that if our torn decisions are wholly undetermined in the manner of TDW-indeterminism, then we author and control them. The first point to note here is that ordinary torn decisions like Ralph's and Jane's are conscious, intentional, and purposeful. In other words, the decisions themselves—and keep in mind that if these decisions are wholly undetermined in the manner of TDW-indeterminism, as we're assuming here, then the decisions themselves are the events that, so to speak, *settle* which of the various live options will be actualized—are conscious, intentional, purposeful events. In particular, they are *conscious doing events*, or *conscious choosing events*. Thus, for example, in Ralph's case, the choice itself *is* a Ralph-consciously-doing event, or a Ralph-consciously-choosing event. The second point to note is that if our torn decisions are wholly undetermined in the manner of TDW-indeterminism, then they flow out of our reasons and thought in a nondeterministically causal way. (Again, the justification for this is simply that the probabilities of the various options being chosen depend on our reasons; i.e., different reason sets give rise to different probabilities here.) And the third point is that if our torn decisions are wholly undetermined in the manner of TDW-indeterminism, then once an agent has moved into a torn state and is going to make a torn decision, nothing external to her conscious reasons and thought has any causal influence over how she chooses. Subconscious reasons don't have any causal influence here; nonmental physical events in the agent's brain don't have any causal influence; alien interveners don't have any causal influence; again, aside from the agent's conscious reasons and thought, *nothing* has any causal influence here.

(Note the reason for the qualifier 'once an agent has moved into a torn state': (a) events external to our conscious reasons and thought can, and very often do, causally influence what our reasons for choosing are [e.g., a math teacher can causally influence the beliefs of her students by showing them a proof]; and so (b) these external factors can [indirectly] causally influence which options we choose in our torn decisions, even if these decisions are wholly undetermined in the manner of TDW-indeterminism. But, of course, this is a general fact about all of our reasons and decisions, whether they're torn or not, and the issue here seems not to matter to what I'm arguing in the present section. The point I'm making here is that if our torn decisions are wholly undetermined in the manner of TDW-indeterminism, then *once an agent has moved into a torn state and is going to make a torn decision*, nothing external to her conscious reasons and thought has any causal influence over how she chooses. Or to put the point a bit differently, we can say that if our torn decisions are TDW-undetermined, then in any given torn decision, nothing external to the agent's conscious reasons and thought has any causal influence, *after the formation of the agent's torn state*, over which of the various reasons-based tied-for-best options is chosen. This follows directly from TDW-indeterminism, which says that when we make torn decisions, the moment-of-choice probabilities of the various live options being chosen match the reasons-based probabilities, and the choice occurs without any further causal input, i.e., without anything else being significantly causally relevant to which option is chosen.[15])

It seems to me that when we combine the three points from the paragraph before last, we get authorship and control, at least in ordinary cases. For instance, if we assume that Ralph's decision was wholly undetermined in the manner of TDW-indeterminism, then we have that (a) Ralph's choice was conscious, intentional, and purposeful—that is, it *was* a Ralph-consciously-choosing event, or a Ralph-consciously-doing event; (b) the choice flowed out of his conscious reasons and thought in a nondeterministically causal way; and (c) *nothing* external to his conscious reasons and thought had *any* causal influence (after he moved into a torn state) over how he chose. But this seems to be enough to give us the result that Ralph authored and controlled the decision in the ordinary intuitive sense that's relevant to the issue of free will—that is, in the sense that it was *Ralph* who made the choice, or who did the choosing, or who settled which option was chosen. Perhaps we can think of it this way: Given that we have (a)–(c), why *wouldn't* we say that Ralph authored and controlled the decision? In this scenario, we seem to get the result that Ralph *actively chose*, and that it was *he* who controlled which option was chosen, because (i) the choice itself *was* a Ralph-consciously-doing event, (ii) it flowed out of his conscious reasons and thought in a nondeterministically causal way, and (iii) at the moment of choice, nothing outside of his conscious reasons and thought had any causal influence over how he chose.

(If you like, we can say that we have here a sort of agent causation, but this is going to reduce to event causation—or more specifically, to [nondeterministic] causation by agent-involving events, in particular, events involving the agent's conscious reasons and thought. Thus, according to standard usage, my libertarian view is not an agent-causal view.[16])

One might object to the argument I've given here by saying something like the following:

> You seem to be embracing a theory of authorship and control, one that formulates a sufficient condition for the applicability of the concepts of authorship and control (but leaves open what the necessary conditions might be). The theory is this:
>
>> (A&C) An agent A has authorship and control with respect to a torn decision D if, but not necessarily only if, (i) A makes D in a conscious, intentional, purposeful way (i.e., D *is* an A-consciously-choosing event); (ii) A's choice flows out of her conscious reasons and thought in a nondeterministically causal way; and (iii) once A moves into a torn state and is going to make a torn decision, nothing external to her conscious

reasons and thought has any causal influence over which option she chooses.

Again, (A&C) seems to be implicit in what you have said so far. But there seem to be counterexamples to it. Suppose, for instance, that an alien implants (conscious) reasons into Tiziana's head and that, a bit later, Tiziana makes a TDW-undetermined torn decision based on these reasons. Then it seems clear that Tiziana didn't author or control this decision. But given what you've argued about torn decisions, (A&C) seems to entail that she did author and control it. (This, of course, is related to your claim a while back that it is perfectly normal for external factors to causally influence what our reasons for choosing are; your view seems to be that this does not destroy authorship or control. Well, you might be right that in *normal* cases, it doesn't; but the Tiziana case suggests that in at least *some* kinds of cases, authorship and control can be destroyed by the presence of external factors that causally influence what our reasons are.)

One might question whether all of the conditions in (A&C) are really satisfied in the Tiziana case; in particular, one might question whether conditions (ii) and (iii) are satisfied, because one might doubt that the implanted conscious reasons are *Tiziana's* reasons. Or alternatively, one might argue that, in fact, Tiziana *did* author and control the decision (though she didn't control what her reasons for choosing were). But I don't want to get into any of these issues, for I have a different response that blocks the above objection before it ever gets off the ground: I am not proposing (A&C) as a conceptual analysis, that is, as a thesis about the meanings of 'authorship' and 'control' that's supposed to provide a sufficient condition for the applicability of the concepts of authorship and control; rather, I intend it (or something like it) to be taken as a claim about when *actual* humans have authorship and control. Thus, since it's reasonable to suppose that in fact, no aliens have implanted any reasons in our heads, the above objection is irrelevant. And indeed, this is how I intend this entire chapter to be read: I am claiming that if *our* torn decisions are, *in fact*, wholly undetermined in the manner of TDW-indeterminism, then they are also, in fact, appropriately nonrandom and L-free.

Given this response to the above objection, one might counterrespond in the following way:

> If you're not giving us a conceptual analysis of authorship and control, then you don't have a theory of what they *are*. So how do you know whether (i)–(iii) are sufficient for authorship and control, even assuming

that we're dealing with "normal cases," that is, cases in which our reasons aren't being influenced by aliens and so on?

I don't have a conceptual theory of what a person is, or what a game is, but I'm still very reliable at distinguishing persons from non-persons and games from non-games. And likewise, I would claim, for authorship and control. For instance, if we focus in on Ralph's decision again, it seems to me that if (i) Ralph chose to move to New York consciously, intentionally, purposefully, and so on, and (ii) his choice flowed out of his conscious reasons and thought in a nondeterministically causal way, and (iii) once Ralph moved into a torn state and was going to make a torn decision, nothing outside of his conscious reasons and thought had any causal influence over how he chose, then (given various plausible empirical assumptions about this being a normal torn decision without anything like alien intervention) we seem to have a scenario that we can recognize as involving authorship and control—that is, the ordinary intuitive kinds of authorship and control that are relevant to the issue of free will. So just as my confidence in the conclusion that Madonna is a person is based not on having a precise theory of what a person is, but rather on my ability to recognize persons when I encounter them, so, too, my conclusion in the present case is based not on having a precise theory of what authorship and control are, but rather on my ability to recognize authorship and control when I encounter them.

There's another point that's worth making here about the above objection and my response to it. In order for us to arrive at an informed theory of what authorship and control are, we *first* need to have the ability to distinguish cases in which authorship and control are present from those in which they're not present. For (a) in order to test our proposed theories (i.e., our proposed conceptual analyses) of authorship and control, we need to have intuitions about whether various kinds of cases involve authorship and control; but (b) to say that we need to have intuitions of this sort is just to say that we need to have the ability to distinguish cases in which authorship and control are present from those in which they're not. Thus, it seems to me that having this ability is *prior* to having a theory of authorship and control. And it follows from this that the above objection to my argument is misguided.[17,18]

3.3.1.2 The argument from phenomenology
The second argument I want to give for the conclusion of this section—that is, the conclusion that if our ordinary torn decisions are wholly undetermined, then we

author and control them—is that it is introspectively satisfying. In other words, this conclusion dovetails with the phenomenology of our torn decisions. Now, of course, introspection and phenomenology can be deceiving; but I want to argue that in the present case, there is only one plausible way that the phenomenology could turn out to be illusory and that this scenario would not undermine my argument. To appreciate this point, let us begin by introspecting on our own torn decisions. When we make decisions like Ralph's and Jane's, does it feel like we author and control them, or does it feel like they just happen to us? For my own part, it feels to me like I'm in control of my own torn decisions, and I think I'm perfectly normal in this respect. I don't think ordinary people make torn decisions—for example, decisions like Jane's, about things like what to order for dessert—and then think, "Wait a minute! How did *that* come out of my mouth?" Perhaps we *sometimes* feel that way, but this is very rare. Usually, when we make torn decisions—everyday torn decisions about things like what to order for lunch, or whether to go to a movie, or how many bottles of wine to buy for a dinner party—we don't think things like "How did *that* come out of my mouth?," because it's part of the experience of torn decision making that these decisions are *ours*. Indeed, we almost always think we *know* how these things come out of our mouths; we think they come out of our mouths precisely because *we* decide to say them. In short, it simply doesn't feel to us like our torn decisions just happen to us; it feels like we can do whatever we want to do when we make torn decisions. That is, it feels like we author these decisions and control which options are chosen.

Now, again, this phenomenology could turn out to be illusory. But let's think for a moment about *how* it could be illusory, about what kinds of scenarios could render the phenomenology false. To this end, suppose I make a torn decision in which I choose some option A over some other option B, and suppose that after I make this decision, it feels to me introspectively as if I authored and controlled the decision. How could this feeling be illusory? It seems to me that the only remotely plausible way that it could turn out to be illusory is if, unbeknownst to me, the decision was generated by—perhaps causally determined by—some event or circumstance in a way that's inconsistent with the claim that *I* authored and controlled the decision. For instance, it could very easily be that my decision was deterministically caused by a wholly nonmental brain event that preceded the decision in my head, and if this were actually the case, then it would seem at least prima facie plausible to suppose that the phenomenology of my torn decision was just mistaken—that is, that *I* (the agent) didn't really author or control the decision.

But we need to remember the argumentative situation we're in here: I am currently arguing that *if* our torn decisions are wholly undetermined in the manner of TDW-indeterminism, then we author and control them; thus, we are assuming in the present section that our torn decisions *are* wholly undetermined. But if my decision was undetermined in this way, then it was not causally influenced by anything external to my conscious reasons and thought. And this seems to eliminate the *only* worry we might have about the accuracy of the phenomenology of my decision. If we know for certain that once I moved into a torn state and was going to make a torn decision, nothing external to my conscious reasons and thought had any causal influence over how I chose—and again, we are assuming here that this is the case—then what else could lead us to say that the phenomenology was mistaken? The answer, it seems to me, is *nothing*. The only remotely plausible way that I could be mistaken in my feeling that I authored and controlled the decision—that is, the only way it could turn out that the intuitive notions of authorship and control don't apply to my decision—would be if it turned out that, unbeknownst to me, my choice was causally determined (or at least causally influenced) by some event or circumstance in an authorship-and-control-destroying way. Thus, since we're assuming here that this is not the case, it seems to follow that the phenomenology is accurate.[19]

Here's another way to think about this point: Suppose that a race of superintelligent neurocognitive scientists studied your brain and told you that, in fact, your own torn decisions are undetermined at the moment of choice in the way we're assuming, so that when you make these decisions, nothing external to your conscious reasons and thought makes you choose as you do. Would you conclude from this that you do not author or control these decisions? It seems to me that it would be downright bizarre to draw that conclusion. Indeed, if I found out that when I make my torn decisions, nothing external to my conscious reasons and thought causally influences how I choose, I would conclude from this that I *do* author and control these decisions. For the worry about a hidden causal influence is the *only* worry I have about whether I author and control my torn decisions. (What other worry is there?) And so it seems to me that if our torn decisions are wholly undetermined in the manner of TDW-indeterminism, then we do author and control them. And this, of course, is just what I wanted to argue in this section.[20]

3.3.1.3 Two objections I've been arguing that if our ordinary torn decisions are wholly undetermined in the manner of TDW-indeterminism, then we author and control them. But one might argue against this thesis in either of the following two ways:

Objection 1 (a.k.a. the "luck objection," or the "chance objection"): Suppose that some agent S is torn between two options, A and B, and eventually chooses A in a torn-decision sort of way. And now suppose that God "rolls back" the universe and "replays" the decision. If the decision is undetermined at the moment of choice, then it seems that the decision might very well go differently the second time around, even if everything about the past—in particular, everything about S and her reasons—remained the same. Indeed, if the decision is wholly undetermined in the manner of TDW-indeterminism, then it seems that if God "played" the decision 100 times, we should expect that S would choose A and B about 50 times each. But given this—given that S would choose differently in different "plays" of the decision, without *anything* about her psychology changing—it's hard to see how we can maintain that S was the author or the source of her decision or that she controlled which option was chosen. It seems to be a matter of *chance* or *luck* what she chose, and to the extent that this is right, it seems that S didn't author or control the decision. At the very least, it seems that the presence of the element of chance or luck here diminishes S's authorship and control. Another way to appreciate the point here is to notice that even if prior conditions don't determine whether S will choose A or B, it might still be that prior conditions determine that there are certain fixed probabilities of A and B being chosen (in particular, if S's decision was wholly determined in the manner of TDW-indeterminism, then both probabilities were around 0.5); but given this, isn't it just a matter of chance or luck whether, in fact, S chooses A or B? And if it's a matter of chance or luck, then it seems that S doesn't author or control the decision. Or again, at the very least, it seems that the presence of the element of chance or luck decreases the amount of authorship and control that S has. (Arguments of this general kind have been mounted in a number of different ways in recent years by a number of different philosophers, including van Inwagen [2002], Fischer [1999], Mele [1999a,b], Haji [1999], Clarke [1995, 2002], O'Connor [2000], Double [1991], G. Strawson [2000], Waller [1988], Bernstein [1995], and Berofsky [2000];[21] many of these arguments, I should say, have been directed against Kane's version of libertarianism.)

Objection 2: If a decision is undetermined, then it isn't determined by the agent's reasons or character; but then at the very least, the agent has less authorship and control than she would have had if her decision had been

Libertarianism Reduces to a Kind of Indeterminacy 93

fully determined by her reasons and character. In short, the looser the connection between the agent's reasons and character on the one hand and her decision on the other, the less authorship and control she has over the decision.

I will begin by responding to objection 1, and in doing this, I want to focus on Ralph's decision to move to New York.[22] The first point I want to make here is that it simply doesn't follow from the fact that Ralph would choose differently in different "plays" of the decision that he didn't author or control his decision. There is no inconsistency in claiming that

(#)   Ralph chooses differently in different plays of the decision,

and

(##)   In each of these different plays of the decision, it is *Ralph* who does the choosing, or who authors the decision and controls which option is chosen.

Thus, if we replayed the decision and Ralph chose to stay in Mayberry in play number 2, it wouldn't follow that it wasn't *him* who chose to move to New York (and who controlled which option was chosen) in play number 1.

Second, and more important, it's not just that there's no inconsistency between (#) and (##); there isn't even any *tension* between the two. Indeed, we can make an even stronger point than this. Given that Ralph is making a *torn* decision, if we take (##) as a hypothesis, then we should *expect* to get (#); that is, if we assume that in each play of the decision, the choice flows from *Ralph*—i.e., that it's *him* who authors and controls the decision—then given that he's torn, we should expect that he would choose differently in different plays of the decision. For consider: Given that Ralph is torn and hence that his conscious reasons don't pick out a unique best option, it would seem very suspicious if he always chose the same way in multiple plays of the decision. If he always chose to move to New York, then it would be plausible to think, "Look, that can't be a coincidence; something must be *causing* him to choose in that way; and since (by assumption) his conscious reasons and thought aren't causing this, it must be something else, for example, a random, nonmental event in his nervous system, or a subconscious mental state." (Of course, you might think that if his choice was determined by a subconscious mental state, then it would still be *Ralph* who authored and controlled the decision. But we will see below [subsection 3.3.2] that at the very least, this would diminish Ralph's control.) On the other hand, if Ralph chose *differently* in different plays of the decision, that would fit perfectly with the hypothesis that the choice is flowing from *him* (or more precisely, from his conscious reasons and thought); for since Ralph is making a torn decision, we know by assumption that he is neutral between his two live options, at least in his conscious thought.

A third point here is this: Just because Ralph's decision was arbitrary or random (or if you like, chancy or lucky) in *some* senses of these terms, it doesn't follow that it was arbitrary or random in the sense that's relevant here. The sense of nonrandomness that's relevant here is the one that's required for free will, that is, the one that involves authorship and control (and possibly other things as well, such as rationality). But it could be that this sort of nonrandomness is compatible with various kinds of randomness. And, indeed, it seems to me that it clearly is. For it could be that (i) *Ralph* chose (or, more to the point, he authored and controlled the decision), and (ii) because he was torn as to which option was best, and because he had to choose (because he believed that choosing right then was better, all things considered, than remaining in a state of indecision), he *just* chose, so that his decision was, in some sense, arbitrary or random, despite the fact that it was *his* choice and that *he* controlled which option was chosen. There is no tension at all between (i) and (ii) here. The fact that Ralph chose randomly or arbitrarily does not undermine the claim that it was *him* who made the choice and who controlled which option was chosen.

A fourth point I want to make here is a response to an assumption that seems to be inherent in the above formulation of the luck objection. The assumption is that if there was a certain fixed probability that Ralph was going to choose to move to New York—more specifically, if there was a 0.5 probability that he would choose to move to New York and a 0.5 probability that he would choose to stay in Mayberry—then it was just a matter of luck that he in fact *did* choose to move to New York. My response: If Ralph's decision was wholly undetermined in the manner of TDW-indeterminism, then (i) it was *his reasons* that caused it to be the case that the probabilities in question were 0.5, and (ii) despite the fact that there were fixed probabilities here, it is still true that the choosing of New York over Mayberry was done *by Ralph* (for as we've seen, if the decision was TDW-undetermined, then it *was* a Ralph-choosing event, and it wasn't causally influenced by anything external to Ralph's conscious reasons and thought). Thus, there's simply no incompatibility between there being fixed moment-of-choice probabilities here and the choice being authored and controlled by Ralph.

These remarks might not seem entirely satisfying as a response to the luck objection. For (a) the version of the luck objection I have responded to here is based on the idea that indeterminacy would either diminish or destroy authorship and control, and (b) one might think of the luck objection as raising a worry about how indeterminacy could *increase* authorship or control. However, I am going to turn to precisely this issue in section 3.3.2. I am going to argue at length there that the right kind of indeterminacy in our torn decisions does increase authorship and/or control. More specifically, I'm going to argue that if our torn decisions are TDW-undetermined, then this increases the authorship and/or control that we have over these decisions.

Let me move on now to objection 2. The central premise of this objection is the following:

> *Principle D*: Determination by conscious reasons is required for full authorship and control, and in general, the looser the connection between the agent's reasons and character on the one hand and her decision on the other, the less authorship and control she has over the decision.

Now, in the present context, it would clearly be question-begging to take this principle as a basic premise without argument. So the question is whether there is any argument in its favor, and I must confess that I can't imagine what such an argument might look like. I admit that if we focus only on cases in which the agent's conscious reasons clearly pick out a unique best option, then Principle D can seem intuitively plausible (and indeed, my view allows for the claim that in such cases, Principle D is true). But as soon as we think about torn decisions, Principle D seems completely implausible. For it entails that regardless of whether torn decisions are determined or undetermined, and regardless of the overall view of free will that we end up endorsing, no human being has ever authored or controlled a torn decision. That strikes me as wildly implausible. If Sandy has to choose between A and B, and if her conscious reasons don't pick out a unique best option, it simply doesn't follow that for this reason alone, she can't author or control the decision between the two. Intuitively, the notions of authorship and control seem to allow for a random selection here, so long as it is *Sandy* who makes the random selection and not something else. (Indeed, while we're at it, we might as well note that, intuitively, the notion of *free will* doesn't seem to require determination by reasons; it seems to make perfect sense to say that Sandy didn't have compelling reasons for choosing A over B but that she chose it of her own free will.)

So it seems to me that in connection with torn decisions, Principle D is counterintuitive. Moreover, as far as I can see, we don't have any good reason for thinking that Principle D is true. And finally, in section 3.3.2, I am also going to provide an argument that entails that Principle D is false. More specifically, I am going to argue there that if our torn decisions are wholly undetermined in the manner of TDW-indeterminism, then we have as much control over them as we do over decisions that are determined by our reasons. And if this is right, then, of course, Principle D is false. So given all of this, I am inclined to conclude that Principle D is false—or, more specifically, that it fails in connection with torn decisions. (I should note, however, that even though Principle D fails for torn decisions, there is very likely still a kind of determination by reasons here, for it is likely that when we make torn decisions, our reasons deterministically cause us to choose from among our reasons-based tied-for-best options. For instance, it seems plausible to suppose that it was causally determined that Ralph was not going to decide to move to Outer Mongolia—that is, that he was going to choose between New York and Mayberry. And this, I think, dovetails with the claim that the decision was *Ralph's*. Moreover, it could also be that there's another sort of determination by reasons here, for as we've seen, it could be that Ralph's reasons deterministically caused the moment-of-choice probabilities of his two live options being chosen to be 0.5 each.)

3.3.2 Why TDW-Indeterminism Increases or Procures Authorship and Control

I want to argue in this subsection for the following theses: (1) If our ordinary torn decisions are wholly undetermined in the manner of TDW-indeterminism, then we have as much authorship and control over them as we could possibly have. (2) If our torn decisions are not undetermined in this way—if, for example, they're causally determined—then we have less authorship and/or control over them than we do in the scenario in which they are TDW-undetermined. Together, these two theses entail that TDW-indeterminism is *freedom-enhancing*—or, more specifically, that it *increases* or *procures* authorship and/or control.

Let me begin by arguing for thesis (1), and once again, let me argue this point by focusing on Ralph's decision. The first point to notice here is this: Because Ralph's decision is a *torn* decision, there is no way to procure more authorship or control for it than it has in the scenario in which it is TDW-undetermined. The fact of the matter is that Ralph's conscious reasons do not pick out a unique best option; but he does have reason to make *some* choice, that is, for not remaining in a state of indecision; thus, it seems clear that Ralph has good reason to *just pick* from among his tied-for-best options (i.e., to pick randomly, or arbitrarily). Given this, it seems that the most we could hope for here, vis-à-vis authorship and control, is that it be *Ralph* who does the just-picking, that is, who makes the random selection from among his tied-for-best options. If the selection is made by an alien intruder, or if it's determined by a nonmental brain event in Ralph's head that triggers the choice, then it is plausible to suppose that in some important sense, Ralph does not author or control the decision. But if the mental/physical event that is Ralph's conscious decision is undetermined in the way we're assuming here, then at the moment of choice, nothing external to Ralph's conscious reasons and thought has any causal influence over his choice; in this scenario, Ralph chooses—consciously, intentionally, and purposefully—without being casually influenced by anything external to his conscious reasons and thought. Thus, it seems that in this case, we do get the result that it is Ralph who does the just-choosing. And so it also seems that in this scenario, we procure as much authorship and control for Ralph as we can, given that he is making a torn decision.

To further appreciate the thesis of the last paragraph—that the libertarian view I'm describing procures as much authorship and control for our torn decisions as is possible—suppose that God told us that we could dictate how the world would be with respect to our torn decisions, and suppose that in deciding how to set things up, the only thing we cared about was maximizing authorship and control. How ought we to proceed? Well, it seems to me that we couldn't ask for anything better than a scenario in which the agent gets to just-choose from among her tied-for-best options without anything external to her causally influencing her choice. For (a) if the choice were anything other than an *arbitrary* selection—that is, anything other than a just-choosing—then the selection procedure wouldn't mesh with the agent's reasons, because her reasons are, by assumption, neutral between her tied-for-best options; and (b) if the just-choosing were done by anything other than the *agent*, then she would lose authorship and control.

In response to this, one might say something like the following: "It would be better to set things up so that people would never be forced to *just choose*—that is, so they would always have good reasons for their choices." I have four things to say in response to this. First, to set things up like this is not to set them up so that we have more authorship or control over our torn decisions; rather, it's to set them up so that we never make torn decisions. Second, it's hard to see why anyone would *want* to set things up like this, because there doesn't seem to be any reason for thinking it undesirable to have to make torn decisions, that is, for thinking that lives without such choices are better, *ceteris paribus*, than lives with them. Indeed, my intuition goes the opposite way: If we never made any torn decisions, if our conscious reasons always picked out unique best options for all our choices, then we could be spontaneous only by being irrational, and that, I think, would be bad; we would be slaves to our reasons in a way that we currently aren't, and so, intuitively, we would have less control—or at any rate, less *spontaneous control*—over our lives than we would if we made some torn decisions in which our choices weren't causally influenced by anything external to our conscious reasons and thought. Third, if we set things up so that people never had torn reason sets, that would be a kind of external control—it would be to *forbid* a certain kind of reason set—and so, intuitively, it would reduce freedom. Finally, the fourth and most important point I want to make here is this: By setting things up so that we never made any torn decisions, we wouldn't be increasing authorship or control at all, because in fact, we do not have more authorship or control over choices that are uniquely picked out by our conscious reasons than we do over torn decisions that are wholly undetermined in the manner of TDW-indeterminism. To appreciate this, consider two Ralphs. $Ralph_1$ is the Ralph we've been considering so far, the Ralph who is torn between his two options and in the end arbitrarily chooses (i.e., has the experience of just-choosing) to move to New York, without anything external to his conscious reasons and thought causally influencing his choice. $Ralph_2$, on the other hand, comes to believe that his reasons for moving to New York are stronger than his reasons for staying in Mayberry and, therefore, decides to move to New York. Does $Ralph_2$ have more authorship or control over his decision than $Ralph_1$? I find it hard to see why we should say that he does. For as we've seen, $Ralph_1$'s decision was a conscious, intentional, $Ralph_1$-doing event; and it flowed out of his conscious reasons and thought in a nondeterministically causal way; and once $Ralph_1$ moved into a torn state and was going to make a torn decision, nothing external to his conscious reasons and thought had any causal influence over how he chose. Thus, it was $Ralph_1$, and nothing else, who chose to move to New York. So I can't see why anyone would say that $Ralph_1$ had any less authorship or control than $Ralph_2$. The difference between the two Ralphs isn't that $Ralph_2$ had more authorship or control ($Ralph_1$, after all, could have done whatever he wanted to); the difference is simply that $Ralph_2$ had compelling reasons for his choice, whereas $Ralph_1$ did not.

Libertarianism Reduces to a Kind of Indeterminacy

It's worth noting that I am disagreeing here with something Kane (1999) has said on this topic. He says that indeterminism diminishes a certain kind of control while increasing another kind. In contrast, I think that (i) given that a decision is a *torn* decision, the sort of indeterminism we're assuming here procures as much control for the agent as is possible (and moreover, we'll see shortly that no deterministic view delivers this much control for our torn decisions), and (ii) if our torn decisions are undetermined at the moment of choice in the way we're assuming here, then we have *just as much* control over them as we do over non-torn decisions in which our reasons determine our choices.

The sort of control that Kane says is diminished by indeterminism is *antecedent determining control*—that is, "the ability to determine or guarantee which of a set of options will occur *before* it occurs" (Kane 1999, 238). One might wonder how I could question Kane's claim that *this* kind of control is diminished by the kind of indeterminism we're assuming here. Let me say two things about this, one relating to point (i) from the preceding paragraph and the other relating to point (ii). The first point is that as long as we're talking about a torn decision, determinism wouldn't deliver antecedent determining control, because it wouldn't be the *agent* who did the prior determining, because before the choice, the agent is torn (at least in his conscious thought, and that seems to be all that matters in connection with Kane's notion of antecedent determining control); thus, in the case of torn decisions, indeterminism doesn't diminish antecedent determining control for the simple reason that we wouldn't have this kind of control anyway. What diminishes antecedent determining control isn't indeterminism, it's *being torn*; if you're not torn (and you're not constrained), then you can have antecedent determining control. Moreover, it's worth noting that even when we're torn, we can still have antecedent determining control *if we want it*. If during dinner someone told Jane that she could have a million dollars if she could say *right then* what she would order for dessert, she could easily do it. Thus, the point is simply that when we're torn, we don't *want* antecedent determining control, because we want to leave our options open.

Moving on to my second point, it might seem that since we don't have antecedent determining control in connection with torn decisions (whether they're undetermined or not), it follows that claim (ii) from the paragraph before last is false; that is, it might seem that we don't have as much control over torn decisions (whether they're undetermined or not) as we do over non-torn decisions in which our reasons determine our choices, because with torn decisions, we don't have antecedent determining control. But I don't think this is the right way to describe the situation. The Ralph$_1$/Ralph$_2$ argument suggests that a lack of antecedent determining control doesn't entail a lack of control, or even a decrease in the amount of control; just because Ralph$_1$ didn't control his choice *in advance*, it doesn't follow that he didn't control the choice, and indeed, it doesn't follow that he had *less* control than he would have had if he would have controlled it in advance. The question of whether an agent has antecedent determining control is a question about *when* an agent has control; it's not a question about *whether* she has control, or *how much* control she has. Thus, if what I've argued about Ralph$_1$ is correct, then what we should say about him, vis-à-vis the issue of antecedent determining control, is that he controlled his decision *at the moment of choice* but didn't control it in advance.[23]

Finally, it's worth noting here that even if we decided to say that a lack of antecedent determining control involves a kind of lack of control, it wouldn't really matter, because antecedent determining control is clearly not required for free will. If an agent S authors and controls a decision at the moment of choice, that's clearly enough authorship and control for free will.

Let me argue now for thesis (2), that is, the thesis that if our torn decisions are *not* wholly undetermined in the manner of TDW-indeterminism—if, for example, they're causally determined by prior events—then we have less authorship and/or control over them than we do in the scenario in which they are wholly undetermined. (If this is true, and if thesis (1) is also true, then it follows that if our torn decisions are wholly undetermined, then this is a freedom-enhancing sort of indeterminism.)

As long as we remember that we're talking here about *torn* decisions, it's easy to see how TDW-indeterminism increases authorship and/or control. Consider, for instance, Ralph's decision. At the moment of choice, he was torn; the sum total of his conscious reasons and thought did not pick out a unique best option, and indeed, he was neutral between two different options, at least in his conscious thought. Now, as we've seen, if Ralph's decision was wholly undetermined in the manner of TDW-indeterminism, so that, at the moment of choice, nothing external to his conscious reasons and thought had any causal influence over which option he chose, then we get the result that Ralph had as much authorship and control over his decision as he could. But if Ralph's decision wasn't undetermined in this way, then we don't get this result. Consider first scenarios in which his decision was completely determined. If Ralph's decision was determined at the moment of choice, then either

(I) it was determined by something external to his conscious reasons and thought,

or

(II) it was determined by his conscious reasons but in a subconscious way, that is, a way that Ralph wasn't aware of.

It couldn't be that the choice was determined by conscious reasons in a way that Ralph was aware of, because we are assuming here that Ralph's decision was a *torn* one; that is, we're assuming that right up to the moment of choice, Ralph felt torn and didn't have any conscious view as to which set of reasons was strongest. Thus, (I) and (II) are the only possible deterministic scenarios here.

Now, in scenario (I), that is, the scenario in which something external to Ralph's conscious reasons and thought determines which option he chooses, it seems that at the very least, Ralph doesn't have as much control as he does in the scenario in which his decision is wholly undetermined in the manner of TDW-indeterminism and, hence, not causally influenced (at the moment of choice) by any factor external to his conscious reasons and thought. For instance, if Ralph's choice was determined by a wholly nonmental neural event in his head, then it seems plausible to suppose that the choice was not authored or controlled by *Ralph*—or, again, at the very least, it seems that this diminishes the amount of authorship and control that Ralph has. Now, I don't want to commit to the claim that *any* scenario in which Ralph's decision was determined by factors external to his conscious reasons is a scenario in which he had no authorship or control over his choice; for instance, one might want to claim that if Ralph's choice was determined by subconscious reasons of his, then it could still be that he had some degree of authorship and control over it, since his subconscious reasons are still *his* reasons, or part of *him*, or some such thing. But it's hard to see how one could maintain that Ralph has as *much* control in this case as he does in the case in which his choice is wholly undetermined in the manner of TDW-indeterminism and, hence, not causally influenced, at the moment of choice, by any factor external to his conscious reasons and thought. It seems that, at the very least, when we move to the case in which Ralph's choice is causally determined by subconscious reasons, he loses some *active* control, or some *conscious* control.

It's more plausible, I think, to claim that determination by subconscious reasons is consistent with *authorship* than to claim that it's consistent with control (or at any rate, with full-blown control). Since Ralph's subconscious reasons are part of him, it seems that if these reasons determine his decision, then there is a clear sense in which he is the *source* of the decision, and so there's at least a case to be made for the claim that he's also the author of the decision. For whatever it's worth, though, my own intuition is that determination by subconscious reasons diminishes both authorship and control, though I think it's clearly *more* damaging to control, in particular, to active, conscious control. (I might also add here that in connection with both authorship and control, it seems pretty clear that determination by subconscious reasons is less damaging than determination by wholly extra-agential factors.)

I should also emphasize here that I am not claiming that determination by subconscious reasons *always* diminishes control; all I am claiming is that this is true in connection with *torn* decisions. There may be cases in which (a) a decision is determined by a subconscious trace of a personal habit and (b) the agent still has full-blown control over the decision. It seems to me, however, that in order to plausibly maintain that a decision like this involved full-blown agential control, it would have to be the case that there were no viable alternatives to the option chosen, that is, no alternatives that were really live options for the agent. And, of course, this is not the case with torn decisions. To bring this point out, let's return to Jane's decision, but let's suppose that she ended up ordering the fruit plate instead of the tiramisu. Moreover, let's suppose in addition that over the years, Jane has developed something of a habit of ordering healthy food, and let's suppose that unbeknownst to her, this habit (or a subconscious trace of it) caused her to order the fruit plate for dessert. If Jane hadn't thought about any other options and had simply ordered the fruit plate, the situation would be different, and it might be plausible to maintain that she had full-blown control over the choice. But we're supposing here that—contra her usual policy, or habit—she was consciously considering the possibility of ordering the tiramisu. She felt torn. And then she had the experience of "just choosing"; she did *not* have the experience of coming to feel that the fruit plate was a better option because it would be better for her health. Given this, it seems to me that if, unbeknownst to Jane, the decision was determined by a subconscious trace of her habit, then she was at least somewhat deluded. Thus, at the very least, she didn't control the decision in the way she *thought* she was controlling it. And so it seems to me that, at the very least, Jane had less conscious control over her decision in this scenario than she would have had if her decision had been TDW-undetermined and, hence, not causally influenced (at the moment of choice) by anything external to her conscious reasons and thought.

(Before leaving the issue of determination by subconscious reasons, I'd like to consider a worry one might have here. In particular, one might think that *all* of our torn decisions, or virtually all of them, are causally influenced by subconscious reasons, or subconscious mental phenomena. The main point I want to make here is that this is irrelevant to what I'm arguing in the present chapter. I'm arguing here that *if* our torn decisions are TDW-undetermined, then they're L-free. But the present worry is that it may be that our torn decisions *aren't* TDW-undetermined [because they're causally influenced by subconscious mental phenomena]. This, of course, is possible; it may be that *none* of our torn decisions is TDW-undetermined. Whether any of them are is an empirical question. Now, in chapter 4, I will argue that this is also a *wide open* question, that as of right now, we have no good reason for favoring either answer to the question. But it's worth noting here that the issue of subconscious reasons [or subconscious weightings of reasons, or compulsions, or whatever] doesn't itself provide a reason to think that none of our torn decisions is TDW-undetermined. Of course, it *may* be that all of our torn decisions are causally influenced by subconscious mental phenomena, but the important point here is that this is a wildly speculative empirical hypothesis and that as of right now we have no good reason to believe it. Notice how strong this hypothesis is; the claim is that *all* of our torn decisions are causally influenced by subconscious mental phenomena—decisions about what to order for dinner, whether to take the freeway or surface streets to work, and so on. I can't imagine why anyone would believe this at the present time.)

In any event, given the above remarks, it seems that in scenario (I)—the scenario in which something external to Ralph's conscious reasons and thought causally determines which option he chooses—Ralph does not have as much control (and probably also doesn't have as much authorship) as he does in the scenario in which his decision is wholly undetermined in the manner of TDW-indeterminism.

Similar remarks can be made about scenario (II), the scenario in which Ralph's decision is determined by his conscious reasons but in a subconscious way, that is, a way he isn't aware of. For present purposes, this case doesn't seem to be importantly different from the case in which Ralph's decision is determined by subconscious reasons. For this is just another case involving causation by nonconscious factors. Thus, once again, it seems that at the very least, Ralph has less active control in this case, or less conscious control, than he does in the case in which his decision is TDW-undetermined and hence not causally influenced (at the moment of choice) by anything external to his conscious reasons and thought.

Thus, it seems that in both scenario (I) and scenario (II), Ralph has less authorship and/or control than he does in the scenario in which his decision is wholly undetermined in the manner of TDW-indeterminism. But these two scenarios are the only deterministic possibilities here, and so it seems to follow that the indeterminism in my model—that is, TDW-indeterminism—procures a degree of authorship and/or control for our torn decisions that can't be had on any deterministic model. In other words, we seem to have the result that if our torn decisions are wholly undetermined in the manner of TDW-indeterminism, then we have more authorship and/or control over them than we would have in any deterministic scenario.

Moreover, it's not just fully deterministic scenarios that give us less authorship and/or control over our torn decisions—it's all scenarios in which our torn decisions aren't wholly undetermined in the manner of TDW-indeterminism. Suppose, for instance, that some factor external to Ralph's conscious reasons and thought probabilistically causally influenced his choice in the sense that it caused the moment-of-choice probability of his choosing New York to be a bit higher than 0.5 and the moment-of-choice probability of his choosing Mayberry to be a bit lower than 0.5 (despite the fact that the reasons-based probabilities were both still 0.5). Then it seems plausible to conclude that, at the very least, Ralph had a bit less conscious control over the choice than he would have had if this external factor hadn't had any causal influence over his choice. In short, it seems that the best-case scenario here—vis-à-vis the issue of maximizing conscious control—is the one in which Ralph's choice was wholly undetermined in the manner of TDW-indeterminism, that is, the one in which nothing external to Ralph's conscious reasons and thought had any causal influence (after he was in a torn state) over which option he chose. (And once again, it seems that subconscious causal influences are less damaging to authorship and control than wholly nonmental causal influences are; but it also seems that subconscious causal influences are at least partially damaging to active, conscious control.)

So we now have an argument for thesis (2), that is, for the claim that if our torn decisions are TDW-undetermined, then we have more authorship and/or control over them than we would have if they weren't TDW-undetermined. But one might object to the argument I've given for thesis (2) by saying something like this:

> Even if you're right that indeterminism is important to procuring authorship and control for torn decisions, the level of authorship and control that's procured here is no greater than the level of authorship and control

that we have in connection with decisions in which our conscious reasons clearly pick out unique best options and deterministically cause those options to be chosen. But this seems problematic, for it seems to follow that a fully deterministic creature who never made any torn decisions—or more precisely, who was such that whenever she made decisions, her conscious reasons always clearly picked out unique best options and deterministically caused her to choose those options—could have as much authorship and control over her decisions as do the indeterministic creatures that you have in mind.

My response to this worry is that it's irrelevant. Even if it's true that there could be certain kinds of deterministic creatures who had as much authorship and control over their decisions as we would have over ours if TDW-indeterminism were true, the fact remains that TDW-indeterminism delivers more authorship and control for *us* than any deterministic (or alternative indeterministic) view does, because it delivers more authorship and control for our torn decisions.

Let me make two points about this response to the above worry. First, it is important to notice how different from us a deterministic creature of the above kind would be. In order for such a creature to have full-blown control over her decisions, it would have to be the case that whenever she made a decision, her conscious reasons always clearly picked out a unique best option and led her to choose that option. It seems to me that the issue of free will and determinism would very likely not even seem problematic or interesting to creatures like this. The idea that determinism might be true would, I think, not be disturbing or depressing to such creatures, because it would seem to them that their decisions *were* determined by their reasons. But we humans aren't like this at all; we routinely make torn decisions, and this, I think, is a large part of the reason why determinism seems to us to generate a problem for free will. And so the fact that my libertarian view delivers more control for our torn decisions than any deterministic view does should not be thought of as an unimportant or trivial result. On the contrary, it is a crucially important result. (I will argue this point more fully in section 3.3.3, where I argue that the sort of freedom I'm describing here is worth wanting, or worth caring about.)

Second, it's important to remember here that TDW-indeterminism doesn't just deliver more authorship and control for our torn decisions than any deterministic (or alternative indeterministic) view does; as we saw above, in my argument for thesis (1), TDW-indeterminism procures as much authorship and control for our torn decisions as it's possible for these decisions to have. In fact, since I've also argued that TDW-indeterminism gives us as much authorship and control over our torn decisions as we have over decisions in which our reasons determine our choices, it seems to follow from what I've argued here that if our torn decisions are TDW-undetermined, then we have as much authorship and control over them as it's possible for us to have over *any* decision.

I have now argued that (1) if our torn decisions are wholly undetermined in the manner of TDW-indeterminism, then we have as much authorship and control over them as we could possibly have, and (2) if our torn decisions are *not* undetermined in this way, then we have less authorship and control over them. Thus, the sort of indeterminism I have in mind is freedom-enhancing; more specifically, it increases or procures authorship and/or control. And this, recall, is exactly what I wanted to argue in the present section.

However, one might not be satisfied with my argument here. For one might think that the particular kind of L-freedom that's being enhanced here is not worth *wanting*, or worth *caring about*. I think this is false; I think this sort of freedom *is* worth wanting, and I want to turn to this issue now.

3.3.3 Why This Sort of L-Freedom Is Worth Wanting

One might object to the argument I've been mounting so far by saying something like this:

> You may be right that there's a certain sort of freedom—or "freedom," as the case may be—that's increased or procured by TDW-indeterminism. But why in the world would anyone *care* about this sort of "freedom"?

We can make this objection more concrete. Indeed, there are a few different arguments one might give for thinking that the sort of freedom I've been describing is *not* worth wanting. In particular, one might argue in one of the following three ways:

Objection 3: The sorts of indeterministic events that you have in mind seem to be little more than neural "blips" that help us get unstuck when we're torn. How could it matter whether these blips are deterministic or indeterministic? Why should we *want* these blips to be indeterministic?

Objection 4: There are certain things that libertarians have traditionally wanted but that your view seems not to deliver. For instance, it seems that libertarians wanted to secure the result that there is a freedom-enhancing indeterminism inherent in *all* of our decisions, including those in which we have good reasons for choosing a specific one of our options. Your view seems not to deliver this. Moreover, it's not clear that it will deliver the result that people are morally responsible for their actions or the result that people are the *sources* of things—or as Clarke (2003, 102) puts it, that they *make a difference* to how things go.

Objection 5: You have said yourself that most torn decisions are relatively unimportant, that is, that they're not life-shaping decisions. So why should we care so much about them?

I will respond to these three objections in turn. And in doing this, I will be trying not just to respond to these three objections but also to provide positive reasons for thinking that the sort of L-freedom I've been describing *is* worth wanting and worth caring about.

I want to start my discussion of objection 3 by constructing a somewhat more detailed version of the objection. One might put the point here in something like the following way:

Suppose that whenever you are about to make a torn decision, a neural signal is sent to a sort of "neural random number generator" in your brain that, so to speak, "flips a neural coin" and sends back another neural signal that determines which option you choose. Intuitively, it seems that it doesn't matter, in connection with the question of whether you author and control your torn decisions, whether this neural random number generator functions in a deterministic or an indeterministic way. And so it seems not to matter whether our torn decisions are determined or undetermined. (Dennett [1978] raises an objection like this to Valerian libertarianism.)

I agree that it wouldn't matter whether a neural "coin tosser" of this sort functioned deterministically or indeterministically—assuming that these "coin tosses" weren't parts of the neural/mental events that *are* our torn decisions. If our best neurocognitive theory suggested that these events were parts of our torn decisions, then I would say something very different about the case. But if it's built into the thought experiment that the neural "coin-tossing" events are *not* parts of the mental events that are our torn decisions—and if we assume (what seems obvious) that such neural "coin-tossing" events would not be parts of our reasons or thought—then it seems to follow that the "coin-tossing" events would be *external determining factors*, whether they were themselves determined or undetermined. Even if these "coin-tossing" events were themselves undetermined, it would still be true that (a) they determine which options we choose in our torn decisions and (b) they are external not just to our torn decisions themselves, but to all of our conscious and unconscious reasons and thought. Thus, on this model, we would not have full-blown authorship or control over our torn decisions; at the very least, we would have less authorship and control in this scenario than we would if our torn decisions were wholly undetermined in the manner of TDW-indeterminism. For again, if our torn decisions are wholly undetermined in this way, then nothing external to our conscious reasons and thought has any causal influence over which of our tied-for-best options are chosen; and as we've seen, in this scenario, we get the result that when we make our torn decisions, *we* are the ones who are doing the choosing, or the selecting. Thus, the conclusion we should draw from the above thought experiment about neural "coin tosses" isn't that it wouldn't matter if indeterminism were true; it's that it wouldn't matter if a certain *kind* of indeterminism were true, namely, the kind inherent in indeterministic neural "coin tosses" of the above kind. But it *would* matter if TDW-indeterminism were true, for as we've seen, TDW-indeterminism is freedom-enhancing.

If, however, our best neurocognitive theory suggested that these neural "coin tosses" were *parts of* our torn decisions, and if these "coin tosses" were undetermined in a way that delivered the result that our torn decisions themselves were undetermined—indeed, wholly undetermined in the manner of TDW-indeterminism—then I think this *would* matter. For in this case, the mental event itself—that is, the decision—would be undetermined, and so, for all the reasons given in the last section, we would have a freedom-enhancing kind of indeterminism.

But now one might press me as follows:

> Why should we *care* about the distinction you're drawing here? Given that we *just choose* when we make ordinary torn decisions like Ralph's and Jane's, why should we care whether these choices are wholly undetermined in the manner of TDW-indeterminism (i.e., whether our choices here are settled by undetermined brain events that are parts of the neural/mental events that are our torn decisions) or whether our choices are causally determined by wholly nonmental brain events that immediately precede our decisions and that are external to our (conscious and unconscious) reasons and thought? In both cases, which option is chosen is settled by a purely physical brain event. Why does it matter whether the event is prior to the decision or part of it? This just doesn't seem to be a difference that matters to what we really care about when we worry about free will and moral responsibility.

Libertarianism Reduces to a Kind of Indeterminacy 109

I just deny this. The difference between these two models is precisely the difference between the decision being made by the *person* (or more specifically, the decision being an action of the person that's not causally influenced, at the moment of choice, by anything outside the person's conscious reasons and thought) and the decision being made, or determined, by something external to the person (or if you'd rather, by something external to the person's overall [conscious and unconscious] reasons and thought). It seems to me that worries like this—like the one in the indented passage just above—are generated by a sort of unnoticed slide into dualism. There seems to be an unspoken assumption here that purely physical brain events are not *agential doings*; and this is how one might be led to the conclusion that if our torn decisions are settled by physical brain events, then it doesn't matter *which* brain events do it. But given the token–token identity theory of decisions, this sort of thinking is confused; for on the token–token view, agential doings *are* physical events, presumably brain events. (Of course, ultimately, they are collections of subatomic events; but insofar as physical events can be "added together" in one way or another, we can say that agential actions are physical brain events; that's what they *are*.) So we can't just lump all brain events together and say, "Who cares which ones settle our torn decisions?" For some brain events are agential doings and others presumably aren't. And as we've already seen, if the brain event that *is* a given torn decision is wholly undetermined in the manner of TDW-indeterminism, then we get the result that it was the *agent* who did the choosing and controlled which option was chosen. So the distinction between the two sorts of brain events in the above indented passage is not a "Who cares?" sort of distinction. Again, it is precisely the distinction between the choice being made by the *person* and the choice being determined by something external to the person (or at the very least, something external to the person's psychology). And this, of course, is a difference that matters to the issues of free will and moral responsibility. Even if, in the end, you think that free will and moral responsibility are compatible with determination by external factors, this is the crucial issue that philosophers have been concerned with.

Finally, one might try to press the general line of attack here in something like the following way:

> Suppose Ralph's decision—or if you'd rather, the neural event that *is* his decision—was wholly undetermined in the manner of TDW-indeterminism. Presumably this means that some of the indeterministic micro-level

events that made up the decision were undetermined. These were brute indeterministic physical happenings. Did Ralph author and control *them*? And is he *responsible* for them?[24]

This strikes me as a rather odd question. Do I own the subatomic particles that make up my car? Well, I suppose there's a pretty clear sense in which I do—at least as long as the particles in question don't get knocked off of the car and hence, remain *parts* of the car. Moreover, whatever we say about my ownership of these particles, one thing seems clear: It would be wrongheaded to argue that I don't own my car, because the car is made up of subatomic particles, and people don't own such particles. The same two points can be made about undetermined torn decisions. I have argued here that if our torn decisions are TDW-undetermined, then we author and control them. Advocates of the above objection want to question this by asking whether people can be said to author and control the subatomic *parts* of these decisions. I have two responses to this. First, whatever we say about the subatomic events in question, I don't see why this should matter to my thesis that Ralph authored and controlled his *decision*. And second, I don't see why we shouldn't say that Ralph authored and controlled the subatomic events that made up his decision. After all, we've already seen that he authored and controlled the decision itself, and the subatomic events in question are just *parts* of the decision. If you like, you can read me here as denying that these subatomic events are "brute" physical happenings—if the word 'brute' is supposed to entail that they're not mental, or some such thing. The subatomic events in question are parts of a Ralph-doing event. That's what they are. So it doesn't seem odd to me to say that Ralph authored and controlled them.

(Notice how crucial it is to my argument that the decision *itself* is undetermined. If a torn decision is determined by a prior nonmental brain event, then as we've seen, that would diminish authorship and control, regardless of whether the nonmental brain event was itself determined or undetermined. But if our torn decisions are wholly undetermined in the manner of TDW-indeterminism, then they're *not* determined by prior nonmental brain events. In this scenario, the only relevant subatomic events are *parts* of the decision, and this is what enables me to respond as I have to the above worries.[25])

Let's move on now to objection 4. The issue here is whether the version of libertarianism I've been articulating delivers certain results that some libertarians might have wanted, in particular, (a) that we humans are morally responsible for our actions; (b) that there is a freedom-enhancing indeterminism inherent in *all* of our decisions, including those in which our conscious reasons clearly pick out unique best options; and (c) that we are the *sources* of things, or that we make a difference to how things go.

It seems to me that my version of libertarianism clearly *does* deliver (c). Insofar as it entails that we author and control our torn decisions, and that these decisions are nondeterministically caused by our reasons, and that nothing external to us has any causal influence, at the moment of choice, over which options we choose in our torn decisions, it seems to follow that we are the *sources* of how we choose in our torn decisions and, hence, that we make a difference to how things go.

Equally clear, I think, is that my libertarian view *doesn't* deliver (b). Or at any rate, I haven't said anything here about how libertarians could deliver (b). I suppose one might try to add to my libertarian view in a way that would enable it to deliver (b), but I'm not going to do this here, because it seems to me that (b) is completely undesirable and that any libertarians who have wanted it have been confused. I will argue this point in section 3.4. More precisely, I will argue that in cases where our conscious reasons and thought clearly and definitely pick out a unique best option (i.e., cases where there's really only one live option for the agent), what we want—or at any rate, what we should want—is causal determination. That is, we should want our reasons to causally determine our choices in these cases. (It might seem that because the sort of freedom-enhancing indeterminism I've been describing is found only in *some* of our decisions—most importantly, torn decisions—this makes it somehow unimportant or insignificant. But when we get to objection 5, we'll see that this is false.)

What about (a)? Does my version of libertarianism deliver moral responsibility? Well, I don't see why it doesn't. If I'm right that it delivers the result that our torn decisions are L-free, then why wouldn't we be morally responsible for them? The worry about moral responsibility, in the domain of free will, is precisely that it may be that (i) moral responsibility requires L-freedom, and (ii) we don't have this sort of freedom. I don't know whether (i) is true (indeed, as we saw in chapter 2, I have my doubts about whether there's even a fact of the matter as to whether (i) is true), but in the present context, it seems not to matter; for since my version of libertarianism entails that (ii) is false, it would seem that this view avoids the above worry about moral responsibility anyway.

I suppose there might be other things, aside from (a)–(c), that some libertarians have wanted and that my libertarian view doesn't deliver. But I can't think of anything that my view doesn't deliver that libertarians *should* want.

Let's move on now to objection 5. The issue here is whether we should care very much about torn decisions, given that most of them are rather unimportant and non-life-shaping. I have two responses to this, one rather unimportant and the other, I think, much more important. The unimportant point is this: *Some* of our torn decisions *are* momentous, life-shaping decisions. Indeed, my own view is that more of our big, life-altering decisions are torn decisions than we might like to admit. But, again, this isn't the main point I want to make. The more important point I want to make might seem rather unimportant when you first hear it, but I want to argue that it is, in fact, very important. The point is this: Torn decisions are important to the issue of free will—to the issue of a free will worth wanting—because of the sheer *number* of them that we make. What I want to suggest is that even if it's true that it wouldn't be a very big deal—wouldn't be worth caring very much about—if some specific (nonmomentous) torn decision was settled not by *me* but by some external, nonmental factor, it *would* be a big deal if this were true of *all* of our torn decisions. I think that I make many, many torn decisions every day. If I weren't in control of whether I had eggs or cereal for breakfast, or whether I exercised before going to work, or whether I went into the office or worked at home, or whether I met my friend Andre for lunch or ate by myself in my office, or whether I worked late or went to a movie, then I wouldn't have control over my *life*. Our lives are shaped, to a very large extent, by a huge plethora of "unimportant" decisions. Big, life-shaping decisions are very, very rare. They might have big impacts on our lives, but I would argue that the so-called unimportant decisions we make have just as big an impact on our lives—simply because we make so many of them. Indeed, I would argue that it's because of *these* decisions—and not because of the handful of big, life-shaping decisions we make during our lives—that the prospect of determinism being true can seem depressing to us. Introspectively, it feels like we have an indeterministic sort of free will that we use every day, all the time; the idea that *all* of this might be an illusion can be very depressing. I frankly doubt that many people would be very upset to learn that while they usually have an indeterministic sort of free will, they in fact didn't have this sort of freedom in connection with the five most important decisions of their lives. In any event, I personally would find this a lot less disturbing than discovering that while I did have an indeterministic sort of freedom in connection with the five most important decisions of my life, I didn't have it at any other time, so that my pretheoretic feeling that I have an everyday sort of indeterministic free will is an illusion. For me, that would be far more depressing.

Libertarianism Reduces to a Kind of Indeterminacy 113

Let me add one more point about all of this. As I noted above, it seems to me that it's *because* we make so many torn decisions that the issue of free will and determinism is important to us. For I think it's because we make so many of these decisions that we have the feeling that we possess an indeterministic sort of free will that enables us to choose whatever we want from a list of genuinely open options. It seems to me that if we didn't make so many torn decisions, then we wouldn't have this feeling. And if we didn't have this feeling, I don't think the issue of free will would be all that important to us. And so it seems to me that procuring L-freedom for our torn decisions—for the huge mass of unimportant torn decisions that we make during our lives—is an important result that's worth caring about.

So it's considerations like these that lead me to think that the sort of L-freedom I've been describing—the sort that's procured or increased by TDW-indeterminism—is worth wanting and worth caring about. In short, it seems to me that this sort of freedom is worth wanting, because (a) if we have it, then we shape the courses of our lives in a significant way, and (b) if we don't have it, then at the very least, we (i.e., us agents) play a less crucial, active role in shaping the courses of our lives.

The conclusion I want to draw, then, based on everything I've argued so far (in section 3.3.1, 3.3.2, and the present section), is that if our torn decisions are wholly undetermined in the manner of TDW-indeterminism, then (a) we author and control these decisions, and (b) the TDW-indeterminacy increases or procures the authorship and/or control, and (c) the kind of indeterminacy-enhanced authorship and control that we get here is worth wanting. But I still need to discuss the issue of rationality as well as the plurality requirements for appropriate nonrandomness. I turn to this now.[26]

3.3.4 If Our Torn Decisions Are Undetermined, Then They Are Sufficiently Rational to Be L-Free

I have spent so much time on authorship and control because I think they are the most important components of appropriate nonrandomness. But I imagine that some readers will grant what I've argued so far—that if our torn decisions are TDW-undetermined, then (a) we author and control them, and (b) the TDW-indeterminacy increases or procures the authorship or control—but claim that I have secured this result only at the cost of making it impossible to maintain that these decisions are rational. For instance, Dennett (1978) argues that Valerian libertarianism is superior to non-Valerian libertarianism by claiming that if the relevant undetermined event occurs after deliberation, then it makes deliberation otiose. And Double (1991) argues that even if non-Valerian libertarian views can salvage control, or authorship, they cannot salvage rationality. In the present subsection, I will dispel these worries by arguing that if our torn decisions are wholly undetermined at the moment of choice, then they are appropriately rational, that is, rational in all the ways that are required for appropriate nonrandomness and L-freedom.

The first thing we need to do is get clear on what the appropriate senses of rationality are. To this end, let me define a few different ways in which a decision can be rational. First, I will say that a decision is *strongly rational* (given the agent's reasons for choosing) if and only if the agent's conscious reasons uniquely pick out the chosen option as the best available option. Second, a decision is *weakly rational* (given the agent's reasons for choosing) if and only if it doesn't run counter to the agent's conscious reasons, that is, if and only if it's not the case that the agent's conscious reasons dictate that the chosen option is worse than other available options; in other words, we can say that a decision is weakly rational if and only if it's consistent with the agent's conscious reasons for choosing.[27] Third, a decision is *teleologically rational* if and only if it is made for (conscious) reasons. Thus, whereas weak rationality is opposed to a certain kind of *ir*rationality, teleological rationality is opposed to a kind of *a*rationality. (We could get more fine-grained in our distinctions here by introducing subconscious reasons. For instance, there could be a decision that was consistent with the given agent's conscious reasons but not her subconscious reasons; or a decision that wasn't made for any conscious reason but was generated by a subconscious reason. We will see below that the introduction of subconscious reasons does not undermine my argument, but for now, I want to ignore this issue.)

Torn decisions are, by definition, weakly rational but not strongly rational. The agent chooses a reasons-based tied-for-best option, and so the choice is consistent with, but not uniquely picked out by, the agent's reasons. Torn decisions are also teleologically rational in at least two different ways (and I should note here that Kane [1985, 1996] has also argued that torn decisions are made for reasons). First, our reasons (and deliberations) serve at least to limit the set of options from which we end up choosing in our torn decisions. For example, Ralph didn't decide to move to Outer Mongolia, and there's a very good explanation for this: He had no reason for so deciding; he had no desire to move to Outer Mongolia. Moreover, as we saw in section 3.2.2, it's plausible to suppose that our reasons play a causal role here, that is, that they play a role in causing it to be the case that in torn decisions, our choices come from among our reasons-based tied-for-best options. Thus, it seems safe to conclude that our torn decisions are teleologically rational in at least this way. But there's also a second way in which ordinary torn decisions like Ralph's are teleologically rational: They are made *in order to satisfy reasons*. Ralph, for instance, decided to move to New York in order to try to become an actor and a football player. He might not have thought that these reasons were compelling reasons for moving to New York, but it's clear that he decided to move to New York in order to try to satisfy these desires of his. And it's worth noting here that if Ralph hadn't had reasons for moving to New York, then he wouldn't have decided to move there.

So torn decisions are weakly and teleologically rational but not strongly rational. Thus, one point I need to argue here is that strong rationality is not required for appropriate nonrandomness or L-freedom. We can appreciate this point very easily. Suppose that someone said the following:

> Jane did not have compelling reasons that uniquely picked out her choice of tiramisu, so she did not choose the tiramisu of her own free will, because her choice was not sufficiently rational.

I think it's pretty clear that this remark would seem downright bizarre to just about everyone. In our ordinary discourse and thought, we simply don't think that because decisions like Jane's aren't strongly rational, they are not free. Thus, strong rationality is not required for the ordinary notion of free will. Now, I suppose one might think that, despite this, libertarians are committed to the claim that strong rationality is required for L-freedom. But this is just false. In general, when it comes to things like rationality, authorship, and control, libertarians are going to maintain that L-freedom requires whatever our ordinary intuitions say is required for ordinary free will. And we need to keep in mind here that libertarians get to dictate what L-freedom requires; after all, it's *their* view. Thus, I think the right thing to say here is that strong rationality is not required for L-freedom.

At this point, we can bring in subconscious reasons and see that they present no problem for my thesis either. Once we acknowledge subconscious reasons, we can define more kinds of rationality. For instance, corresponding to weak, strong, and teleological rationality, we can define three more kinds of rationality as follows: A decision is *con-or-subcon-teleologically rational* if and only if it is made for a (conscious or subconscious) reason; a decision is *con-and-subcon-weakly rational* (given the agent's reasons for choosing) if and only if it's not the case that the agent's total reason set (including her conscious and subconscious reasons) dictates that the chosen option is worse than other available options; and a decision is *con-and-subcon-strongly rational* (given the agent's reasons for choosing) if and only if the agent's (conscious and subconscious) reasons uniquely pick out the chosen option as the best available option. But (a) teleological rationality entails con-or-subcon-teleological rationality, and therefore, since our torn decisions have the former sort of rationality, they also have the latter. And (b) con-and-subcon-strong rationality is clearly not required for L-freedom or the ordinary notion of free will; it's clearly not the case that in order for Ralph's decision to count as free, or L-free, he has to have had subconscious reasons that dictated that moving to New York was his best option. And likewise, (c) con-and-subcon-weak rationality isn't required either; even if Ralph had subconscious reasons for staying in Mayberry, so that, overall, his conscious and subconscious reasons favored Mayberry over New York, it seems clear that since he believed that his reasons were neutral between his two options, his decision was still sufficiently rational to count as L-free, and free in the ordinary sense.[28]

So given that torn decisions are weakly and teleologically rational, and given that strong rationality isn't required for appropriate nonrandomness or L-freedom, can I now conclude that torn decisions are sufficiently rational to be appropriately nonrandom and L-free? Well, one might object to my drawing this conclusion here on the grounds that there might be a fourth kind of rationality that is (a) required for L-freedom but (b) not possessed by torn decisions. But I find it hard to believe that there really is such a kind of rationality. I say this for two related reasons.

The less important of the two reasons is that I just don't think much rationality at all is required for a decision to be L-free, or free in the ordinary sense. A decision can be irrational in all sorts of ways and still be L-free and ordinary-language free. We have no problem with the sentence 'She chose of her own free will, but she chose irrationally'. On the other hand, the sentence 'She chose of her own free will, but she didn't author or control her choice' seems incoherent to us. And this suggests that rationality is just not as central to the notion of free will, or the notion of L-freedom, as authorship and control are. In fact, I even have doubts about whether weak and teleological rationality are required. Here's a pair of prima facie arguments for thinking they might not be:

> (i) Suppose that Sally is deliberating about whether to take a job and comes to believe that her reasons for refusing the job outweigh those for taking it (and suppose that she has not overlooked any forgotten or sub-

conscious reasons). But suppose that when she calls to turn the job down, she is suddenly overcome by a feeling that she ought to take it, and she acts on this impulse and decides on the spur of the moment to accept the job. Prima facie, it seems plausible to say that this decision is not weakly rational; but this does not seem to be a reason to deny that it is L-free, or ordinary-language free.

(ii) Suppose that Floyd is reading a book and he suddenly decides to go for a walk, simultaneously, perhaps, with his acquiring a desire to go for a walk. Prima facie, it seems at least somewhat plausible to say that this decision is not teleologically rational; but again, it's not clear that if this were true, it would give us a reason to deny that the decision was L-free, or ordinary-language free.

I will not pursue these prima facie arguments here, because in the present context, it doesn't matter whether weak or teleological rationality is required for L-freedom, because we've already seen that our torn decisions *are* weakly and teleologically rational. But considerations like these suggest that not much rationality is required for L-freedom, or ordinary-language freedom. It *may* be that weak and teleological rationality are required (i.e., that in order for a decision to be free, or L-free, it has to be made for a reason and it cannot flagrantly run counter to the agent's consciously remembered reasons for choosing), but it seems unlikely that any more rationality than this is required. Again, a decision can be irrational in all sorts of ways and still be L-free and ordinary-language free.[29]

The second and more important reason why I doubt that there is a fourth kind of rationality that is (a) required for L-freedom but (b) not possessed by torn decisions is this: When we reflect on actual torn decisions like Ralph's and Jane's, it seems intuitively that they just *are* rational enough to count as free. Indeed, both of these decisions seem *very* rational. In the first place, there doesn't seem to be much that Ralph or Jane could have done to have been more rational (would it have been more rational for Jane to have stared at her waiter until she believed that she had compelling reasons for one of her options?); and second, if we compare torn decisions to decisions that are fully determined by reasons, the only kind of rationality that the former seem to lack is strong rationality, which we've already seen is not required for L-freedom (or for ordinary-language free will).

(The observation that ordinary torn decisions like Ralph's and Jane's can be very rational—indeed, the most rational thing to do in a given situation—gives us a response to a worry that one might have about these decisions, a worry that's related to the issue of contrastive explanations. Taking Jane's decision as an example, it seems clear that we cannot give a contrastive explanation of why, given all of her reasons, she ordered tiramisu rather than a fruit plate. But in the present context, this just doesn't seem to matter. It seems that Jane's decision was rational anyway.)

I conclude, then, that ordinary torn decisions are appropriately rational, that is, rational enough to fulfill the rationality requirement for appropriate nonrandomness. And notice that I argued this point independently of any claims about whether our torn decisions are undetermined. Thus, the conclusion holds regardless of whether our torn decisions are undetermined, and so we have the result that *if our torn decisions are undetermined in the way we're assuming here, then they are rational in an appropriate sense of the term*. And this, of course, is just what I wanted to establish in this section.

Before going on, I want to respond to Dennett's claim that libertarians require indeterminacy prior to the formation of intention, for otherwise, deliberation will be rendered pointless. He says:

> It would be insane to hope that after . . . deliberation had terminated with an assessment of the best available course of action, indeterminism would then intervene to flip the coin before action. (Dennett 1978, 51)

I have already hinted at how we can respond to this worry, for in arguing that Ralph's decision was teleologically rational, I argued that his reasons were relevant to his choice, and we can maintain that his deliberation was relevant to his choice in essentially the same way. We can say that Ralph's choice was made *in the light of* his deliberation and reasons. Deliberation left him with the feeling that two of his options (moving to New York and staying in Mayberry) were better than all the others (e.g., moving to Outer Mongolia) and that he was torn between these two options. Given this, there could have been three appropriate responses to the deliberation: (a) just choose to move to New York; (b) just choose to stay in Mayberry; and assuming there was no deadline that would force an immediate choice, (c) just choose to deliberate some more. So by going with (a), Ralph didn't do anything that made his deliberation otiose (or that ignored his reasons). Moving to Mongolia would have been inappropriate, given his deliberation and reasons; but choosing to move to New York in a torn and perhaps undetermined-at-the-moment-of-choice sort of way was not inappropriate at all; indeed, given his deliberation and his reasons, it makes perfect sense. In short, even if Ralph's decision was undetermined at the moment of choice and, hence, not determined by his reasons or deliberation, it doesn't follow that his reasons or deliberation were irrelevant to the choice, and in fact they weren't, because they succeeded in limiting his options to two, providing reasons for both of these options, and delivering the assessment that the two options were equally appealing.

3.3.5 Plural Authorship, Control, and Rationality
So far I have argued that if our torn decisions are wholly undetermined in the manner of TDW-indeterminism, then (a) they are sufficiently rational to count as L-free; (b) we author and control them; (c) the indeterminacy in question increases or procures the authorship and/or control; and (d) the indeterminacy-enhanced authorship and control that we get here is worth wanting. The last thing I need to argue is that if a torn decision is wholly undetermined, then it satisfies the requirements for plural authorship, control, and rationality—that is, there is at least one unchosen option that the person in question could have chosen such that if she had, then she still would have authored and controlled the decision, and it still would have been sufficiently rational to be L-free. This is easy to appreciate. Consider the case of Ralph. Given that his decision was wholly undetermined at the moment of choice, if he had made a torn decision to stay in Mayberry instead of making a torn decision to move to New York, then we could say the same thing about this decision that I have said here about his decision to move to New York: By the reasoning used in section 3.3.1, it would have been authored and controlled by Ralph, and by the reasoning used in section 3.3.4, it would have been sufficiently rational to count as L-free. The crucial point to notice here is that as long as we're dealing with torn decisions, plural authorship, control, and rationality are no harder to come by than one-way authorship, control, and rationality.

(One might think that libertarians of the sort I have in mind need to establish not just that we have plural authorship and control over our torn decisions, but that we have plural *indeterminacy-enhanced* authorship and control over these decisions. But once again, this would not be hard to argue. If Ralph had decided to stay in Mayberry, I could still have argued—using the reasoning in section 3.3.2—that he had an indeterminacy-enhanced variety of authorship and control over his decision.)

My conclusion, then, is that if any of our ordinary torn decisions are wholly undetermined in the manner of TDW-indeterminism, then they are L-free; more specifically, (a) they are not just undetermined but also appropriately nonrandom—in particular, we (plurally) author and control them, and they are (plurally) sufficiently rational (in particular, they are [plurally] weakly and teleologically rational)—and (b) the authorship and/

or control (and, hence, the appropriate nonrandomness) are enhanced by the TDW-indeterminacy.

(Given this conclusion, we have a response to what is undoubtedly the most important objection to libertarianism, i.e., the argument that libertarianism could not be correct because of the tension between indeterminism and appropriate nonrandomness, in particular, because it seems that the insertion of an undetermined [and, hence, presumably *random*] event into a process could not increase the *non*randomness of that process. But there is another well-known argument that has been leveled against libertarianism, and it is worth noting that the version of libertarianism that I have been describing here has no problem at all with this second argument. The argument I have in mind is based on the claim that libertarianism leads to an unacceptable regress because it entails that in order for a decision to be L-free, the agent in question has to have been responsible for her character being the way it was when it produced the given decision; and that in order for the agent to have been responsible for her character being the way it was when it produced the given decision, she has to have (a) had an earlier character that produced the later character and (b) been responsible for the genesis of this earlier character; and so on. [See, for instance, G. Strawson 2000 for a statement of this argument.] Given what I have already said, it should be obvious how libertarians of the sort I have in mind can respond to this argument; they can simply point out that there is nothing in their version of libertarianism that says that in order for a decision to be L-free, the agent in question has to have been responsible for her character being the way it was when it produced the given decision. Libertarians of the sort I have in mind don't commit to this thesis because they don't need to. Indeed, we'll see in the next section [in connection with the case of Brandy] that there are good reasons for libertarians to *reject* this thesis. As we've seen, the only thing libertarians need to commit to is the thesis that our ordinary torn decisions are, *in fact*, undetermined at the moment of choice in the manner of TDW-indeterminism; for we have found here that if our torn decisions are undetermined in this way, then they are also, *in fact*, L-free.)

3.4 Non-torn Decisions

I will not try to argue this point here, but I think that my thesis applies not just to torn decisions, but to various other kinds of decisions as well. For instance, I think my thesis applies to Buridan's-ass decisions. (I defined Buridan's-ass decisions in section 3.2.1; they are just like torn decisions except that the reasons for choosing the various tied-for-best options are the *same* reasons. E.g., if you are in a grocery store and you want to buy a can of tomato soup and there are two cans of the same kind on the shelf, then in connection with each can, you have a reason for picking it; but the reason for picking the first can and the reason for picking the second can are one and the same reason; in particular, in both cases, the reason is just that you want to eat the given kind of soup.) For reasons very much like the reasons I have given here concerning torn decisions, I think that if Buridan's-ass decisions are wholly undetermined in the manner of TDW-indeterminism, then they are L-free. Moreover, I think that a similar point could probably be argued in connection with certain kinds of decisions that aren't weakly or strongly rational (e.g., Sally's spur-of-the-moment decision, if it's not weakly rational), and I think that if we in fact make decisions that aren't teleologically rational (e.g., spontaneous, no-real-reason decisions like Floyd's), then, again, a similar point could probably be argued about these decisions as well. In particular, I think it could probably be argued that if decisions like these are appropriately undetermined at the moment of choice, then they are L-free. Now, the sort of indeterminism that would be required for full-blown L-freedom in these cases would be a bit different from the sort that's required in connection with torn decisions; some thought would have to be put into what exactly would be required here, but in both cases, the main thing that would be required is that the decision not be causally influenced, at the moment of choice, by any external factors. But, again, I won't pursue any of this here.

However, I would like to say a few words about two different kinds of decisions, namely, (i) decisions in which the agent's conscious reasons clearly pick out a unique best option and deterministically cause that option to be chosen, and (ii) decisions in which the agent decides while *leaning* toward one or more options among a set of live options. I think that decisions of both of these kinds can be free in the ordinary sense of the term (indeed, I think they can be free in this sense even if the ordinary concept of free will is a libertarian concept and, hence, incompatible with full-blown determinism); and I think that libertarians should allow that decisions of these two kinds can be L-free. Libertarians can do this by defining their terms in something like the following way.

First, we can say (as we have been saying all along) that a *person* is L-free if and only if she makes at least some decisions that are such that (a) they are both undetermined and appropriately nonrandom (where this involves at least [plural] authorship and control and perhaps also [plural] weak and/or teleological rationality), and (b) the indeterminacy is relevant to the appropriate nonrandomness in the sense that it increases or procures the nonrandomness. And second, we can say that in order for a *decision* to be L-free, it needs to have been made by an L-free person, and it needs to have been appropriately nonrandom, but it does not necessarily have to have been undetermined. In connection with decisions that *are* undetermined, appropriate nonrandomness will again require (plural) authorship and control and perhaps also (plural) weak and/or teleological rationality; and in connection with decisions that are *not* undetermined—i.e., that are determined—appropriate nonrandomness will require (at least one-way) authorship and control, (at least one-way) weak or strong rationality, and (at least one-way) teleological rationality.

Given this, we can specify a few different kinds of decisions that can be L-free, provided that they are made by L-free persons. The following is a (possibly complete[30]) list of such decision types (and keep in mind that I am not claiming here that all of these types are instantiated in the actual world):

1. Torn decisions that are wholly undetermined in the manner of TDW-indeterminism. (This, of course, is the case I've discussed at length in this chapter. Note, too, that as we saw in section 3.2.2, a torn decision could also be partially undetermined and, because of this, partially L-free. But in this section, I'm ignoring the issue of partial L-freedom and concentrating on full-blown L-freedom.)

2. Buridan's-ass decisions that are wholly undetermined in the manner of TDW-indeterminism.

3, 4. *Maybe*: Certain kinds of decisions that aren't teleologically rational (e.g., spontaneous, no-real-reason decisions like Floyd's) and certain kinds of decisions that are neither weakly nor strongly rational (e.g., Sally's spur-of-the-moment decision, if it's not weakly rational), provided that they are appropriately undetermined at the moment of choice and authored and controlled by the agent in question. (Note the 'maybe' qualifier here; all I'm saying is that it *might* be that decisions like these could be appropriately nonrandom and L-free; in both cases, I think there are a number of issues that would need to be thought through before we could confidently say that decisions of the given type could be appropriately nonrandom and L-free.)

5. Decisions in which the agent's conscious reasons and thought clearly and definitely pick out a unique best option and deterministically cause that option to be chosen. (In other words, in cases of this kind, the agent is not torn, and indeed, it would not even be correct to say that the

agent is leaning toward one option among many, for this would imply that there are other live options; in decisions of this kind, there is really only one live option, at least as far as the person's conscious reasons and thought are concerned.) Decisions like this will (typically) be appropriately nonrandom in the sense that they will be (one-way) authored and controlled by the agent, (one-way) weakly and strongly rational, and (at least one-way) teleologically rational. (I will discuss decisions of this kind in more detail below.)

6. Decisions in which (a) the agent is leaning toward one or more options among a set of live options and (b) which option is chosen is appropriately undetermined at the moment of choice (I'll say more about this shortly).

7. Decisions in which (a) the agent is leaning toward one option among a set of live options, and (b) which option is chosen is appropriately *determined* at the moment of choice (again, I'll say more about this shortly).

I have already discussed type-1 decisions at length. I won't discuss decisions of types 2–4 here, but I want to say a few words about decisions of types 5–7.

Before I discuss these types of decisions, however, I want to point out that this way of setting things up is consistent with everything I've said so far. Libertarianism is still defined here as the view that human beings are L-free, and L-freedom is still defined in the same way I've been defining it all along. In reading earlier sections of this chapter, it might have seemed that on the view I have in mind, a decision is L-free if and only if *it* is undetermined and appropriately nonrandom and so on; but I never said that. What I did say is that if a *torn* decision is appropriately undetermined, then it is also appropriately nonrandom and L-free; and I also said that if a torn decision is causally determined, then at the very least, this diminishes its appropriate nonrandomness; but it doesn't follow from this that the same is true of all decisions or that a decision can't be both determined and L-free at the same time.

Let me now say a few words about type-5 decisions, that is, decisions in which our conscious reasons and thought clearly and definitely pick out a unique best option and deterministically cause that option to be chosen. In particular, I want to explain why it's plausible for libertarians to maintain that if we are L-free persons (i.e., if we do make some decisions that involve a freedom-enhancing sort of indeterminism), then type-5 decisions (or at any rate, typical type-5 decisions) should count as L-free.[31]

Before giving my argument for this claim, I should note that I do *not* have in mind the argument that Kane (1996) uses in this connection and that, by now, can probably be thought of as a standard libertarian argument for the claim that a decision can be causally determined and still be L-free. Kane's idea, in essence, is that a decision can be derivatively L-free if it is causally determined by the agent having a certain character (or a certain psychological state, including certain reasons for choosing) that was formed, or partially formed, by prior decisions of the agent that were directly L-free in the sense that they involved a freedom-enhancing sort of indeterminism. Again, this is not what I have in mind here. I think it's plausible for libertarians to maintain that a decision that was causally determined by the given agent's reasons could be L-free even if it *wasn't* the case that these reasons were produced by previous L-free choices of the agent. For instance, suppose that Brandy is in a restaurant that has only three items on the menu, a salmon dish, a mushroom dish, and a beef dish; and suppose that Brandy likes beef very much but doesn't particularly like mushrooms or salmon; and finally, suppose that Brandy orders the beef dish and that this choice was causally determined by her having the above preferences. It seems that, usually, preferences like these are not the products of previous decisions made by the agent in question; of course, there might be *some* cases where people come to have preferences like these because of past decisions, but it would seem implausible to claim that this is universally true, and so we can suppose for the sake of argument that in this particular case, Brandy's preferences are *not* the products of previous decisions that she has made. Still, it seems to me plausible for libertarians to claim that as long as Brandy is an L-free person (i.e., as long as some of her other decisions involve a freedom-enhancing sort of indeterminism), and as long as we're dealing here with a typical case (i.e., a case that doesn't involve anything bizarre like preference manipulation by Martians), Brandy's causally determined decision to order beef should count as L-free. (And note that I'm not saying here that libertarians should claim that Brandy's decision *is* L-free, in some predefined sense; since 'L-free' is a term of art, libertarians can define it however they like; thus, my claim here is that it makes good sense for libertarians to set things up so that Brandy's decision counts as L-free.) Let me try to explain why I say this.

I have three arguments here. First, the stance I have in mind seems to dovetail with the ordinary concept of free will—even if that concept is a libertarian concept. Second, this stance seems to dovetail with the concerns that motivate libertarianism in the first place. And third, when we find ourselves in situations like Brandy's—situations in which our conscious reasons and thought clearly and definitely pick out a unique best option—the best-case scenario, relative to the desire that we author and control these decisions, is the scenario in which our reasons causally determine our choices. Let me begin with the first argument.

Suppose that the ordinary concept of free will is a libertarian concept, so that free will is incompatible with determinism. And now suppose that determinism is in fact false and that libertarianism is true; that is, suppose that we all make numerous decisions that involve a freedom-enhancing sort of indeterminism. Finally, consider Brandy's causally determined decision to order beef, and ask yourself (from within the context of the above suppositions) whether Brandy's decision is free in the ordinary sense of the term. It seems to me that it clearly is. In this scenario, Brandy is a person with genuine free will who routinely makes decisions that involve a freedom-enhancing sort of indeterminism. And now she finds herself in a situation where she really wants to order beef; there is just no contest for her about what to order for dinner, and so she does just what she wants to do—she orders beef. It seems clear that in this case, we should say that Brandy's decision is free; the fact that it was causally determined by her reasons doesn't undermine this claim at all, even assuming an overall libertarian conception of free will. Thus, it seems to me that if the ordinary notion of free will is a libertarian notion, then it's a libertarian notion that allows that Brandy's causally determined decision is free. And so I think that libertarians ought to say that Brandy's decision is L-free. (And I might add here that part of the reason that it seems right to say that Brandy's decision is free in this scenario is that it seems right to say that she authored and controlled her decision—in the ordinary intuitive senses that are relevant to the issue of free will.)

My second argument for the claim that libertarians can plausibly maintain that type-5 decisions like Brandy's can be L-free, despite the fact that they're causally determined, is generated by thinking carefully about the concerns that motivate libertarianism in the first place. The idea that determinism might be true can seem disturbing or depressing to us, and the reason, I think, is that it can seem to follow from determinism that we are something like puppets. If it was already determined before any of us were born that our lives would take the exact courses that they in fact take, then it can seem that we don't have free will in any interesting or worthwhile sense. But let's suppose for the sake of argument that determinism is in fact false and, indeed, that every day, we all make numerous decisions that involve a freedom-enhancing sort of indeterminism. Then the worries about determinism being true entirely evaporate. And now, from within the context of this assumption, let's suppose (what seems very plausible) that we sometimes find ourselves in situations like Brandy's, situations in which we have to make decisions and our conscious reasons clearly pick out unique best options. Given this, and given that many of our other decisions involve a freedom-enhancing sort of indeterminism, so that we are L-free persons, would anyone be disturbed or depressed by the idea that in situations like this—situations in which our conscious reasons and thought clearly and definitely pick out unique best options—our reasons deterministically cause the reasons-based best options to be chosen?

Well, one might respond here by pointing out that people sometimes do choose (and *want* to choose) in ways that fly in the face of their better judgments—for example, when someone who's trying to quit smoking gives in to temptation and has a cigarette. But this just isn't a case in which the person's conscious reasons and thought clearly and definitely picked out a unique best option; for this person obviously had competing reasons and multiple live options. Now, this isn't to say that the decision was a torn decision—the person might have been leaning toward one of her two options—but the decision wasn't a type-5 decision, that is, a decision in which the agent's conscious reasons and thought clearly and definitely picked out a unique best option. Thus, decisions like this are not relevant here, for I'm simply not talking about them. I'm talking only about type-5 decisions, that is, decisions like Brandy's. Brandy just doesn't have any desire at all to order the mushroom dish or the salmon dish; she just clearly wants the beef dish—period. Given this, my claim here is that if we assume that many of our other decisions involve a freedom-enhancing sort of indeterminism, so that we are L-free persons, then there is nothing disturbing or depressing about the idea that, *in cases like Brandy's*, our decisions are determined by our reasons. And so it seems to me that libertarians would not be saying anything that runs counter to the spirit of their overall program if they said that type-5 decisions like Brandy's can be L-free, despite the fact that they're causally determined, provided that we are already L-free persons, that is, provided that some of our other decisions involve a freedom-enhancing sort of indeterminism.

This leads naturally into my third argument for thinking that libertarians can plausibly maintain that type-5 decisions like Brandy's can be L-free. The third argument just takes the conclusion of the second argument and pushes it one step further: It's not just that there is nothing disturbing or depressing about the idea that in cases like Brandy's, our decisions are determined by our reasons; it's that determination by reasons

Libertarianism Reduces to a Kind of Indeterminacy

is what we *want* here—or at any rate, it's what we *should* want, and this includes libertarians. My argument for this is that it is only through determination by reasons that we can get a guarantee that, in cases like Brandy's, we author and control our decisions. For if our reasons *don't* determine our choices in cases like this, then that just opens the door to the possibility of things going wrong, from the agent's own point of view. In these cases, the agent's overall conscious reason set clearly picks out a unique best option. Again, Brandy *wants* to order the beef dish—period; she doesn't have any desire at all to order anything else. So if her reasons don't determine her choice here, then that just opens the door to the possibility of something happening against Brandy's wishes; for example, it opens the door to the possibility of a decision to order salmon occurring in Brandy's head, against her wishes. Thus, it seems to me that if we were able to set things up however we wanted to in cases like this, and if our main concern in doing this was to set things up in a way that guaranteed that it would be *us* who made these decisions—or who authored and controlled the decisions—then the best way to do this would be to set things up so that our choices were determined by our reasons. By doing this, we would get a guarantee of authorship and control, because we would be eliminating the possibility of things going wrong in something like the above way. And so because of this, it seems to me very plausible for libertarians to maintain that type-5 decisions (i.e., decisions in which the agent's conscious reasons and thought clearly and definitely pick out a unique best option and deterministically cause that option to be chosen) can be appropriately nonrandom and L-free.

(A few people have asked me, in connection with the argument I've been running here, how the fact that our torn decisions are undetermined and L-free [if they are] could make it the case that *other* decisions of ours—in particular, causally determined decisions like Brandy's—are L-free. But this way of putting things misrepresents the view I've got in mind. It's not that the indeterminacy in our torn decisions somehow *makes it the case* that these other decisions are L-free—in the sense of altering their status. The idea is rather that the indeterminacy in our torn decisions *makes it the case that we are L-free persons*, and given this, it makes good sense to set things up so that the term 'L-free' applies to these other decisions as well. It's also worth remembering here the point I made in section 3.3.3 about the sheer number of torn decisions we make. If our torn decisions are L-free in the way described above, then we are, so to speak, routinely and abundantly L-free. The point I'm making here is that, given this, and for the reasons listed above, it makes sense to say that decisions like Brandy's are L-free as well. Finally, I should note here that I do not think this point is particularly important. If they wanted to, libertarians could also set things up so that type-5 decisions didn't count as L-free, and then they could argue—using some of the above points—that it doesn't matter that these decisions aren't L-free.)

Let's move on now to decisions of types 6 and 7, both of which involve cases in which the agent decides while leaning toward one or more options among a set of live options. Decisions like these are, in a certain way, in between torn decisions and type-5 decisions. There is a spectrum of possible cases here, ranging from pure torn decisions on the one hand (i.e., cases where the agent's conscious reasons and thought are neutral between the various tied-for-best options) to pure non-torn decisions on the other (i.e., type-5 decisions, where the agent's conscious reasons and thought clearly and definitely pick out a unique best option); in between are cases where the agent's conscious reasons and thought don't clearly pick out a unique best option but where the agent (in her conscious reasons and thought) is leaning toward one or more of the live options, so that the reasons-based probabilities of these options being chosen are higher than those of the other live options.

It seems to me plausible for libertarians to maintain that decisions involving leanings of this kind can be fully L-free. Indeed, it seems to me that there are two different possible scenarios here that are consistent with the idea that these decisions are L-free. The two possible scenarios correspond to decisions of types 6 and 7 on the above list. One of them involves causal determination by reasons, and the other involves an appropriate kind of indeterminism. In the indeterministic scenario (type-6 decisions), the moment-of-choice probabilities of the various live options being chosen match the reasons-based probabilities. For instance, suppose that Sam's conscious reasons and thought favor option A over option B by a 70–30 margin (of course, it's pretty artificial to hang precise numbers on the strengths of a person's reasons in this way, but this is really just a device for getting clear about what we ought to say about different kinds of cases); and suppose that a deadline forces Sam to choose while in this 70–30 state; then it could be that Sam's reasons cause it to be the case that the moment-of-choice probabilities of A and B being chosen are 0.7 and 0.3, respectively, given the complete state of the world and all the laws of nature, and the choice occurs without any further causal input, that is, without anything else being significantly causally relevant to which option is chosen. It seems to me that it would be appropriate for libertarians of the sort I've been describing to maintain that if we make decisions like this, then they are fully appropriately nonrandom and fully L-free. (Of course, libertarians would need to *argue* that if decisions like Sam's are undetermined in the above way, then they're L-free; but the argument I would give here would be analogous to the one I've given in this chapter for the claim that if our torn decisions are wholly undetermined in the manner of TDW-indeterminism, then they are L-free.)

In the deterministic scenario, on the other hand (type-7 decisions), which option is chosen is causally determined by the fact that the agent is leaning toward a specific option. For instance, there could be a case in which a deadline forces Sam to decide while in a 70–30 state and his reasons deterministically cause him to choose option A (because his reasons favor A by a 70–30 margin). Once again, it seems to me that it would be plausible for libertarians to maintain that if we make decisions of this kind, then they are fully L-free (provided that we are L-free persons, i.e., provided that some of our other decisions are undetermined and L-free). My argument for this claim is analogous to my argument for the claim that libertarians should say that type-5 decisions can be L-free.[32] Thus, whereas type-6 decisions are analogous to type-1 decisions, that is, to wholly undetermined torn decisions, type-7 decisions are analogous to type-5 decisions, that is, decisions that are straightforwardly determined by the agent's reasons.[33]

In contrast to both of these cases, it would seem plausible for libertarians to maintain that if a deadline forced Sam to decide while in a 70–30 state, and if something wholly external to him and his reasons (e.g., a nonmental brain event that preceded the decision in his head) deterministically caused a specific option to be chosen, then the decision would not be L-free (or at the very least, it wouldn't be full-blown L-free). And, likewise, it would also seem plausible for libertarians to maintain that if something wholly external to Sam and his reasons probabilistically causally influenced his decision in the sense that it altered the moment-of-choice probabilities, away from 0.7 and 0.3 to something else, say, 0.8 and 0.2, or 0.6 and 0.4, then the decision would be at least partially non-L-free.

Finally, it is worth noting that libertarians don't need to claim that any of the decision types on the above list are required for the truth of libertarianism; that is, they don't need to claim that there is some type on the above list that is such that we need to make some decisions of that type in order to be L-free. All that's required here is that some of our decisions are such that (a) they are both undetermined and appropriately nonrandom, and (b) the indeterminacy procures or increases the nonrandomness. Thus, since many of the decision types on the above list involve a freedom-enhancing indeterminism of this kind, no one of these types is required. Nonetheless, I think torn decisions are the most interesting and important of these types, and that's why I've concentrated on them. Moreover, as I pointed out in section 3.2.2, it seems plausible to suppose that if we make any L-free decisions, then some of our torn decisions are L-free. For (a) it seems beyond doubt that we all make torn decisions very often, and (b) the kinds of indeterminacy that are required in the various cases are all fairly similar, and so it seems plausible to suppose that if the appropriate kind of indeterminacy is present in any of these cases, then it's probably present in cases of torn decisions as well. And given this, it's plausible to maintain that the question of whether libertarianism is true comes down to the question of whether some of our torn decisions are L-free. And as I've argued at length in the present chapter, the question of whether our torn decisions are L-free—or full-blown L-free—comes down to the question of whether they're appropriately undetermined, that is, wholly undetermined in the manner of TDW-indeterminism.

3.5 Where We Stand

We have found in this chapter that the question of whether libertarianism is true (i.e., the question of whether human beings are L-free) reduces to the question of whether any of our torn decisions are wholly undetermined in the manner of TDW-indeterminism. In other words, it reduces to the question of whether TDW-indeterminism is true. (We also saw that if any of our torn decisions are not undetermined in this way, then there is also a question about whether they are partially undetermined and, if they are, to what extent they are; but as I pointed out in section 3.2.2, in the present context, we don't need to worry about this further question.)

But I haven't argued here that any of our torn decisions *are* wholly undetermined; that is, I haven't argued that TDW-indeterminism is true, and so for all that's been said here, it could be that human beings are not L-free and hence that libertarianism is false.

In chapter 4, I will argue that there are no good arguments, empirical or a priori, for or against TDW-indeterminism. In short, we will see that we don't have any rational reason whatsoever for taking sides here—i.e., that it's a wide open (empirical) question whether TDW-indeterminism is true or false and, hence, that it's a wide open (empirical) question whether libertarianism is true or false.

4 Why There Are No Good Arguments for or against Determinism (or Any Other Thesis That Would Establish or Refute Libertarianism)

It is far better to remain silent and appear a fool than to open your mouth and remove all doubt.
—Mark Twain[1]

4.1 Introduction

We saw in chapter 2 that (a) the metaphysical issue inherent in the problem of free will and determinism comes down to what I called the which-kinds-of-freedom-do-we-have question, and (b) this question reduces largely, though perhaps not entirely, to the question of whether human beings are L-free, that is, the question of whether libertarianism is true.[2] Moreover, in chapter 3, we found that (c) the question of whether human beings are L-free comes down to the question of whether some of our torn decisions are undetermined in a certain specific way. In the present chapter, I will argue that there are no good arguments for or against the sort of indeterminacy that's needed here. Thus, if the arguments of chapter 3 and the present chapter are cogent, then, as of right now anyway, we do not have any good arguments for or against the libertarian thesis that humans are L-free.

(The notion of a *torn decision* was defined in chapter 3; briefly, it is a decision in which the person in question (a) has reasons for two or more options and feels torn as to which set of reasons is strongest, i.e., has no conscious belief as to which option is best, given her reasons; and (b) decides without resolving this conflict and, thus, has the experience of "just choosing" from a list of reasons-based tied-for-best options. See section 3.2.1 for a more thorough discussion of this notion.)

As we saw in chapter 3, L-freedom requires some of our torn decisions to be undetermined in a very specific way. In particular, what's needed is that the following empirical hypothesis be true:

TDW-indeterminism: Some of our torn decisions are wholly undetermined at the moment of choice, where to say that a torn decision is wholly undetermined at the moment of choice is to say that the moment-of-choice probabilities of the various reasons-based tied-for-best options being chosen match the reasons-based probabilities, so that these moment-of-choice probabilities are all roughly even, given the complete state of the world and all the laws of nature, and the choice occurs without any further causal input, that is, without anything else being significantly causally relevant to which option is chosen.

Let me note three things about TDW-indeterminism (all of which were discussed in greater detail in chapter 3, section 3.2.2). First, it requires indeterminacy *at the moment of choice*. This means that the version of libertarianism I'm working with is *non-Valerian*. (Recall that a non-Valerian version of libertarianism is simply one that places the important indeterminacy at the moment of choice, whereas a Valerian version of libertarianism is one that places the important indeterminacy *prior* to the moment of choice.) Because I think non-Valerian versions of libertarianism are superior to Valerian versions (my reasons for this emerged in chapter 3), the arguments of the present chapter are couched in terms of the issue of moment-of-choice indeterminacy; but it should be noted that in the context of the present chapter, this is relatively unimportant, because almost everything I say here could be reformulated in a way that would make it relevant to Valerian libertarianism as well.

The second point I want to make about TDW-indeterminism is that it is consistent with the thesis that the mere *occurrences* of our torn decisions are determined (and also with the thesis that when a torn decision is made, it is causally determined that the person in question will choose from a specific list of options, namely, her reasons-based tied-for-best options, and that the moment-of-choice probabilities of these options being chosen are all roughly even). What must be undetermined, in order for a torn decision to be undetermined in the relevant sense, is precisely *which option is chosen*—or more precisely, which of the reasons-based tied-for-best options is chosen. Thus, for example, if you're buying a soda and you make a torn decision to buy a Coke rather than a root beer, then it would be OK—that is, it would be consistent with the thesis that the decision was undetermined in the relevant sense—if it was determined (by your reasons) that you were going to choose between Coke and root beer, so long as it wasn't determined that you were going to choose Coke.

The third and final point I want to make about TDW-indeterminism is that it requires some of our torn decisions to be *wholly* undetermined, as opposed to partially undetermined, at the moment of choice. This is the upshot of the clause about the moment-of-choice probabilities matching the reasons-based probabilities and the choice occurring without anything else being significantly causally relevant to which option is chosen. (In contrast to this, we can say that a torn decision is *partially* undetermined at the moment of choice if (a) nothing causally determines which option is chosen, but (b) the moment-of-choice probabilities of the various reasons-based tied-for-best options being chosen are altered to some extent, away from the reasons-based probabilities, due to some sort of causal input.)

What I argued in chapter 3 is that if any of our torn decisions are wholly undetermined at the moment of choice in the manner of TDW-indeterminism, then they are also L-free, so that the question of whether libertarianism is true comes down to the question of whether TDW-indeterminism is true. (We also saw in chapter 3 that some libertarians might want to claim, in addition, that if any of our torn decisions are partially undetermined at the moment of choice, then they're also partially L-free; but as I pointed out there, in the present context, we don't need to worry about the issue of partial indeterminacy and partial L-freedom.)

In the present chapter, I want to motivate the thesis that we do not currently have any good arguments for or against TDW-indeterminism. In other words, I want to motivate the idea that the question of whether TDW-indeterminism is true is a wide open question. And, of course, if this is true, then—given the conclusion of chapter 3—it follows that the question of whether libertarianism is true (i.e., the question of whether humans are L-free) is also wide open.

(I think there are also parallel arguments that suggest that we currently have no good reason to believe or disbelieve the thesis that some of our torn decisions are *partially* undetermined. Now, given what I say here about the limiting case of TDW-indeterminism, it will be pretty obvious how these parallel arguments about partial indeterminism would go, and indeed, some of the reasoning behind these arguments will be evident here. But I will not bother to spell out these arguments explicitly.)

Since TDW-indeterminism is an empirical hypothesis about the workings of the physical world, it is unlikely that there are any good a priori arguments here. Nonetheless, one sometimes hears arguments that might seem to deliver a priori reasons for endorsing or rejecting TDW-indeterminism. Thus, I will begin by saying a few words to undermine these a priori arguments (or allegedly a priori arguments, as the case may be). In particular, in section 4.2, I will consider and refute an a priori argument that seeks to establish determinism (and hence, if cogent, would refute TDW-indeterminism); and in section 4.3, I will consider and refute an (allegedly) a priori argument that seeks to establish libertarianism (and hence, if cogent, would provide good reason to endorse TDW-indeterminism).

Then in section 4.4, I will move on to consider empirical arguments, and I will spend much more time on this. Now, I will not argue every point that would really need to be argued in order to fully justify the claim that there are no good empirical arguments for or against TDW-indeterminism. In particular, I am simply going to assume that there are no good empirical arguments in *favor* of TDW-indeterminism, and I am going to concentrate on the question of whether there are any good empirical arguments *against* it. The reason I make this assumption is that I think it's more or less obvious that there aren't any good arguments here; at any rate, I don't know of any attempts to mount an empirical argument for anything like TDW-indeterminism, and (given our current state of knowledge) I can't imagine how one might proceed in trying to do this. In contrast to this, however, there are numerous strategies that one might use to try to argue *against* TDW-indeterminism; in particular, one might try to do this by arguing in favor of any one of a number of different kinds of determinism. In section 4.4, I will define several varieties of determinism, and I will argue that we do not have any good (empirical) reason to believe any of them; moreover, I will also argue that we don't have any good (empirical) arguments directed explicitly against TDW-indeterminism itself. Thus, if we combine this with the plausible assumption that there are no good empirical arguments in *favor* of TDW-indeterminism, and if I'm right that there are also no good *a priori* arguments for or against TDW-indeterminism, it follows that the question of whether TDW-indeterminism is true is a wide open question. And, hence, given the arguments of chapter 3, it also follows that the question of whether libertarianism is true is wide open.

Before moving on, I want to make four general points. First, I just said that I'm going to argue that, at present, we have no "good arguments" for any of the various kinds of determinism I'll be discussing. If you interpret expressions like 'good argument' and 'good reason' weakly, you might take this claim to be stronger than I intend it to be. By a good argument, I mean a *compelling* argument, or an argument that, all things considered, gives us a rational reason to believe the conclusion, or something along these lines. Thus, my central claim here is that, as of right now, all things considered, we ought (rationally) to remain neutral on the question of whether any of the relevant kinds of determinism are true. But in saying this I do *not* mean to suggest that there are no considerations that provide any coherent rationale—or any arguments that ought to be taken seriously—for any of these kinds of determinism.

The second point I want to make here is that since this chapter provides a sort of survey—in particular, since it covers a variety of arguments for several different deterministic theses—I will not be able to go into as much depth on any of the various issues as I would like. This is a bit unfortunate, but it's just an unavoidable constraint on survey pieces like this.

Third, one might be thinking that the conclusion of the present chapter is somewhat uninteresting because it's already widely accepted that we don't have any good reason to believe determinism. But I am not just going to argue that we have no good reason to believe universal determinism; I'm also going to argue that we have no good reason to believe some much weaker versions of determinism. Since libertarianism requires a very specific kind of indeterminism (namely, TDW-indeterminism), it can be refuted not just by universal determinism, but by some much weaker theses, for example, claims to the effect that all of our conscious decisions are significantly causally influenced (not necessarily genuinely determined) by prior events in certain kinds of freedom-damaging ways. What I'm going to argue here is that we have no good reason to believe any of the deterministic theses—or any of the "pseudo-deterministic" theses, as the case may be—that would rule out L-freedom. And this, I think, is not something that people already believe.

Finally, in saying that we have no good reason to endorse or reject TDW-indeterminism, I am not saying that we have no good reason to endorse or reject any other theses, theses that one might think are related to TDW-indeterminism. For instance, my stance here has no bearing whatsoever on the status of hypotheses (due to people like Penrose, Hameroff, and Stapp[3]) about the importance of quantum mechanics to consciousness. For all I will argue here—and I'll comment on this below, in section 4.4.4.1—it may be that we have good reason to reject such hypotheses. My thesis is concerned only with the causal determinacy of the neural events that are our torn decisions. Again, my claim is simply that we currently have no good reason to endorse or reject TDW-indeterminism.

4.2 An A Priori Argument for Determinism (and, Hence, against TDW-Indeterminism)?

It's pretty hard, I think, to come up with an a priori argument for determinism that's even remotely plausible. But I have sometimes heard people give arguments along the following lines:

Determinism must be true because we cannot conceive of physical events "just happening." If you set up two physical systems in *identical* ways, and if you perform the *exact* same experiment on them, then you will get the same result in both cases. If you get different results in the two different cases, then you must not have done things in exactly similar ways in the two cases; that is, there must have been hidden differences between them. For if you really set them up in the exact same way, you *couldn't* get two different results, because things don't just happen. We can't even conceive of two physically identical processes leading to two different results. Therefore, indeterministic just-happenings are impossible.

It is important to note that this is supposed to be an a priori argument; the claim is that indeterminism is *impossible* because it is inconceivable. Now, there are, of course, empirical arguments that try to establish the claim that there is good observational evidence suggesting that, in *fact*, in this world, things don't "just happen" in indeterministic ways. We will discuss these arguments below, but here we are concerned with the a priori argument that indeterministic just-happenings are inconceivable and, hence, impossible.

One might attack this argument by denying that inconceivability (by us humans) entails impossibility or even falsity. I won't pursue this line here. Instead, I simply want to point out that, in fact, we *can* conceive of events occurring indeterministically. Indeed, it's easy to describe possible worlds in which *all* physical laws are indeterministic, or probabilistic, so that all events are at least partially undetermined. Or to take it one step further, I have no trouble imagining a world with no laws whatsoever, except for a very general law stating that the world's matter reorganizes itself sometimes. In the world I have in mind, physical matter sits in one state, unchanging, until a world-shift occurs (at an undetermined time), and at such moments, all the matter in the world suddenly and instantaneously and for no reason shifts into another state; so for instance, the matter in my right arm might suddenly come together with some of the matter in the Eiffel Tower to form a velvet-canvas painting of Don Knotts, hovering in space in a distant region of the universe.

I suppose that one might object here by saying that we can't really conceive of *how* this would happen. But I'm not sure what it even means to talk about *how* something *just happens*. Isn't the point of saying that it "just happens" that there isn't a *how* there at all? Moreover, even if there is a how here, I'm not sure we couldn't imagine it, and even if we couldn't, it's not clear that we can do any better at conceiving of how an event could occur deterministically—that is, how one event could "force" another event to occur. (Indeed, Hume seems to want to say that we *can't* conceive of this. I certainly don't want to commit to this Humean thesis, but I will say that if one of these things is harder to conceive of, it is probably deterministic occurrences, since they seem more substantive and positive—they are physical *forcings*, whereas indeterministic occurrences are just occurrences without full-blown physical forcings.) But I'm disinclined to get into arguments over any of these points. Instead, I would just like to point out that it doesn't matter whether we can conceive of "how" events could just happen, for the fact remains that we can clearly conceive of worlds in which events *do* just happen, and indeed, as we'll see below, one of the standard views among physicists and philosophers of physics is that, in fact, some actual events do occur without deterministic causes.

4.3 An A Priori Argument for Libertarianism (and, Hence, in Favor of TDW-Indeterminism)?

There is a famous argument for the truth of indeterminism and libertarianism that traces back at least to Kant and has been endorsed in contemporary times by Peter van Inwagen (1983). If this argument is cogent, then it presumably gives us a good reason to believe TDW-indeterminism, or something very much like it, since (as we saw in chapter 3) there's good reason to think that libertarianism is true only if TDW-indeterminism is true. In any event, the argument I've got in mind can be put in the following way:

(1) People are at least sometimes morally responsible for their actions. (Or alternatively, we can say that during the entire history of the world, at least one sentence of the form 'S ought to do A' has been literally true; e.g., it seems that during World War II, the sentence 'Hitler ought to stop killing Jews' was true.) But

(2) Moral responsibility requires indeterminism and L-freedom. (Or alternatively, if some sentence of the form 'S ought to do A' is true, then the corresponding sentence of the form 'S is L-free to do A' is also true.) Therefore,

(3) At least some of our actions are undetermined and we are at least sometimes L-free. (Or alternatively, during the history of the world, at least one sentence of the form 'S is L-free to do A' has been true.)

Many philosophers, I think, would say that this is an a priori argument. In the end, I do not think it is, because I think premise (1) is best thought of as an empirical claim (and, indeed, I think that (2) is partially empirical). But the question of whether this argument is a priori or not doesn't really matter. What I want to show is that the argument isn't cogent, that is, that it doesn't provide any good reason at all—a priori or not—for believing indeterminism or libertarianism. (There are, of course, other a priori arguments that philosophers have used to try to establish libertarianism, but I don't know of any others that have any sort of currency today, and for good reason—none of these other arguments is even initially plausible, at least in my opinion. Thus, I will not pursue any of these other arguments here.[4])

The argument in (1)–(3) is pretty clearly valid. Thus, if we're going to try to block this argument, we've got to claim that either (1) or (2) is false. Now, I don't think either of these premises is obviously false, and indeed, I think that each of them, taken in isolation, could be motivated in ways that are at least somewhat plausible. But I want to argue that, given our current epistemic situation, it would be wrongheaded for us to endorse both (1) *and* (2). I begin my argument here by arguing for the following thesis:

If-(2)-Then-No-Argument-for-(1): If premise (2) is true, and if we have good reason to believe this, then we have no good reason to believe premise (1); that is, if moral responsibility requires indeterminism and L-freedom, and if we have good reason to believe this, then we have no good reason to believe that we humans are morally responsible for our actions.

I want to argue for this thesis by formulating an initial argument for it, and then giving an objection to that argument, and then finally, explaining how the objection can be answered. The initial argument can be put like this:

Suppose that (2) is true and that we have discovered good reason to believe this thesis, that is, good reason to believe that moral responsibility requires indeterminism and L-freedom. Then this would be a discovery that moral responsibility is a lot harder to come by than we might have thought. Indeed, in this scenario, the hypothesis that we humans are morally responsible for our actions would be extremely controversial. For if we had good reason to believe (2), then in order to motivate the claim that we are morally responsible creatures—that is, in order to motivate (1)—we would have to motivate the claim that we are L-free. For after all, (2) just says that moral responsibility requires L-freedom. So if we assume (2), it seems that an argument for (1) would have to include an independent argument for indeterminism and libertarianism. Thus, since, presumably, we don't have

No Good Arguments for or against Determinism 139

any such independent argument for indeterminism and libertarianism, it follows that if (2) is true, and if we have good reason to believe (2), then we have no good reason to believe (1).

One might object to this argument in the following way:

> You seem to be assuming that the only way to motivate premise (1)—the thesis that we are morally responsible for our actions—is to list all of the requirements for moral responsibility and then argue that we satisfy these requirements. But this is not the only way to motivate premise (1). And what's more, it should be clear that defenders of the argument in (1)–(3) would not want to motivate it in this way; for on their view, one of the requirements for moral responsibility is L-freedom, and so in order to motivate premise (1) in this way, they would need to provide an independent argument for libertarianism; but since the point of the argument in (1)–(3) is itself to motivate libertarianism, they are clearly not going to want their argument for (1) to include an argument for libertarianism. But there is another way in which defenders of the argument in (1)–(3) could try to motivate premise (1). They could try to argue that we have good reason to believe that (1) is true—that is, that humans are morally responsible for their actions—*regardless of what this requires*. And it should not be thought that this is implausible on its face, for we seem to have reasons of this sort all the time. For instance, I seem to have good reason to believe that I am a person regardless of what personhood requires. And so one might think that we have good reason to believe that we are morally responsible for our actions regardless of what moral responsibility requires. And if we do have such reasons, then if we also came up with independent reasons for thinking that moral responsibility requires L-freedom, then we could conclude that we are L-free.

But how could defenders of the argument in (1)–(3) *motivate* the claim that we have reason to believe that (1) is true regardless of what it requires? As far as I can see, the only plausible strategy they might pursue here would be to say something roughly like this:

> *(1)-Is-Pretheoretic*: The belief that premise (1) is true—that is, that we are morally responsible for our actions—is a pretheoretical, commonsense belief that we naturally have, and this belief can survive a process of reflective equilibrium and count as justifiable provided that it doesn't conflict with any other better-established theses that we come to believe.

Taken in isolation, I think this stance toward (1) is fairly plausible. However, it seems to me that we can adopt this stance only if we don't also endorse (2), or have good reason to endorse (2). We can appreciate this point in two different ways.

First, if we came to have good reason to endorse (2)—that is, to suppose that moral responsibility requires indeterminism and L-freedom—then this would show that the pretheoretic belief that we are morally responsible for our actions *is* in danger of conflicting with other theses that we have come to endorse for good reasons, namely, premise (2) and the thesis that we do not presently have any good empirical evidence for indeterminism (and the thesis that any good reason to believe indeterminism would have to involve empirical data about the actual causal behavior of physical objects and could not be derived from pretheoretic beliefs that we have about our status as moral beings). In short, the point here is that if we had good reason to believe (2), then our pretheoretic belief that (1) is true would be brought into question; more specifically, (1) would be shown to be the sort of hypothesis that requires substantive empirical evidence and cannot be a justifiable pretheoretic belief.

Let's move on now to the second way of motivating the idea that we can endorse *(1)-Is-Pretheoretic* only if we don't also endorse premise (2). Suppose that premise (1)—the claim that we are morally responsible for our actions—*is* a justifiable pretheoretic belief. Then, of course, this requires the concept of moral responsibility to be a concept of a sort that allows for justifiable pretheoretic beliefs here. One sort of concept that could do this is a *kind* concept. The concept of water is a kind concept, and accordingly, it allows for justifiable pretheoretic beliefs. We use the term 'water' to refer to the stuff in our pipes and lakes and so on, regardless of what that stuff turns out to be. Thus, because of this, people can have justifiable pretheoretic beliefs to the effect that the stuff in our pipes and lakes and so on is water. Likewise, if 'morally responsible' were something like a kind term (or if it were some sort of family-resemblance term, like, for instance, 'game'), then we might well be able to have justifiable pretheoretic beliefs to the effect that we are at least sometimes morally responsible for our actions. But notice that if 'water' were *not* a kind term, then things might be different here. In particular, if the concept of water required some specific chemical structure, then one could not have a justifiable pretheoretic belief that the stuff in our pipes and lakes and so on was water; on the contrary, one would need to have empirical evidence for the thesis that that stuff really did have the required sort of chemical structure. And the same goes for moral responsibility. If the concept of moral responsibility required causal indeterminism, then one could not have a justifiable pretheoretic belief that we are morally responsible for our actions; on the contrary, one would need to have empirical evidence for the thesis that our actions and decisions really are causally undetermined in the required way. Thus, if we *do* have a justifiable pretheoretic belief that we are morally responsible for our actions, then moral responsibility does not require indeterminism and L-freedom. In short, the point here is that you cannot have it both ways. You cannot claim that the applicability of a concept C has substantive empirical requirements that are not apparent in ordinary observation (things like a specific chemical structure, or causal indeterminism) and *also* claim that we have justifiable pretheoretic beliefs to the effect that various ordinary things in our environment are instances of the concept C. These two claims just don't go together. But this is precisely what the argument in (1)–(3) tries to do.

This gives us an argument for a thesis that's actually a bit stronger than *If-(2)-Then-No-Argument-for-(1)*; in particular, it gives us an argument for this:

> If we currently have good reason to endorse (1), then (2) is false; that is, if we currently have good reason to believe that we are morally responsible for our actions, then moral responsibility does not require L-freedom. And equivalently, if (2) is true, then we have no good reason to endorse (1); that is, if moral responsibility requires L-freedom, then we have no good reason to suppose that we are morally responsible for our actions.

But given this, it would clearly be wrongheaded for us to endorse both (1) *and* (2). And so it follows that the argument in (1)–(3) does not give us a good reason to endorse libertarianism.

There is a more general point to be made here. Putting aside the question of whether the argument in (1)–(3) is itself an a priori argument, it seems clear that no purely a priori argument could establish or refute determinism or indeterminism or TDW-indeterminism, because these are all contingent hypotheses about the workings of the physical world (and they are all pretty clearly consistent and nontautologous). So let's turn now to empirical arguments.

4.4 Empirical Arguments?

As I pointed out above, I will assume here that as of right now, we do not have any good empirical reason for endorsing TDW-indeterminism (see section 4.1 for a brief discussion of this point as well as a definition of TDW-indeterminism). In this section, I will argue that there is likewise no good empirical reason for *rejecting* TDW-indeterminism.

There are several different strategies one might use to try to argue against TDW-indeterminism. First, one could try to argue for *universal determinism*, the view that all events are causally determined by prior events together with physical laws. (Clearly, this would do the trick, because universal determinism entails that torn decisions are determined, and hence that TDW-indeterminism is false.) Second, one could try to argue for *macro-level determinism*, the view that whatever we say about micro-level events, all macro-level events are determined. (Again, this would suffice, because our torn decisions are neural events and so they are macro-level events.) Third, one could try to argue for what we might call *virtual macro-level determinism*, the view that while it may be true that some macro-level events are strictly undetermined (because they are composed of micro-level events, some of which are undetermined), it is also true that all macro-level events are virtually determined—that is, that in every macro-level situation (or experiment), there is a specific possible outcome or event such that prior circumstances together with causal laws make it overwhelmingly likely that the given event will occur. In other words, the idea here is that while there may be some micro-level indeterminacies, these all "cancel out" or "disappear" before we get to the macro level, presumably because macro-level phenomena are composed of such large numbers of micro-level phenomena. (Clearly, virtual macro-level determinism would undermine TDW-indeterminism, because it entails that all torn decisions are virtually determined—i.e., that for any torn decision, there is a unique option X such that it is overwhelmingly likely that X will be chosen.) Fourth and fifth, one could zero in even more, not just to the macro level, but all the way to the neural level; that is, one could try to argue for *neural determinism*, the view that all neural events are determined, or for *virtual neural determinism*, the view that all neural events are virtually determined in the above sense. Sixth and seventh, one could narrow one's attention even further and try to argue for *torn-decision determinism* or *virtual torn-decision determinism*. And finally, eighth, one could try to give a direct argument against TDW-indeterminism itself.

If we had a reason to endorse any of the above versions of determinism or virtual determinism, that would give us a reason to reject TDW-indeterminism. But I will argue in this section that we don't have any good (empirical) arguments for any of these versions of determinism or virtual determinism. In section 4.4.1, I argue that there are no good empirical arguments for universal determinism; I concentrate here on issues in quantum mechanics. In section 4.4.2, I argue that there are no good empirical arguments for macro-level determinism or virtual macro-level determinism; I concentrate here on an inductive argument put forward most notably by Honderich. In section 4.4.3, I argue that there are no good empirical arguments for neural determinism or virtual neural determinism; I concentrate here on issues in neuroscience. And in section 4.4.4, I consider what I think are the most plausible strategies one might use to mount an empirical argument in favor torn-decision determinism or virtual torn-decision determinism or against TDW-indeterminism in particular, and I argue that none of the arguments here is good. In particular, I consider (i) an argument based on the work of the physicist Max Tegmark (Tegmark's argument is directed against the Penrose-Hameroff quantum-computer view of the brain, but it's been taken by others to raise a problem for the sort of indeterminism required for libertarian freedom); (ii) an argument based on the work of Benjamin Libet; and (iii) a cluster of arguments based on the many psychological studies showing that much of our behavior is significantly causally influenced by factors that we have no conscious access to. I have in mind here studies related to situationism, confabulation, and the slowness of consciousness; I do not deny that these studies show that nonconscious factors are more important to the causation of our behavior than we might like to admit; my claim will simply be that these studies don't give us good reason to reject TDW-indeterminism.

In arguing that there are no good arguments for any of the above versions of determinism or virtual determinism, I do not mean to suggest that I think there are good arguments *against* these views. In fact, I don't, and in a few places, I say a bit about this, though I don't need this result here, because the existence of such an argument wouldn't entail an answer to the question of whether TDW-indeterminism is true anyway (although an argument against virtual torn-decision determinism would certainly be a step in the direction of an argument for TDW-indeterminism). In any event, the fact that there aren't any good arguments for or against any of the various versions of determinism or virtual determinism is, I think, important; for it drives home the point, which I will be trying to make, that all of these questions are wide open.

4.4.1 Arguments for Universal Determinism?

Since macro-level events are exhaustively composed of bunches of micro-level events, it seems that the question of whether universal determinism is true boils down to the question of whether all micro-level events are determined.[5] Now, one might think it possible to motivate universal determinism without looking at any evidence concerning micro-level events, because one might think that our experience with macro-level events already suggests that *all* events are determined. But I will respond to arguments of this sort in section 4.4.2; we will see there that our experience with macro-level events doesn't even provide a good reason for thinking that all *macro-level* events are determined (or virtually determined), let alone that *all* events are determined. What I want to argue in the present section is that there isn't any empirical evidence concerned explicitly with micro-level phenomena that suggests that universal determinism is true, because there isn't any such evidence that suggests that all micro-level events are determined. (What I say in this section will be mostly unoriginal, and it will probably be familiar to many readers; but it's worth going through this material, because it will be relevant in later sections, especially section 4.4.4.1, where I discuss Tegmark's work. I will be brief.)

It used to be widely believed that all micro-level events are determined, but the emergence of quantum mechanics (QM) has undermined this belief. The first point to be made here is that QM contains probabilistic laws; it tells us, for instance, that if an electron is spin-up in the x-direction, then it is in a *superposition* state with respect to its spin in the orthogonal direction y—where this is a kind of indeterminate state, a sort of "hovering between" spin-up and spin-down—and if we measure the electron for spin in the y-direction, then there is a 0.5 probability that it will be spin-up and a 0.5 probability that it will be spin-down. It's important to realize that these superposition states cannot be understood epistemologically, in terms of observer ignorance. It's not that the electron is already spin-up or spin-down in the y-direction (prior to our measurement of its spin in that direction) and that we just don't know which it is; the electron isn't spin-up or spin-down in the y-direction prior to measurement. There is a very strong argument for this due to Kochen and Specker (1967).[6] Thus, on the standard view, the superposition state is physically real, and the measurement process involves a *collapse*—what's known as a collapse of the wave function—into a spin-up or a spin-down state.

(By the way, it should also be noted here that superposition states are very *weird*. If you don't know what spin is, you could miss this point in connection with the above example; but quantum systems can also be in superposition states with respect to more familiar properties, such as position. Suppose that a box is exhaustively partitioned by regions A and B. An electron can be in the box (in some sense) but not in region A and not in region B, for it can be in a superposition of *in A* and *in B*. QM does not tell us what exactly this means, and no one really understands it; it is best to think of it as a physically real state of the electron that physicists do not yet understand—at least in terms of having a physical "picture" of what the superposition state *is*.)

Of course, the fact that QM contains probabilistic laws of the above sort does not, by itself, undermine determinism, because determinists could maintain that there are *hidden variables* that determine whether a given electron that's spin-up in the x-direction will be spin-up or spin-down if measured for spin in the y-direction. But the problem is that there is no good evidence for the existence of hidden variables of this kind, and so, for all we know, it could just as easily be that when electrons that are spin-up in the x-direction are measured for spin in the y-direction, nothing determines whether they become spin-up or spin-down in the y-direction; in other words, it might be that these are strictly undetermined events. Now, this is not to say that we have good reason to endorse an indeterministic view of this kind; rather, it's to say that as of right now, we have no good reason to reject this sort of view. So there is an open question here about whether processes of the above kind are deterministic. To answer this question, we need to solve what's known as the problem of measurement. To solve the problem of measurement is to provide an adequate theory of what happens during quantum measurements, or more precisely, during wave-function collapses. What we have for such processes is a probabilistic predictive formalism that is extremely accurate, statistically speaking, when applied to large numbers of measurements of the same kind. But there is no widely accepted theory of what's going on—in terms of a physical "picture," or as physicists might want to put it, a dynamical description—in particular cases. More specifically, there is no widely accepted view on the question of whether wave-function collapses are deterministic or indeterministic, and more importantly, there is no good *evidence* for either answer to this question. (By the way, it's important to note here that there is no good reason to think that measurements are required for wave-function collapses; indeed, it's plausible to suppose that the physical processes involved in wave-function collapses occur in the absence of measurements and observers, and so the problem of measurement might more aptly be called the problem of wave-function collapses.)

In a nutshell, the point here is that we don't know whether or not all quantum events are determined, because we don't know how to interpret the probabilistic mathematical formalism of QM. There are some deterministic interpretations out there, and there are some indeterministic interpretations, but as of right now, we don't have any good argument (in particular, we don't have any good empirical evidence) for any of these interpretations.[7] The two main deterministic interpretations of QM are the hidden-variables interpretation inherent in Bohm's theory and the many-worlds interpretation (actually, it's not entirely clear that the many-worlds interpretation should be thought of as deterministic, but I won't pursue this issue here).[8] Bohm's theory is not just an interpretation of QM; it is an alternative theory, empirically distinct from standard QM. Now, in domains that we are currently able to investigate experimentally, Bohm's theory and standard QM predict the same results; but the predictions of the two theories could in principle diverge in new domains—in particular, as Bohm and Hiley (1993, 347) put it, in "a subquantum domain in which the laws of quantum theory would break down." But so far, we have not been able to test whether or not Bohm's theory is correct.

As for the many-worlds interpretation, the situation is even worse, because it's not clear that we could *ever* have any evidence for it. The many-worlds interpretation says, in a nutshell, that every time there is a collapse of a wave function, the world splits into numerous worlds in which the collapse goes differently. For instance, in the above scenario in which an electron that's spin-up in the x-direction is measured for spin in the y-direction, the world splits into two worlds, one in which the electron is spin-up in the y-direction and one in which it's spin-down. We happen to be in one of these worlds, but we have doppelgängers in the other world. To see why we do not—and probably could never—have any good reason to believe the many-worlds interpretation, consider the following view, which can be opposed to the many-worlds view:

> *One Indeterministic World (OIW)*: The probabilities generated by QM correspond to propensities of quantum systems to behave in certain ways when measured for certain observable quantities; thus, to return to the example used above, if we take a bunch of electrons that are spin-up in the x-direction and measure them for spin in the y-direction, half will be spin-up and half will be spin-down; but for any *single* electron of this sort, whether it collapses into a spin-up state or a spin-down state in such a measurement situation is not determined by anything—it just happens.

The problem with the many-worlds interpretation is that according to that view, our world—that is, the world we live in—is just as it would be if some interpretation along the lines of OIW were correct. What distinguishes the many-worlds interpretation from OIW-type interpretations is its claim that there are *other* worlds in which the various collapses go differently. But as of right now, we have no evidence whatsoever for believing in these other worlds (and it seems likely that we could never have such evidence). Therefore, as of right now, we have no good reason to endorse the many-worlds interpretation.

So at present, we don't know whether QM should be interpreted deterministically or indeterministically. Thus, we don't have any good reason to endorse or reject the idea that all quantum events are determined. And so we don't have any good reason to endorse or reject universal determinism. Or at any rate, we have no good reasons here that are based on considerations having to do explicitly with micro-level phenomena; it is of course conceivable that there is some argument based on our experience with macro-level phenomena for endorsing universal determinism, but I will argue in the next section (4.4.2) that, in fact, there is no good argument of this sort either.

4.4.2 Arguments for Macro-level Determinism or Virtual Macro-level Determinism?

People sometimes try to argue for macro-level determinism by means of an inductive generalization. We might put the argument here in the following way:

(1) All of the macro-level events that we have encountered in our lives have been causally determined by prior events together with causal laws. Therefore,

(2) Macro-level determinism is true—that is, all macro-level events are determined.

One might also try to motivate universal determinism in the same way. Ted Honderich tries to do this in the following passage (2002, 462):

> In my life so far I have never known a single event to lack an explanation in the fundamental sense, and no doubt your life has been the same. No spoon has mysteriously levitated at breakfast. There has been no evidence at all, let alone proof, of there being no explanation to be found of a particular event. On the contrary, despite the fact that we do not seek out or arrive at the full explanations in question, my experience and yours pretty well consists of events that we take to have such explanations. If we put aside choices or decisions and the like—the events in dispute in the present discussion of determinism and freedom—my life and yours consists of nothing but events that we take to have fundamental explanations. Thus, to my mind, no general proposition of interest has greater inductive and empirical support than that all events whatever, including choices or decisions and the like, have explanations.

In the present section, I will argue that this sort of reasoning is misguided. I will concentrate on the argument in (1)–(2), arguing that our experiences don't even motivate macro-level determinism (and, of course, it follows from this that they don't motivate universal determinism either). Moreover, after undermining the argument in (1)–(2), I will undermine an analogous inductive argument for virtual macro-level determinism.

The problem with the (1)–(2) argument for macro-level determinism is very simple: Premise (1) is unmotivated, wildly controversial, and question-begging. We encounter all sorts of macro-level events that seem as though they might be undetermined—or more accurately and importantly, that are such that we have no idea whether they are determined or not—for example, coin tosses, the appearances of unsightly facial blemishes on the mornings of proms, events in which a person contracts chicken pox from someone else, events in which macro-level measuring devices reveal quantum wave-function collapses, human decisions, chimp decisions, parakeet decisions, temper tantrums, fallings in love, cars running out of gas after being run for 314 miles rather than 314.0001 miles, etc., etc., etc. Now, of course, determinists have a story to tell about how it *could be* that events like these are deterministic; for instance, they can claim that if, say, Jack and Jill were both exposed to chicken pox and only Jack fell ill, this would not undermine determinism, because it could very easily be that there were hidden physical variables at work in the situation (e.g., factors having to do with the physical well-being of Jack and Jill, or the duration of their exposures, or whatever) that determined that Jack would contract the disease and Jill would not. And likewise for events of the other kinds listed above: Determinists can say that events like coin tosses and decisions might be deterministic, even if they seem random to us, because it might be that there are hidden determining factors at work in such cases. I agree; for all we know, it *might* be that events of the above kinds are fully determined. But in the present context, this is entirely irrelevant. What determinists need, in order for the argument in (1)–(2) to have any force, is not a story about how it *could be* that events of the above kinds are determined; what they need is a positive argument for the claim that, in fact, such events *are* determined.

Perhaps an analogy will help make this point. Suppose Jane claims that all adult humans secretly hate God and tries to argue for this inductively, inferring it from the claim that every adult we've ever encountered has harbored such a hatred. And suppose that Peter responds by pointing out that we have in fact observed many adult humans who seem not to hate God, for example, the various church goers in the world. Will Jane accomplish anything by pointing out that it *could be* that all of these people attend church only to hide their hatred of God from their neighbors? Certainly not. What Jane needs, if her inductive argument is to provide a good reason to believe her conclusion, is a positive argument for the claim that all the apparent nonhaters of God that we have observed are, in fact, really God haters. Likewise, what advocates of the (1)–(2) argument for macro-level determinism need to argue is that macro-level events that seem as though they might be undetermined—events like coin tosses and decisions—are in fact determined. Providing an account of how it *could be* that such events are determined accomplishes exactly nothing in the present context.

I take it that determinists have no response to this, i.e., that they do not have an argument of the required sort. The argument they used to give is that any apparently indeterministic behavior of macro-level systems must really be deterministic, because such systems are made up of micro-level systems whose behavior is deterministic. But this argument is no good, because as we've seen, we currently have no more reason to believe micro-level determinism than macro-level determinism.

I suppose one might respond here by claiming that every time we go looking for deterministic explanations, we find them. But this is just false. It's not just that we don't currently have deterministic explanations of these phenomena; it's that we haven't the foggiest idea how to proceed in trying to construct and justify such explanations.

What about virtual macro-level determinism? Well, there is an inductive argument for this view that is exactly analogous to the (1)–(2) argument. We might put this argument in the following way:

(1') All of the macro-level events that we have encountered in our lives have been either determined or virtually determined. Therefore,

(2') Virtual macro-level determinism is true—that is, all macro-level events are either determined or virtually determined.

But this argument is flawed in the same way that the (1)–(2) argument is flawed. In short, the problem is that (1') is unmotivated, controversial, and question-begging. There are lots of macro-level events—for example, coin tosses, quantum-measurement events, decisions, and so on—that, for all we know, might be neither determined nor virtually determined. In order for virtual macro-level determinists to motivate an inductive argument of this sort, they would need to provide positive reasons for thinking that events like coin tosses and decisions and quantum measurements are, in fact, either determined or virtually determined. But at present, there is simply no good reason to believe this.

There is a second empirical argument—distinct from the inductive arguments in (1)–(2) and (1')–(2')—that one sometimes hears for universal determinism, or macro-level determinism, or virtual macro-level determinism. In a nutshell, the argument is that we have to assume that some sort of determinism is true in order to account for the success we have had in science, or for the regularity we have found in nature. But the existence of indeterministic processes—indeed, macro-level undetermined events that aren't even virtually determined—is perfectly consistent with regularity and the success of science. Of course, indeterminism is not consistent with *complete* regularity (if by that, we mean determinism), but there is no good reason to think that the physical world is completely regular; in particular, it's clear that the success of science doesn't require complete regularity, or determinism. To begin with, in a somewhat-but-not-completely-regular world, there can of course be statistical causal laws, for example, laws of the form '80 percent of A-type events cause B-type events'. But there can also be *universal* causal laws in such worlds, and for two different reasons. First, even if there are some indeterministic causal processes, other processes may be deterministic, and so we can have deterministic laws that govern these deterministic processes (e.g., the Schrödinger equation is a deterministic law governing quantum behavior). Second, and more interestingly, even if *all* causal processes involved some indeterminism, there could still be true universal causal laws, for such laws could, so to speak, *gloss over* the indeterminacies involved in the processes in question. For instance, suppose that A-events always cause B-events but that they cause different *kinds* of B-events—say, B_1-events, B_2-events, and B_3-events—and that which kind of B-event occurs in the wake of a given A-event is indeterministic. Then 'All A-events cause B-events' will be a true universal causal law of nature, even if there are indeterminacies involved in all A-to-B causal chains. For instance, it may be that 'Untreated rabies causes death' is universally true, even if there are indeterminacies involved in all death-by-rabies processes; for the term 'death' is so broad that it could gloss over the differences between a variety of different possible death-by-rabies processes. (Note, though, that 'death' isn't so broad that it makes the above law uninteresting; indeed, if you had rabies and didn't have access to any treatment, this law would probably be more interesting to you [if that's the right word] than any more detailed law on the same subject.)

So I don't think the success-of-science argument is any better than the Honderich-style inductive argument, and indeed, the above remarks seem to suggest that we don't have any empirical evidence for determinism, or macro-level determinism, or virtual macro-level determinism. What drives arguments like Honderich's, it seems to me, is not any actual evidence, but rather a deeply ingrained dogma that some kind of determinism is true.

People have long assumed that everything can be explained, that if we perform an experiment twice and get two different results, then there must have been hidden differences that we did not detect between the two physical systems on which we performed the experiments. But the fact of the matter is that we do not have any good reason to believe this. This is the lesson—or at any rate, one of the lessons—of quantum mechanics; it has taught us that for all we know, there may be indeterministic processes at work in nature. In short, the deep-seated belief that people have had in determinism (and the thesis that all events can be explained) is just a dogma. It may be true, but we do not have any good reason to believe it (or to disbelieve it).

It is worth pointing out in this connection that Honderich's own wording of the inductive argument suggests that there is a sort of dogma at work here. He says: "my life and yours consists of nothing but events that *we take* to have fundamental explanations" (emphasis added). I agree that people very often *take* macro-level events (which seem as though they might be undetermined) to have deterministic explanations, but it does not follow from this that these events do have such explanations or that we have any good reason to suppose that they do.

4.4.3 Arguments for Neural Determinism or Virtual Neural Determinism?

We have seen in sections 4.4.1 and 4.4.2 that for all we know, it may be that universal determinism, macro-level determinism, and virtual macro-level determinism are all false. That is, it may be that there exist macro-level events that are neither determined nor virtually determined. Despite this, however, one might think we have reasons for endorsing neural determinism or virtual neural determinism. For one might think that even if there are some macro-level events that are neither determined nor virtually determined, there are reasons for thinking that neural events could not be among them. In this section, I will refute an argument for neural determinism, and in the process, I will argue that, at present, there are no good arguments for neural determinism or virtual neural determinism, because current neuroscientific theory (and the existing empirical evidence) are perfectly consistent with the falsity of these theories, that is, with the thesis that some neural events are neither determined nor virtually determined.

(The argument for neural determinism that I will refute here is due to Honderich. One might also try to use some recent calculations by Max Tegmark to construct an argument for neural determinism, or virtual neural determinism; but Tegmark's work is more naturally and commonly seen as generating an argument against indeterministic views of *mental* processes, and so I will discuss his work in section 4.4.4, in connection with torn-decision determinism.)

Honderich (1988, chapter 5) claims to have an empirical argument for neural determinism. In particular, he argues for two theses that he thinks motivate neural determinism. The two theses are (a) that "Mental and neural events are intimately connected—each specific type of mental event somehow necessarily occurs with a simultaneous specific type or types of neural event" (1988, 269), and (b) that "Neural events are the effects of standard causal sequences," that is, of "prior neural or other bodily events" (1988, 288).

But in fact, these theses don't motivate neural determinism. Thesis (a) is clearly consistent with neural indeterminism. Honderich thinks that thesis (a) creates a problem for dualistic views of the mind, and he seems to think that indeterministic views of the mind have to be dualistic. But, of course, this is false. There is no reason for neural indeterminists or libertarians to endorse dualism, and indeed, the version of libertarianism described above involves a commitment to a token–token mind–brain identity theory, and it's perfectly consistent with type–type identity theories that entail thesis (a). So, again, thesis (a) poses no threat to the kind of indeterministic view that we're concerned with here.

Similar remarks apply to thesis (b). Most of what Honderich says here does little more than motivate the idea that there's nothing "spooky" about brain processes—in particular, that the brain is not causally influenced by weird, "nonstandard," or immaterial forces. Again, this is something that neural indeterminists can and should accept. They can say that neural causation is just like other kinds of physical causation. The only difference between neural determinists and neural indeterminists is that the latter think that some neural events aren't causally determined by prior events. But this doesn't mean they think there is something unusual going on in the brain, because they can of course say that there are lots of non-neural events that aren't causally determined either—for instance, quantum events, quantum-measurement events, unsightly-facial-blemish events, and so on.[9]

Now, there is one reading of thesis (b) according to which it *is* incompatible with neural indeterminism; in particular, if 'standard causal sequence' means *deterministic causal sequence*, then obviously, thesis (b) is little more than a rewording of neural determinism. And, indeed, it's obvious that this is what Honderich has in mind. But the problem is that he doesn't have any *argument* for thesis (b) on this reading. His discussion motivates nothing stronger than the claim that the brain is a physical, causal system. There isn't a shred of evidence given for the claim that all of the causation involved in the brain is deterministic causation. The only thing he says on this topic is that neuroscientists understand causation as deterministic causation. He writes (1988, 292):

> there is no doubt that neuroscience everywhere uses the intuitive and standard conception of a causal circumstance and effect, such that the former necessitates the latter.

But this claim is just straightforwardly false. Or at any rate, the claim that neuroscience treats all neural processes deterministically is straightforwardly false; what the standard neuroscientist's conception of causation is, I don't know, and as far as I can see, it doesn't matter. Current neuroscientific theory treats a number of different neural processes probabilistically, and any decent textbook on neuroscience will point this out. For instance, synaptic transmission and spike firing are both treated probabilistically. One textbook (Dayan and Abbott 2001, 179, 9) puts these points as follows:

> (I) ... [synaptic] transmitter release is a stochastic process. Release of transmitter at a presynaptic terminal does not necessarily occur every time an action potential arrives and, conversely, spontaneous release can occur even in the absence of the depolarization due to an action potential.
>
> (II) Because the sequence of action potentials generated by a given stimulus varies from trial to trial, neuronal responses are typically treated statistically or probabilistically. For example, they may be characterized by firing rates, rather than as specific spike sequences.

It is worth noting that some aspects of the indeterminacies in both of these processes are caused by the indeterminacy inherent in another process, namely, the opening and closing of ion channels, which are essentially little gates that let charged ions in and out of cells. Now, to be sure, by treating these processes probabilistically, neuroscientists do not commit themselves to the thesis that, in the end, they are genuinely indeterministic. But the important point here is that they aren't committed to determinism either. The question of whether these processes are genuinely indeterministic simply isn't answered by neuroscientific theory. Indeed, it is a standard view among those who work in this area that for at least some of these processes (e.g., the opening and closing of ion channels), this isn't even a neuroscientific question, because it is already clear right now that there could not be deterministic neuroscientific explanations of the phenomena. In other words, the idea is that (a) from the point of view of neuroscience, these processes might as well be undetermined, but (b) it *could* be that there are underlying deterministic *physical* explanations of the phenomena. Thus, the question of whether there actually are such explanations is not a neuroscientific question at all; it is rather a question of physics, because the issue comes down to questions about the behavior of the elementary physical particles involved in the neural processes.

That this is a standard view among those who work in this area is an empirical claim. My reason for believing it arises out of private correspondences I have had on this point with a few neuroscientists. Dayan, for instance, says that "people would argue that there are good thermal reasons to think that [the opening and closing of ion channels] is truly random. Thus, short of philosophical debates about hidden variables for all forms of randomness in physics, this is some fundamental randomness for which people nearly have evidence." And Sebastian Seung, a neuroscientist at MIT, says that "The question of whether [synaptic transmission and spike firing] are 'truly random' processes in the brain isn't really a neuroscience question. It's more of a physics question, having to do with statistical mechanics and quantum mechanics." And finally, Christof Koch, a Cal Tech neuroscientist, says: "At this point, we do not know to what extent the random, i.e., stochastic, neuronal processes we observe are due to quantum fluctuations (à la Heisenberg) that are magnified by chemical and biological mechanisms or to what extent they just depend on classical physics (i.e., thermodynamics) and statistical fluctuations in the underlying molecules."[10]

It seems, then, that standard neuroscience is *consistent with* neural determinism but that it doesn't come close to entailing (or, indeed, to providing any reason at all to endorse) neural determinism or even virtual neural determinism. In short, the claim that current neuroscientific theory gives us reason to believe neural determinism or virtual neural determinism is just straightforwardly false.

So, returning to Honderich, I agree with his claim that the brain is an ordinary physical system involving ordinary causal processes. What I deny is that it follows from this that these processes are deterministic. As far as I can see, Honderich just hasn't given any evidence at all for the claim that all brain processes—which, granted, are ordinary, physical, causal processes—are deterministic. And it should be noted that the point here goes beyond a refutation of Honderich's argument; given what we've seen here about current neuroscientific theory, it seems safe to conclude that as of right now, there is no good empirical reason to believe neural determinism or virtual neural determinism.

4.4.4 Arguments for Torn-Decision Determinism, or for Virtual Torn-Decision Determinism, or against TDW-Indeterminism?

Let us now focus our attention all the way down to the level of torn decisions. Even if there are no good empirical arguments for universal determinism, macro-level determinism, virtual macro-level determinism, neural determinism, or virtual neural determinism, one might still think there are good empirical reasons for believing torn-decision determinism or virtual torn-decision determinism—or, more specifically, for rejecting TDW-indeterminism, the thesis that's actually needed for libertarianism to be true. In this section, I will consider what I think are the strongest arguments for these claims, and I will argue that none of them is cogent. In particular, in subsection 4.4.4.1, I respond to an argument that arises out of the work of Max Tegmark; in subsection 4.4.4.2, I respond to an argument that arises out the work of Benjamin Libet; and in subsection 4.4.4.3, I respond to a collection of arguments that arise out of various psychological studies suggesting that much of our behavior is determined by nonconscious phenomena.

4.4.4.1 The argument from Tegmark's work Tegmark (2000) has given an argument that some people have taken as providing strong reason for doubting the existence of any indeterminacies that are relevant to mental events like torn decisions. Tegmark advertises his argument as a refutation of the Penrose-Hameroff view that the brain acts as a quantum computer and that this is centrally important to consciousness (see Penrose and Hameroff 1995, and Hameroff and Penrose 1996); but the argument is really an argument against a specific thesis that's inherent in the Penrose-Hameroff theory, namely, the thesis that there are neural superposition states in the brain that undergo wave-function collapses due to neural processes. The Penrose-Hameroff theory involves two central ideas. The first, proposed by Hameroff, is that tubulin proteins residing within neurons could, in theory, take on superposition states. Tubulin proteins make up the walls of microtubules, which are tiny hollow cylinders that (along with other structures) make up the "skeletons," or "internal scaffoldings," of neurons. Hameroff's idea is that since tubulin proteins can take on two different shapes, namely, *extended* and *contracted*, they could in principle be in extended-contracted superposition states. The second idea in the Penrose-Hameroff model is that tubulin-protein superpositions are inherently unstable and, therefore, subject to wave-function collapses—or objective reductions, or self-collapses—brought on by a quantum-gravity mechanism suggested by Penrose. Tegmark's argument is aimed not at the specific idea that there are tubulin-protein superpositions that self-collapse due to a Penrose-style quantum-gravity mechanism, but rather at the more general claim that there are neural superpositions, or macro-level brain-state superpositions, that undergo wave-function collapses due to neural processes. The argument, in a nutshell, is that because the brain is so warm and wet, neural superpositions could not survive long enough to be affected by neural processes. More specifically, Tegmark argues that (a) because of the brain's temperature, and because of disturbances within the brain caused by things like ions and water molecules, any neural superpositions that might obtain within the brain would decohere due to the destructive influence of environmental "noise" within about 10^{-13} seconds; but (b) neurons function, at the fastest, on a time scale of about 10^{-3} seconds; and so (c) even if there are neural superpositions, they could not avoid decoherence for a long enough period of time to undergo self-collapse.

This argument has been taken to show that there couldn't be any quantum indeterminacies that matter to mental processes like decision making. For instance, David Hodgson (2002, 107) says that Tegmark's argument, if cogent, shows that "in systems as massive, hot, and wet as neurons of the brain, any quantum entanglement and indeterminacies would be eliminated within times far shorter than those necessary for conscious experiences." If this is right, then Tegmark's argument provides some motivation for virtual torn-decision determinism. For (a) as of right now, it seems plausible to suppose that the best hope for torn-decision indeterminism is the existence of quantum indeterminacies in the brain, and (b) on the above reading of Tegmark's argument, it suggests that even if there are quantum indeterminacies in the brain, they disappear quickly and aren't relevant to mental events like torn decisions.

But I want to argue that even if Tegmark's argument is cogent—even if it succeeds in refuting the Penrose-Hameroff view[11]—it doesn't show that there are no quantum indeterminacies in the brain that are relevant to mental events like torn decisions. What his argument shows is that there couldn't be any neural indeterminacies of a certain, specific kind, namely, indeterminacies based in macro-level brain-state superpositions that undergo wave-function collapses due to neural processes. But Tegmark's argument does not show that there couldn't be any neural indeterminacies that involve *micro*-level superpositions and wave-function collapses. More specifically, for all Tegmark has argued, it could be that the following model is true:

The neural-dependence-on-micro-indeterminacy model of neural/mental indeterminacy: (i) There are some neural events that are such that some of their constituent micro-level events are undetermined; and (ii) for some of these neural events, some of their macro-level features (e.g., whether there's a synaptic transmission or a neural firing) depend on the outcomes of the constituent indeterministic micro-level events in such a way that prior to the occurrence of the neural event in question, there was a significant probability of its being different, so that the neural event is not only not determined, but also not virtually determined; and (iii) in some cases of this sort, if the undetermined neural event(s) go one way, then there is one sort of mental event (or set of mental events), and if they go another way, then there is a different sort of mental event (or set of mental events). Finally, it could be that in some cases of this sort, (a) if the undetermined micro-level events go one way, we get one neural event (call it N_1), whereas if they go another way, we get a different neural event (call it N_2); and (b) N_1 and N_2 are both torn decisions, but in N_1 the agent in question chooses one of her reasons-based tied-for-best options, whereas in N_2 she chooses another.

Clearly, this model could be true even if there are no such things as macro-level superpositions or macro-level wave-function collapses (and even if the brain is not a quantum computer). Thus, it could be true even if Tegmark's argument is entirely cogent. And so Tegmark's argument should not be thought of as establishing the claim that there couldn't be any quantum indeterminacies that are relevant to mental events like torn decisions. It is rather an argument for the thesis that there couldn't be any neural indeterminacies of a certain, specific kind, namely, indeterminacies involving macro-level brain-state superpositions that undergo wave-function collapses due to neural processes.

It's worth noting that whatever others have said, Tegmark himself seems to think that his argument is consistent with the thesis that there are indeterminacies in the brain that survive to the macro level. He writes (2000, 11):

> For the neural network community, the implication of our result is . . . [that] there is no need to worry about the fact that current simulations do not incorporate effects of quantum coherence. The only remnant from quantum mechanics is the apparent randomness that we subjectively perceive every time the subject system evolves into a superposition . . . , but this can be simply modeled by including a random number generator in the simulation. In other words, the recipe used to prescribe when a given neuron should fire . . . may have to involve some classical randomness to correctly mimic the behavior of the brain.

And later, in talking about "the degrees of freedom that constitute the subject," Tegmark says that "there is nothing quantum-mechanical about their equations of motion (except that they can be stochastic)." So, clearly, Tegmark's point is *not* that neural processes are deterministic, for he allows that they can be indeterministic and, indeed, that these indeterminacies result from quantum phenomena. Moreover, it's also not his point that neural processes are virtually determined, for clearly, he thinks the indeterminacies matter to the behavior of the brain—hence, the use of the random number generator to mimic brain behavior. And finally, since on this view the indeterminacies matter to the behavior of the brain—to what neural events occur—they could presumably matter to what mental events occur and, in particular, to which options we choose in our torn decisions. So, it doesn't seem that Tegmark's point is that there are no quantum indeterminacies that are relevant to mental processes. His point is that we do not have to use the theory of quantum mechanics in studying cognitive processes (and that the brain is not a quantum computer, as Penrose and Hameroff suggest).

The neural-dependence-on-micro-indeterminacy model that I formulated above gives us a kind of neural indeterminacy that's consistent with Tegmark's argument but still relevant to mental events like decisions. But it's important to note that I am not claiming that we have good reason to endorse this model. All I'm saying is that as of right now, we have no good reason to doubt it. At any rate, Tegmark's argument doesn't give us a reason to doubt it, and as far as I know, we don't have any good reason at all. (Note, too, that my stance here is made more plausible by the arguments of section 4.4.3, which show that current neuroscientific theory and the existing empirical evidence are perfectly consistent with the existence of neural events that are neither determined nor virtually determined.)

It's also important to note how *weak* the neural-dependence-on-micro-indeterminacy model is. In formulating this model, I have tried to capture the most general version of the idea that there are neural/mental indeterminacies that are based in micro-level indeterminacies; that is, I have tried not to give any details about how the view might be filled in, and so I have located what is, I think, the weakest version of the view. And again, my claim is simply that, as of right now, there is no good reason to disbelieve this view.

Having said how my stance here is weak, though, I should also point out something that libertarians who endorsed this stance would be committed to. In order for a libertarianism of the sort described in chapter 3 to be true, it needs to be the case that some of our torn decisions are undetermined *at the moment of choice*. So not just any scenario that involves neural dependence on micro-level indeterminacy will do here. In particular, if the relevant undetermined micro-level event(s) are prior to, and not part of, the torn decision, we will not procure the required sort of indeterminacy. The undetermined micro-level event(s) need to be *part(s) of* the torn decision, so that the decision itself (in particular, which option is chosen) is undetermined. Now, this is not to say that the undetermined micro-level events need to be simultaneous with the *whole* of the decision; as long as they are parts of the decision, it would be OK (i.e., consistent with chapter-3-style libertarianism) if the decision continued for a period of time after the completion of the undetermined micro-level events. But this issue raises an important point: There is no guarantee that in every case there will be a clearly right answer to the question of whether the relevant undetermined micro-level events were (a) prior to the relevant neural/mental event, i.e., the torn decision, or (b) part of that event. There could be cases where it would clearly be best to say that the relevant micro-level events were prior to the relevant neural/mental event, and there could be cases where it would clearly be best to say that the former were part of the latter; but there could also be cases where there was no clearly right answer to the question, because the cutoff between what was prior to the decision and what was part of it was vague. And, of course, given the arguments of chapter 3, this would mean that there was no clearly right answer to the question of whether the decision was L-Free.

In any event, it seems to me that for the reasons given above, Tegmark's results do not give us any good reason to think that any of our torn decisions are determined or virtually determined. Indeed, his results seem to be perfectly consistent with the libertarian thesis that some of our torn decisions are wholly undetermined in the manner of TDW-indeterminism.

4.4.4.2 The argument from Libet's work Benjamin Libet has produced some results that have been taken to generate a problem for free will. In particular, his work seems to generate a problem for the sort of indeterminism that's required for L-freedom. The story here begins with a neuroscientific discovery that goes back to the 1960s. It was discovered then that voluntary decisions are preceded in the brain (by as much as a second) by a slow change in electrical potential; this electrical shift, which is recordable on the scalp, is known as the *readiness potential* (see Kornhuber and Deecke 1965, and Deecke, Grotzinger, and Kornhuber 1976). Building on this work, Libet has tried to establish an exact timeline for the readiness potential, the conscious intention to act, and the act itself (see Libet et al.

1983, and Libet 2002). His results suggest that the readiness potential appears about 350–400 milliseconds before the conscious, experienced intention to act, and about 550 milliseconds before the act itself. (It should be noted here that the decisions Libet worked with were trivial; subjects were told to flick their wrists at arbitrary times—whenever they felt an urge to do so—and in connection with these actions, Libet timed the onset of the readiness potential and the conscious intention to act.)

These data have been taken to raise a serious problem for free will. For instance, Henrik Walter (2001, 249) writes: "Libet's . . . findings immediately evoked the query. If we are not aware of our intentions until after the neural machinery for starting the act has already been warmed up, is free will just an illusion?" And Max Velmans (1991, 658) says that Libet's work "suggests that conscious volition may be one output from the (prior) cerebral processes that actually select a given response." More specifically, Libet's results seems to generate a problem for libertarian views that are based on TDW-indeterminism. For TDW-indeterminism seems inconsistent with the idea that our torn decisions are determined prior to the moment of conscious volition, and, to use Walter's way of putting things, Libet's findings seem to suggest that the "neural machinery for starting an act" is already up and running before the agent's conscious thought enters the picture.

To make things a bit more precise, one might argue from Libet's findings to the rejection of TDW-indeterminism in something like the following way:

(1) Conscious decisions are preceded by nonconscious brain processes (namely, the readiness potential) and are, in fact, nonconsciously initiated; and

(2) These nonconscious brain processes are presumably *not parts of* the conscious decisions in question. Therefore, it seems likely that

(3) Torn decisions are at least causally influenced by prior-to-choice nonconscious brain processes, and so they are not wholly undetermined in the manner of TDW-indeterminism (and they might even be determined, or virtually determined, by prior-to-conscious-choice brain processes).

One might try to attack this argument by questioning (1) or (2); for instance, one might argue that the lag between conscious decisions and reported awareness of conscious decisions is longer than Libet allows for; thus, one might in this way try to defend the idea that conscious decisions are simultaneous with the relevant brain events after all. But I do not want to pursue this strategy here. Instead, I want to argue that even if (1) and (2) are true, they do not give us any good reason to accept (3).

The first point to note here is that we don't know what the *function* of the readiness potential is. Indeed, because we don't know what its function is, we don't know whether it's even present in real-life torn decisions (as opposed to trivial laboratory decisions about things like wrist flicks). But the more important point here is that even if the readiness potential is present in torn decisions, we don't know what its purpose is. In particular, it would be an unmotivated assumption to suppose that, in torn decisions, the readiness potential is part of a causal process that's relevant to which option is chosen. There are plenty of other things the readiness potential could be doing, aside from this. One way to appreciate this is to recall (from chapter 3, and from section 4.1 of the present chapter) that libertarianism and TDW-indeterminism are perfectly consistent with the idea that various things involved with our torn decisions might be causally determined. In particular, a torn decision could be TDW-undetermined and L-free even if it was determined in advance that (i) a torn decision would occur, (ii) the choice would come from among the agent's reasons-based tied-for-best options, and (iii) the moment-of-choice probabilities of these options being chosen were all roughly even. The only thing that needs to be undetermined, in order for a torn decision to be TDW-undetermined and L-free, is *which option is chosen*. Given this, here are two stories that libertarians and TDW-indeterminists could tell about what the readiness potential might be doing (there are other stories as well—see, e.g., Mele 2006—but these two will do):

Model A: It might be that (a) the readiness potential is part of the causal process leading to the *occurrences* of torn decisions, and this has nothing whatsoever to do with which option is chosen; and (b) which option is chosen is in fact wholly undetermined in the manner of TDW-indeterminism. (A similar point, though a bit different, has been made by Haggard and Eimer—see, e.g., Haggard and Eimer 1999 as well as Haggard's contribution to Haggard and Libet 2001.[12])

Model B: It might be that (a) the readiness potential is part of the process whereby our reasons cause our decisions; and (b) in connection with torn decisions, this process doesn't determine which option is chosen; rather, it deterministically causes it to be the case that the choice will come from among the agent's reasons-based tied-for-best options (and perhaps also that the moment-of-choice probabilities of these options being chosen are all roughly even).

Of course, the views contained in models A and B are controversial, and as of right now, I don't think we have any good reason to endorse either of them. But the important point here is that as of right now, we don't seem to have any good reason to reject them either; in particular, the available evidence concerning the readiness potential doesn't give us any good reason to reject them. More generally—and in the present context, this is the really important point—as of right now, there is no reason to think that, in torn decisions, the readiness potential is part of a causal process that's relevant to the issue of which tied-for-best option is chosen. There is simply no evidence for this, and so the existence of the readiness potential doesn't give us any reason to suppose that, in torn decisions, which option is chosen is causally influenced, prior to the moment of conscious choice, by nonconscious processes.

Notice that I'm not just claiming that TDW-indeterminism is *consistent* with the available evidence concerning the readiness potential. By itself, that wouldn't be a very compelling defense, since all sorts of ludicrous theories—for example, the theory that evil Martians planted dinosaur bones in the ground to trick us into believing that the Earth is older than it really is—are consistent with the existing evidence. My claim here is that the evidence concerning the readiness potential doesn't even increase the probability that TDW-indeterminism is false. The thesis that in torn decisions, the readiness potential is part of a causal process that determines which option is chosen is *no more likely*, given our evidence, than, for example, Model B is. So the evidence concerning the readiness potential just doesn't give us any reason at all to reject TDW-indeterminism.

Finally, I should also note here that Libet himself is an indeterminist and that he thinks conscious thought could play a role in decision making. But Libet's way of making room for consciousness delivers much less control for the agent than models A and B do. On Libet's view, an agent's conscious will can influence a decision by vetoing the whole process—that is, by stopping the decision from being made, after the readiness potential has appeared. But models A and B deliver more control for the agent; indeed, by separating the issue of which option is chosen from other causal processes involved in torn decisions, both of these models seem to deliver full-blown control for the agent. I might add, though, that I think Libet's point is important as well, for it brings out the fact that the available evidence concerning the readiness potential is perfectly consistent with the idea that a person can have libertarian-style control over a decision about whether to make a given decision at a given time or remain in a state of indecision.[13]

4.4.4.3 Arguments from psychology There are a number of different psychological studies that generate doubts about human free will. For instance, there are studies that suggest that:

1. Consciousness is sluggish—that is, conscious awareness of various actions and processes lags behind the processes themselves (see, e.g., Velmans 1991 and Wegner 2002).
2. People are often mistaken about why they perform various actions and, indeed, confabulate reasons for their actions. (There is a mountain of evidence for this; see, e.g., Festinger 1957.)
3. Our actions and behaviors are often significantly influenced by situational factors that, intuitively, seem relatively unimportant (see, e.g., Isen and Levin 1972 and Milgram 1969; and for a discussion, see Nelkin 2005).
4. Conscious choices can be causally influenced by magnetic stimulation to the brain (see Brasil-Neto et al. 1992).

I think these studies are important and that they reveal all sorts of interesting and often depressing facts about humans. But I don't think they give us any good reason to reject TDW-indeterminism. In general, the problem is that these studies either (a) don't tell us anything at all about torn decisions or (b) don't tell us anything universalizable about them. Let me say a bit about this.

In connection with point 1, the evidence concerns processes for which, intuitively, it's not surprising that awareness lags behind action—things like the processing of incoming speech and knee-jerk reactions in emergency situations (e.g., the jerking of a steering wheel to one side to avoid hitting a child who has suddenly run in front of your car). Whatever we end up saying about cases like these, there is no evidence right now that in torn decisions, consciousness lags behind the actual selection of one of the reasons-based tied-for-best options.[14]

In connection with 2 and 3, there are a number of points to make. First, while there is overwhelming evidence for the thesis that much of our behavior is causally influenced by factors to which we have no conscious access, most of the studies here are irrelevant to our question, because they concern actions and behavior that aren't prefaced by conscious decisions (and certainly aren't prefaced by *torn* decisions). This is a point that is too infrequently noticed in discussions of what these studies tell us about free will. The fact of the matter is that very few of our actions are prefaced by conscious decisions. (And this, by the way, is good; imagine what a nightmare it would be to have to consciously will all your actions. Your inner monologue during a stroll might go something like this: "Move the left foot forward; OK, now the right; easy going—not too far with that foot—land right there, just before the hole," and so on.) Libertarianism and TDW-indeterminism are concerned with cases involving conscious decisions, in particular, torn decisions—that is, cases in which we feel torn, pause for at least a moment, and then consciously and intentionally choose one of our tied-for-best options. Very few of the experiments related to points 2 and 3 have any bearing at all on these cases. On the other hand, I think it's fair to say that the sum total of all the experiments here provides ample evidence for thinking that at least sometimes—and perhaps very often—our torn decisions are causally influenced by nonconscious factors. I don't think anyone who knows the psychological literature would want to deny this. But the point I want to make here is that libertarians don't *need* to deny it. All they need to do is endorse TDW-indeterminism, which says only that *some* of our torn decisions are not inappropriately caused by nonconscious factors. (It might be better to say that libertarians need to maintain that a *significant percentage* of our torn decisions are TDW-undetermined—or something along these lines; but to repeat a point I made in chapter 3, it seems plausible to assume that there is a fair amount of regularity here, so that if any of our torn decisions are TDW-undetermined, then many of them are.)

In any event, this point is important; for as interesting and important as the various psychological experiments here are, they don't come close to motivating the conclusion that *all* of our torn decisions are causally influenced by nonconscious factors in ways that are inconsistent with TDW-indeterminism. Think of a typical day: You might make torn decisions about whether to have eggs or cereal for breakfast, whether to exercise before going to work, whether to go to your office or work at home, whether to take the freeway or surface streets to work, whether to meet a friend for lunch or eat in your office to get more work done, whether to work late or go to a movie, and so on. Does the psychological literature really suggest that *none* of the decisions that we make of this kind is TDW-undetermined? The answer, I think, is that it does nothing of the sort. The evidence that we currently have seems perfectly consistent with the thesis that a significant percentage of our torn decisions are TDW-undetermined.

Finally, the Brasil-Neto study mentioned in point 4 might seem particularly relevant to TDW-indeterminism, because it's directly concerned with something like torn decisions (subjects were told to raise either their left or right fingers when they heard clicks, and unbeknownst to them, their choices were correlated with whether the left or right sides of their brains were magnetically stimulated[15]). But in fact, this study doesn't undermine

TDW-indeterminism at all. The study is a sort of real-life version of the various alien-manipulation thought experiments that philosophers often discuss. But even if aliens can manipulate our torn decisions, it doesn't follow that when aliens aren't present, our torn decisions aren't TDW-undetermined and L-free.

So I don't think any of the arguments or considerations discussed in this section give us any good reason to reject TDW-indeterminism (or to endorse torn-decision determinism or virtual torn-decision determinism). Moreover, I don't know of any other arguments here that are even initially promising. Thus, it seems that as of right now, we have no good empirical reason for doubting the thesis that some of our torn decisions are wholly undetermined in the manner of TDW-indeterminism.

In sum, then, the situation is this: The arguments in sections 4.4.1 through the present section (4.4.4) suggest that there are no good empirical arguments against TDW-indeterminism; and as I pointed out in section 4.1, it seems pretty clear that there are also no good empirical arguments in *favor* of TDW-indeterminism; and finally, as we saw in sections 4.2-4.3, it seems that there are also no good a priori arguments for or against TDW-indeterminism. Thus, the overall conclusion of this chapter is that as of right now, we have no good reason to believe or reject TDW-indeterminism. (And, of course, if we combine this with the conclusion of chapter 3—that the question of whether libertarianism is true comes down to the question of whether TDW-indeterminism is true—then we obtain the result that we have no good reason to believe or reject libertarianism either.) The bottom line on TDW-indeterminism is that we just don't know anywhere near enough about brain processes right now to know whether our torn decisions are fully determined or partially determined or wholly undetermined in the manner of TDW-indeterminism. So the rational thing to do is to remain silent. This might make us appear foolish or ignorant, but we should resist the temptation to open our mouths and espouse a theory; for it seems to me that any theory we could come up with now (and any evidence we might put forward in support of such a theory) would seem hopelessly primitive to anyone who knew the truth about brain processes and would very likely remove all doubt (in the minds of any knowers of the truth) about our foolishness and ignorance.

4.5 Where We Stand

We found in chapter 2 that the metaphysical issue inherent in the problem of free will and determinism comes down to what I called the which-kinds-of-freedom-do-we-have question. We also found there that the which-kinds-of-freedom-do-we-have question reduces largely (though not entirely—more on this in a moment) to the question of whether libertarianism is true—that is, the question of whether human beings are L-free. Moreover, in chapter 3, we found that the question of whether humans are L-free comes down to the purely empirical question of whether some of our torn decisions are wholly undetermined in the manner of TDW-indeterminism—that is, to the question of whether TDW-indeterminism is true. (We also saw in chapter 3 that if any of our torn decisions are not wholly undetermined in the manner of TDW-indeterminism, then there is also a question about whether they are partially undetermined at the moment of choice and, if they are, to what extent they are.) Finally, in the present chapter, we have found that we currently have no good reason to accept or reject TDW-indeterminism (and it seems pretty clear that parallel considerations show that we also have no good reason to take any stand on the question of whether any of our torn decisions are partially undetermined at the moment of choice).

Thus, if we combine the conclusions of chapters 3 and 4, we obtain the result that the libertarian question—that is, the question of whether human beings are L-free—comes down to a wide open empirical question about the moment-of-choice causal determinacy of the neural events that are our torn decisions. Moreover, if we add the conclusion of chapter 2 to this—that is, if we add the result that the metaphysical issue inherent in the problem of free will boils down largely to the libertarian question—then we seem to get the result that the metaphysical issue inherent in the problem of free will reduces to the same wide open empirical question about the causal histories of our torn decisions. But we need to add two different caveats or provisos to this conclusion, because, again, we cannot say that the metaphysical issue inherent in the problem of free will reduces *entirely* to the libertarian question.

The first proviso here is that the libertarian question is not the only controversial subquestion of the which-kinds-of-freedom-do-we-have question. For instance, as I pointed out in chapter 2, one might think that recent studies in psychology throw doubt on the idea that our actions and decisions are as responsive to our reasons as they seem to be, introspectively. And given this, one might think there are important, controversial questions about the degree to which human beings possess various compatibilist kinds of freedom that require reasons responsiveness.[16] (My own view here is that while it is no doubt true that we are often less reasons responsive than we might have taken ourselves to be, pretheoretically, and while there are indeed interesting and important questions about the *degree* to which we are reasons responsive, it is still pretty clear that our actions and decisions are at least sometimes responsive to our reasons in the ways that are required for the relevant kinds of compatibilist freedom.) But whatever we say about this, it's important to note that the substantive open questions here—questions about the degree to which we are reasons responsive—are *empirical* questions. And what's more, I think this point can be generalized, so that even if the which-kinds-of-freedom-do-we-have question doesn't reduce entirely to the libertarian question, we still get the result that it reduces to empirical questions about human beings (in particular, it would seem, to questions about our decision-making processes and the causal histories of our decisions).

Let me turn now to the second caveat or proviso that needs to be noted in connection with my claim that the metaphysical issue inherent in the problem of free will boils down (largely) to the libertarian question. It could be that at some time in the future, someone will formulate a kind of freedom (call it *X-freedom*) that is both (a) distinct from L-freedom (and from the various other kinds of freedom that philosophers have so far come up with) and (b) controversial in the sense that it is not obvious whether human beings possess it. If this happened, then in addition to the question of whether humans are L-free (and in addition to questions about whether we possess various kinds of reasons-responsiveness-freedom), there would be another controversial subquestion of the which-kinds-of-freedom-do-we-have question, namely, the question of whether humans are X-free. However, I would argue (although I won't do it here) that just like the question of whether we are L-free, this new question would have to be an *empirical* question (unless it was factually empty). For I would argue that if the sum total of all the empirical facts about human beings didn't settle the question of whether or not human beings were X-free, then there simply wouldn't be any fact of the matter as to whether humans were X-free. But the argument for this claim will have to wait for another occasion.

In sum, then, my stance here is that (a) the metaphysical issue inherent in the problem of free will reduces to the which-kinds-of-freedom-do-we-have question; and (b) the which-kinds-of-freedom-do-we-have question reduces largely to the libertarian question; and (c) the libertarian question reduces to a wide open empirical question about the causal histories of our torn decisions, namely, the question of whether any of these decisions are wholly undetermined in the manner of TDW-indeterminism; and (d) in connection with the use of the word 'largely' in point (b), if there are any other controversial subquestions of the which-kinds-of-freedom-do-we-have question, aside from the libertarian question, then they too come down to empirical questions about the nature of human decision-making processes—for example, questions about the degree to which our decisions are causally influenced by our reasons.

Now, I do not mean to suggest here that these empirical questions about our decision-making processes are the only interesting questions that are relevant to the philosophical topic of free will. As we saw in chapter 2, this is not the case. Most notably, the following two questions are also of central concern to philosophers:

(I) What is free will? (Or if you'd rather, what is the correct analysis of the notion of free will, or the correct definition of the expression 'free will'?)

(II) Which kinds of freedom (or "freedom") are required for moral responsibility?

But as we saw in chapter 2, these two questions are essentially irrelevant to metaphysical questions about the nature of human beings and human decision-making processes. Thus, the presence of questions (I) and (II), in philosophical discussions of free will, does not undermine the claims I made in the last paragraph about the metaphysical component of the problem of free will; that is, it doesn't undermine claims (a) through (d).

Of course, being told that questions (I) and (II) aren't about the nature of human beings, or human decision-making processes, does not tell us what they *are* about. As we saw in chapter 2, there are multiple views that one might endorse of what these questions are about, or of the kinds of facts that determine which answers to these questions are correct. One view here is that (I) and (II) are straightforwardly empirical questions about ordinary-language meaning, or folk usage and intentions. Now, of course, there are other views one might endorse here as well, but I think it can be argued (though, admittedly, I haven't argued it in this book) that all the different kinds of facts that might be relevant here—that might be relevant to determining which answers to questions (I) and (II) are correct—are either physical-empirical facts or logical facts.

If I'm right about this, then it would seem that all of the important philosophical questions about free will reduce to empirical questions and logical questions. And if this is right, then depending on what we mean when we say that a given problem is a *metaphysical* problem, it might just be a confusion to think of the problem of free will as a metaphysical problem. If a metaphysical problem is just a problem *about the world*, or something like that, then of course, the problem of free will is a metaphysical problem. But if a metaphysical problem is supposed to be somehow different from the kinds of problems that we address in the empirical sciences, then if what I've argued here is correct, then the problem of free will is *not* a metaphysical problem. It's just a really hard empirical problem.

Finally, I think it can be argued that the point here generalizes to other so-called metaphysical questions and problems. More specifically, I think it can be argued that all so-called metaphysical questions boil down to questions that are either (a) straightforwardly empirical questions about the nature of the physical world, or (b) straightforwardly logical questions, or (c) factually empty questions, that is, questions to which there are no correct answers.[17] If this is right, then there is no subject matter for metaphysics, distinct from the subject matters of the empirical and logico-mathematical sciences; that is, there are no distinctly metaphysical *facts*. But again, the argument for this sweeping thesis will have to wait for another occasion.

Notes

1 Introduction

1. Some of the many people who have endorsed compatibilist views of free will (and/or moral responsibility) are: Hobbes (1651), Locke (1689), Hume (1748), Hobart (1934), P. F. Strawson (1962), Aune (1967), Frankfurt (1969, 1971), Watson (1975), Lehrer (1976), Lewis (1981), Dennett (1984), Berofsky (1987), Dworkin (1988), Vihvelin (1988, 1991), Wolf (1990), Fischer (1994), Fischer and Ravizza (1998), Wallace (1994), Kapitan (1996, 2000), and Bok (1998). In addition, compatibilist views have been developed, but not endorsed, by Double (1991) and Mele (1995).

2. For a good overview of some of the most prominent compatibilist conceptions of free will and responsibility, see Haji 2002.

3. Some of the philosophers who have endorsed libertarian views of one kind or another are: Bramhall (1655), Reid (1788), Chisholm (1964a, 1995), Taylor (1966, 1974), C. A. Campbell (1967), Wiggins (1973), Thorp (1980), Nozick (1981), van Inwagen (1983), Kane (1985, 1996, 1999), Rowe (1987), Donagan (1987), Ginet (1990, 2002), O'Connor (1993, 2000), Clarke (1993, 1996), McCall (1994), Goetz (1997), McCann (1998), and Ekstrom (2000). In addition, libertarian views have been developed, though not endorsed, by Dennett (1978), Mele (1995), and myself (1999, 2004).

4. Of course, 'indeterminacies' can be used to refer not just to undetermined events but also to indeterministic states of affairs. Suppose, for instance, that there's no determinate fact of the matter as to whether Tim is bald. Then one might describe this situation by saying that there is an *indeterminacy* here. But this, of course, is not what I'm using the word 'indeterminacies' to refer to here. I am using this term to refer to events that aren't causally determined.

5. Broad (1952), G. Strawson (1986), and Pereboom (2001) have all endorsed views that are more or less equivalent to this. In addition, Double (1991) and Smilansky (2000) have endorsed views that are similar but a bit different.

2 Why the Compatibilism Issue and the Conceptual-Analysis Issue Are Metaphysically Irrelevant

1. So libertarianism is being defined here as the view that human beings are L-free. As we saw in chapter 1, some people would define it as the view that (a) humans are L-free and (b) the notion of L-freedom provides an accurate definition of 'free will'. But this is not how I'm using the term here, because (as we'll see) I want to keep metaphysical theses like (a) separate from semantic theses like (b).

2. I argued in chapter 1 that free will is compatible with FE-determinism if and only if it's compatible with determinism. Nothing very important will turn on this issue here, but for the sake of simplicity, I will assume it's true. And given this, the compatibilism question can be couched in traditional terms, i.e., in terms of the compatibility of free will and determinism, rather than free will and FE-determinism.

3. Humean freedom and Frankfurtian freedom were defined in chapter 1. See also Hume 1748 and Frankfurt 1971.

4. This is a tricky issue. The traditional view is undoubtedly naive about how philosophers' intuitions can be altered by their training and theorizing. But the idea that empirical semanticists should trust the results of intuition-pumping polls seems questionable as well. One problem here is that (a) a bit of training seems to be required to teach people how to play the thought-experiment-intuition game, but (b) this training can alter what we want to study. So getting at "the unaltered intuitions of ordinary folk" can be very difficult. Another problem is that it is relatively easy to get different answers from ordinary folk, in connection with controversial semantic questions, by simply altering the wording of the questions we ask them.

5. Parfit (1995) endorses a view similar to this in connection with the issue of personal identity.

6. Actually, let me say just a few words about the view that 'free will' is a kind term that picks out the sort of freedom that's inherent in normal human choices, whatever that turns out to be. To see how implausible this view is, notice how different 'free will' is from kind terms like 'water'. 'Water' denotes the stuff in our lakes and pipes and so on, whatever that stuff turns out to be. So if we discovered (in this world) that that stuff isn't H_2O, that it's really XYZ, then it would follow that water is XYZ; it certainly wouldn't follow that there is no such thing as water. Or to use a different example, if we discovered that the things we call "cats" are really Martian robots, this would not be a discovery that there are no such things as cats (assuming that 'cat' is a kind term); rather, it would be a discovery that all cats are robots. But 'free will' doesn't work like this. Suppose we discovered that all our choices were controlled by Martians via remote control. If 'free will' were a kind term, it would follow that free will consists in being controlled by Martians. But, of course, that's wrong. If we discovered that Martians were controlling all our choices, that

Notes 173

would be a discovery that we don't have free will. So it seems that 'free will' is not a kind term.

7. Van Inwagen (1983, section 6.3) has mounted an argument like this for the claim that human beings are L-free.

8. Note, however, that while the worth-wanting question is not relevant to the which-kinds-of-freedom-do-we-have question, the latter question might be relevant to the former. For one might think that the kind of freedom that we actually have is worth wanting, and so one might think that we have to determine which kinds of freedom we've got in order to fully answer the worth-wanting question.

9. Given the arguments of people like Kripke and Putnam, it seems beyond doubt that kind terms like 'water' are rigid designators. But it doesn't follow from this that they're directly referential, or that they don't express concepts, because they could express rigidified, indexical concepts; e.g., one might take the concept expressed by 'water' to be something like *the stuff that's (actually) in our lakes and pipes and so on, i.e., the stuff that we standardly call 'water', whatever that stuff turns out to be*. Similarly, one might think that the concept expressed by 'free will' is something like *the sort of freedom that's (actually) at work when we humans make the kinds of choices that we ordinarily call 'free', whatever that turns out to be*.

10. See, e.g., Hume 1748, Austin 1961, Chisholm 1964b, Lehrer 1966a, 1968, Aune 1967, Ayers 1968, Falk 1981, Sanford 1991, and White 1993. And for an overview of the literature, see Berofsky 2002.

11. Recent compatibilist analyses of free will and/or moral responsibility have been proposed by, e.g., P. F. Strawson (1962), Frankfurt (1971), Watson (1975), Dworkin (1988), Wolf (1990), Double (1991), Fischer (1994), Fischer and Ravizza (1998), Wallace (1994), Mele (1995), and Bok (1998). For an overview, see Haji 2002.

12. The classical statement of this argument is given in van Inwagen 1975. Other early statements of the argument appear in Ginet 1966, 1980, Wiggins 1973, and Lamb 1977. And other relevant works include Greenspan 1976, Narveson 1977, Gallois 1977, Foley 1979, Lewis 1981, Slote 1982, Fischer 1983, 1994, van Inwagen 1983, 2002, Horgan 1985, Widerker 1987, Vihvelin 1988, 1991, 1995a,b, Ginet 1990, Kapitan 1991, 1996, 2002, Nathan 1992, O'Connor 1993, 2000, Ekstrom 1995, 1998, 2000, McKay and Johnson 1996, Kane 1996, and Crisp and Warfield 2000. For a good overview of the literature on this argument, see Kapitan 2002.

13. For instance, Fischer (1994) thinks the argument shows that moral responsibility is compatible with determinism but not that free will is compatible with determinism.

14. The classical statement of this argument is given in Frankfurt 1969. Other relevant works include Blumenfeld 1971, van Inwagen 1978, 1983, Fischer 1982, 1994, 2002, Kane 1985, 1996, Stump 1990, 1999, Widerker 1991, 1995a,b, Haji 1992,

1993, 1999, Lamb 1993, Clarke 1994, Zimmerman 1994, Glannon 1995, Ginet 1996, McKenna 1997, Wyma 1997, Copp 1997, J. K. Campbell 1997, Fischer and Ravizza 1998, Mele and Robb 1998, Otsuka 1998, Hunt 2000, and Pereboom 2001. For a good overview of the literature on this argument, see Fischer 2002.

15. What's controversial and what philosophers actually argue about in connection with the various analyses of free will is not whether they are compatible or incompatible with determinism, but whether they capture the concept of free will. For instance, we don't find compatibilists and incompatibilists arguing about whether Humean freedom is compatible with determinism, but we do find them arguing about whether Humean freedom provides a correct analysis of the notion of free will.

3 Why the Libertarian Question Reduces to the Issue of Indeterminacy

1. See, e.g., Fischer and Ravizza 1998 on the topic of compatibilism and reasons responsiveness.

2. See Hobbes 1651, Hume 1748, and Hobart 1934.

3. Actually, one might think of the luck objection as a *version* of the main objection I'll be discussing, i.e., the objection based on the idea that nonrandomness can't be increased by the presence of random events.

4. When I speak of "the moment of choice," I do not mean to suggest that I think choices occur instantaneously; on the contrary, I think our decisions are very likely temporally extended events, i.e., events that are spread out in time.

5. Two points: First, van Inwagen (1983) and the later Chisholm (1995) have developed event-causal libertarian views, but I do not include them here, because as far as I can tell, neither of these views involves a commitment to non-Valerianism (or, for that matter, to Valerianism). Second, some people, e.g., Clarke (2002), have taken Ekstrom's view to be Valerian; but I think this is because her terminology is confusing. She places the important indeterminism in *preference formation*, and on the most standard philosophical usage, this would suggest that it is located prior to decision making. But for Ekstrom (2000, 107), decision making is a *kind* of preference formation—it produces preferences concerning what we want to do—and it is here that she places the important kind of indeterminism. So I think that Ekstrom is a non-Valerian libertarian, and in private correspondence, she has endorsed this interpretation.

6. Libertarians needn't maintain that *all* of our torn decisions are undetermined, because they're claiming only that we make *some* L-free decisions. I suppose one might claim that the real question is whether *many* of our torn decisions are undetermined, since it would hardly vindicate libertarianism if it turned out that exactly one human decision was L-free; but I will assume that there is some degree of regu-

larity here, so that if any of our torn decisions are undetermined, then many of them are.

7. There might be some mental phenomena for which some version of nonspecificism is plausible. For instance, it's plausible to suppose that George W. Bush believes that 13.712 is greater than 9.3 and also that 13.721 is greater than 9.3; and it's plausible to suppose that his having these beliefs supervenes on neural phenomena; but it would be implausible to maintain that different neural phenomena are relevant in the two different cases, and so one might think it misguided to try to specify precisely which neural state in Bush's head *is* his belief that 13.712 is greater than 9.3. Whatever you think of this argument and nonspecificist views of mental *states* like beliefs, there is no reason at all to endorse a nonspecificist view of mental *events* like decisions. Decisions might be spread out across the brain, and they might lack clear (i.e., perfectly well-defined) beginnings and endings, but this is true of all sorts of events that we think are physical events. For instance, lunar eclipses might be best thought of as being spread out over large regions of space, and they might lack clear beginnings and endings, but it seems pretty clear that they *are* physical events and that they have at least fuzzy locations in spacetime. And likewise, it would seem, for decisions. A similar point can be made about eliminativism: Even if you think it plausible to endorse eliminativist views with respect to *some* (alleged) mental phenomena, it does not seem plausible to endorse an eliminativist view of *decisions*, because 'decision' seems to be a natural kind term, and if it is, then neuroscience could no more establish that there are no such things as decisions than zoology or chemistry could establish that there are no such things as cats or water.

8. As long as the eliminativist allows that when humans have the experiences that we call decisions, there are neural events occurring that, so to speak, "correspond" to these decisions, I could define libertarianism and run my argument in terms of these neural events, regardless of whether they count as *decisions*. And as for nonspecificism, we would first need to get clear on what it would mean to say that our torn decisions are causally undetermined on this view; as long as this claim made sense, I could run my argument in terms of whatever it is that would be undetermined on this view. Now, if the claim of indeterminacy couldn't be made sense of on this view, then the whole point of my argument would evaporate. But I think it's pretty far-fetched to suppose that some such version of nonspecificism is true.

9. Of course, there is also a continuum of conceptually possible cases in which the *reasons-based* probability of Ralph choosing to move to New York moves away from 0.5 and ranges from 0 to 1. But these cases don't involve torn decisions; rather, they are cases that involve *leanings* of the sort discussed in section 3.2.1 (a torn decision, recall, is defined as a decision in which the reasons-based probabilities of the various live options being chosen are all roughly even). For the time being, I am ignoring decisions involving leanings of this sort, but I will return to them in section 3.4.

10. Given the complexity of the brain, one might wonder what the odds are, in any given torn decision, of it being the case that the moment-of-choice probabilities of the various tied-for-best options being chosen are all exactly even. But it's important to keep in mind that what's really needed here, in order for TDW-indeterminism and libertarianism to be true, is that some of our torn decisions are such that the moment-of-choice probabilities are all *roughly* even. If the moment-of-choice probabilities in some two-option torn decision were .51 and .49, that would presumably not undermine the L-freedom of the choice in any significant way. So the real question here is whether our torn decisions are causally influenced in a *significant* way by factors external to our conscious reasons and thought. And we are going to find in chapter 4 that, as of right now anyway, there is no good reason for thinking that they are. More specifically, we are going to find that there is no good reason to doubt the TDW-indeterminist claim that some of our torn decisions are not significantly causally influenced by external factors.

11. We'll see in section 3.4 that if libertarians set things up properly, they can maintain that decisions that are determined by our reasons can also be L-free. But this will require that we also make some decisions that involve a freedom-enhancing indeterminism, and these are going to be either torn decisions or decisions of one of the other kinds I have in mind in the text. I will discuss this in more detail in section 3.4; for now, we can ignore this point.

12. I suppose one might also object here that it might be that human beings just don't make very many torn decisions, compared with these other kinds of decisions. But I already addressed this worry in section 3.2.1.

13. Depending on your view of probabilistic causation, you might want to say that there is a noncausal element in probabilistic causation and, hence, that there is a noncausal thread in event-causal libertarian views of the sort I'm describing. For you might maintain that probabilistic causation is just deterministic causation of probabilistic states that then issue by chance—i.e., in an uncaused way—into one possible outcome or another (see, e.g., Hausman 1998). Thus, an event-causal libertarian of the sort I have in mind might want to say that if S chose A over B in a torn decision, and if this choice was wholly undetermined in the manner of TDW-indeterminism, then (a) S's reasons deterministically caused it to be the case that the moment-of-choice probabilities of A and B being chosen were both 0.5, and (b) the fact that S ended up choosing A over B (or if you'd rather, the fact that S's choice had the property of being an A-over-B choice) was uncaused. As far as I can see, libertarians of the sort I have in mind don't need to take a stand on the question of whether there is in fact a noncausal element of this kind in their event-causal view. Indeed, it seems to me that the question of whether there's such a noncausal element in this view might just be terminological.

14. Kane first introduced conditions of this sort in Kane 1985, where he called them *duality* conditions. In Kane 1996, he called them plurality conditions.

15. One might think that the claim being made here—that if a torn decision is wholly undetermined in the manner of TDW-indeterminism, then *at the moment of choice*, nothing external to the agent's conscious reasons and thought has any causal influence over how she chooses—is still too strong. One might try to argue this by pointing out that various things are causally necessary for the decision to occur at all—e.g., blood flow to the brain. But to repeat a point I made above, even if a torn decision is wholly undetermined in the manner of TDW-indeterminism, it could still be that the mere *occurrence* of the decision is causally determined. The only thing that needs to be undetermined, in order for a torn decision to count as wholly undetermined, is *which option is chosen*. Thus, I haven't said anything here that's inconsistent with the claim that the occurrences of our torn decisions are determined and that things like blood flow to the brain are causally necessary for their occurrences. All I'm saying is that if a torn decision is wholly undetermined, then (at the moment of choice) nothing external to the agent's conscious reasons and thought is causally relevant to *which option is chosen*. And this is true. Again, it follows from the definition of 'wholly undetermined'.

16. According to standard usage, it is built into the definition of 'agent-causal view' that agent causation is not reducible to event causation. But it has always seemed to me an important feature of event-causal libertarianism that (if properly formulated) it can provide an intuitively pleasing conception of agent causation in event-causal terms. This point has also been made by Ekstrom (2000, ix), the later Chisholm (1995), and Kane (2002b); they all characterize themselves as providing event-causal accounts of agent causation, though, I should note, their accounts are different from mine.

17. I suppose one might worry that there might be *multiple* notions of authorship or control that might be relevant here. Perhaps. But I don't think there's any good reason to suppose that there are multiple notions of authorship or control that are (a) relevant to the issue of free will and (b) sufficiently different to yield the result that ordinary torn decisions are (if wholly undetermined) authored or controlled in one of the relevant senses but not the other. Thus, until someone actually produces two such notions of authorship or control, I think it's safe to assume that there's just one relevant notion of both authorship and control (or more precisely, that if there are multiple notions here, they will either both be present or both be absent in the relevant cases we're considering).

18. The remarks in the text also provide a response to another worry the reader might have. One might object as follows:

> You argued in chapter 2 that conceptual analysis is essentially irrelevant to metaphysical questions about the nature of human beings. But you are engaged here in conceptual analysis of the notions of authorship and control, and you are taking this to be relevant to a metaphysical question about humans, namely, the question of whether we're L-free.

But as the remarks in the text make clear, I do not take myself to be doing conceptual analysis here. I am not providing a theory of what authorship and control *are*. Rather, I am arguing that the ordinary notions of authorship and control—the ones that are relevant to the issue of free will—are applicable in certain scenarios. More specifically, I'm arguing that if our ordinary torn decisions are wholly undetermined in the manner of TDW-indeterminism, then the ordinary notions of authorship and control apply to them. (I suppose one might also mount an objection of the above kind based on the claim that I'm providing a conceptual analysis of *free will*; in particular, one might think I'm claiming here that the ordinary notion of free will requires authorship and control. Well, for whatever it's worth, I think the ordinary notion of free will probably does require authorship and control, but this is completely irrelevant to the arguments of this chapter. I am not trying to establish any claims here about the ordinary notion of free will. What I'm doing is (a) *stipulating* that *L-freedom* involves authorship and control, and (b) arguing that if TDW-indeterminism is true, then we actually *have* authorship and control [and L-freedom] with respect to at least some of our torn decisions.)

19. One might object that (i) we could discover that unbeknownst to me, via some nonconscious process (e.g., a subconscious "weighting" of reasons, or some such thing), my conscious reasons *themselves* deterministically caused me to choose A over B; and (ii) in this scenario, the phenomenology of my decision would be mistaken. But once again, this possibility is ruled out by our hypothetical assumption that my decision was wholly undetermined in the manner of TDW-indeterminism. Remember, a decision counts as wholly undetermined in this sense only if the moment-of-choice probabilities of the various live options being chosen are all even, or at least roughly even; but this condition is clearly not met in cases of the above kind. (It's also worth noting here that nonconscious processes of the above kind would, on the way I'm carving things up, already count as external causal influences.)

20. One might think that we shouldn't trust our intuitions and introspections about the status of our own decisions, because we're so wedded to the idea that we're free that our judgments here are biased. But unless someone can think of another worry about the reliability of our introspections, aside from the worry about hidden external causes, I'm inclined to think that our biases here just don't matter.

21. There are important differences between the various formulations of this argument; e.g., van Inwagen used it to attack the notion of agent causation, whereas O'Connor thinks the problem can be solved by invoking agent causation.

22. I should say in advance that some of the points I make here in response to the luck objection are similar to points made by Kane, who has also responded to the luck objection; see, e.g., Kane 1999. Moreover, for another response to the luck objection, see Ginet 2007.

23. The reason Kane thinks that a lack of antecedent determining control involves a kind of lack of control is that he thinks of torn decisions in terms of efforts of will. The idea here is this: If Ralph is *trying* to decide to move to New York (and also trying to decide to stay in Mayberry), and if he doesn't have antecedent determining control, then he can't guarantee the success of his effort, and that's a kind of lack of control. But I think it's a mistake to think of Ralph as trying to do two different things. He's simply torn between two different courses of action, and his so-called lack of antecedent determining control is just a manifestation of the fact that he is, for the time being, keeping his options open. Now, in *some* cases, it does make sense to think of torn decisions in terms of efforts of will—e.g., cases in which someone is trying to quit smoking. In cases like this, I think it makes sense to say that the agent lacks a certain kind of control; but this isn't a problem for my view; this is simply what we should say about such cases, regardless of the theory we endorse. When someone's really *trying* to quit smoking, and she keeps failing because of an uncontrollable desire, the right thing to say about her, regardless of whether determinism or indeterminism is true, is that she is not fully in control and not fully free.

24. Mylan Engel expressed a worry like this to me.

25. It might sometimes be difficult to tell whether a subatomic event was prior to or part of a torn decision. Indeed, it's at least conceptually possible that there are cases in which there is no definite fact of the matter as to whether a given subatomic event was prior to or part of a torn decision. I will discuss this in chapter 4.

26. There's another response that one might make to the objections of this section, i.e., objections having to do with the issue of whether the sort of L-freedom I've been describing is worth wanting. One might think these objections are irrelevant. For one might argue that (a) whatever we say about whether this sort of L-freedom is *worth* wanting, it seems pretty clear that most people *do* want it, or something like it; and (b) this is already enough to motivate the claim that the question of whether humans have this sort of L-freedom is important and worth investigating. I don't know whether claim (b) is true—actually, I'm not sure there's even a fact of the matter as to whether (b) is true—but for whatever it's worth, it seems to me that claim (a) is pretty obviously right. Most people, I think, would be depressed to learn that all of their torn decisions were determined by factors external to their conscious reasons and thought. For instance, if it came out that neuroscientists could predict the outcome of human torn decisions before they occurred, most people would find this disturbing or depressing. And this suggests that there is an important sense in which most people want it to be the case that their torn decisions are not determined by external factors. Indeed, I think this would be true even if people became convinced that the notions of free will and moral responsibility were compatible with determinism. We just do have a desire for the metaphysical facts to be indeterministic, regardless of what we say about moral responsibility.

27. When I say that a decision is consistent with a given agent's conscious reasons, all I mean is that it's not the case that the agent's conscious reasons dictate that the chosen option is worse than other available options. Now, one might worry that if the agent's conscious reason set is inconsistent (e.g., because it contains inconsistent beliefs), then none of her decisions is consistent with her conscious reasons and, hence, none of them is weakly rational, no matter how irrelevant the inconsistency in the person's reason set might seem to a given decision. There are a few different ways one might respond to this worry. First, one might argue that on the above conception of what it is for a decision to be consistent with a set of conscious reasons, it is in fact possible for a decision to be consistent with an inconsistent reason set (because inconsistent reason sets don't dictate everything that they entail). Or, second, one might simply alter the definition of 'weakly rational' to avoid this problem; e.g., one might say something like this: a decision is weakly rational iff either (a) the agent's conscious reason set is consistent and the decision is consistent with that reason set in the above sense, or (b) the agent's conscious reason set is inconsistent, but for all of the reasonable ways of doing away with the inconsistency, the resulting reason set would be consistent with the decision in the above sense. Of course, much would need to be said about the notion of a *reasonable way of doing away with an inconsistency*, but I will not go into this here.

28. A similar argument applies to decisions that fly in the face of reason sets that include reasons that are conscious in the sense of being accessible to the agent but that were simply forgotten during deliberation and choice.

29. One idea I've toyed with is that while an individual decision can be simultaneously irrational and L-free, for a *person* to be L-free, it must be the case that some of her decisions are rational. Thus, if all of Sally's decisions were like the one described in the text, we might want to deny that she was L-free, or ordinary-language free. One way to develop this idea would be to begin by defining the notion of an L-free person and then to define the notion of an L-free decision in terms of that. I will return to this latter idea in section 3.4, but I will not tie it in with the above issue about requiring rationality at the level of the person but not the decision. There is no need for me to take a stand here on the question of whether this is the right way to proceed in connection with the issue of what is required, in terms of rationality, for L-freedom.

30. I can't right now think of any other decision types that could be L-free, but there may be others that I'm not thinking of, and I am not committed in any way to the thesis that this list is in fact complete.

31. Two points. First, the reason I say only that *typical* type-5 decisions can be counted by libertarians as L-free is that it's easy to dream up science-fiction examples of type-5 decisions (made by L-free persons) that aren't appropriately nonrandom; for instance, if a Martian inserted reasons into my head that then caused me to make some decision D, then even if I'm ordinarily L-free, we would presumably

not want to say that I authored or controlled D, or that D was L-free. Second, one might think that most cases in which our actions are caused by our reasons do not involve *decisions* at all—and, hence, don't involve type-5 decisions. For instance, my reasons might cause me to get up and get a drink of water without my ever *deciding* to do so. I have no problem with this, for I am simply not talking here about cases like this; I am talking only about cases that involve mental events that could reasonably be thought of as decisions. (I should note, however, that libertarians might want to go on to claim that we can have a kind of freedom in cases of this other kind as well—i.e., cases in which we act for reasons but don't make decisions. I will not try to say what this sort of freedom consists in, but for whatever it's worth, it does seem plausible to me to suppose that we can have a kind of freedom in these cases [and indeed that we can be morally responsible for actions of this kind].)

32. Actually, in connection with type-5 decisions, I had three different arguments, and I would not use them all here. The first and second arguments can be used in connection with type-7 decisions, but not the third.

33. There's a difference between type-6 and type-7 decisions that's worth noting. In type-6 decisions, the agent can be leaning toward *more than one* of the live options; e.g., if S is trying to decide between A, B, and C, and if her reasons favor A and B over C by a 40–40–20 margin, and if S is forced to decide while in this state, then it seems to me that libertarians can claim that if the moment-of-choice probabilities match the reasons-based probabilities, then the choice is fully L-free (and I think they can also claim that if the moment-of-choice probabilities of A and B being chosen are both 0.5, then the decision is L-free). But type-7 decisions occur only in cases where the agent is leaning toward a specific option, and her reasons deterministically cause that option to be chosen.

4 Why There Are No Good Arguments for or against Determinism (or Any Other Thesis That Would Establish or Refute Libertarianism)

1. I actually don't know where (or even if) Mark Twain said this, and one sometimes sees the quote attributed to others, e.g., Abraham Lincoln.

2. As I've pointed out in previous chapters, I am using 'libertarianism' to denote the thesis that human beings are L-free. Some use it to denote the thesis that (a) humans are L-free, and (b) the notion of L-freedom provides a good definition of 'free will'. But this is not how I'm using the term here.

3. See Penrose and Hameroff 1995, Hameroff and Penrose 1996, and Stapp 1993, 1998.

4. Probably the most well known of these other arguments is the one formulated by Malcolm (1968). But this argument is extremely implausible, because it is inconsistent with materialistic views of the mind.

5. If any micro-level events are undetermined, then obviously, universal determinism is false. And if all micro-level events are determined, then it would seem that universal determinism must be true. Now, one might try to defend the idea that there could be macro-level indeterminacies that aren't based in micro-level indeterminacies; indeed, this idea has been defended by Ilya Prigogine (see, e.g., Prigogine 1996). But this is pretty hard to swallow. For if we assume for the sake of argument that all micro-level events are determined, and if we also assume (what seems beyond doubt) that all macro-level events are composed entirely of micro-level events, then it seems to follow that all macro-level events are determined. Now, of course, I don't think that whenever a macro-level event is composed of a bunch of micro-level events that have some property F, the macro-level event also has F. Obviously, this is false: A speech can be long-winded even if all of its constituent micro-level events are non-long-winded. But the property of being causally determined by prior events doesn't seem like the property of being non-long-winded in this respect. It seems more like the property of being located in California. Anyway, that's how it seems to me. But, of course, I don't need to defend this claim here, because the position I'm trying to motivate is perfectly consistent with the idea that there are indeterminacies that arise for the first time at the macro level, i.e., that aren't based in micro-level indeterminacies.

6. The argument is a geometrical proof of the claim that if the probabilistic laws of QM are correct (and there is overwhelming empirical evidence for them), then no electron could possibly have a determinate value of spin for every direction in space at the same time.

7. It is sometimes said that deterministic interpretations of QM are ruled out by Bell's (1964) theorem. This is false. See, e.g., Earman 1986, chapter 11, in this connection. It is, I think, also sometimes thought that the so-called Copenhagen interpretation (which traces back to the thought of Niels Bohr and is indeterministic) is something like the "standard interpretation" of QM, and one might infer from this that we have good reason to accept it. But it's just not true that, today, the Copenhagen interpretation is widely accepted by those who do serious work on the foundations of quantum mechanics; and more importantly, as far as I know, there is no good reason at all to accept it.

8. The many-worlds interpretation is due to Everett 1957; see also DeWitt 1970. The idea behind Bohm's theory was first hinted at in print by de Broglie (1930), probably also has some roots in Einstein's thinking, and was first developed into a full-blown theory by Bohm (1952); it has also been given very nice presentations by Bell (1982) and Albert (1992). Finally, it's worth noting that while Bohm's *theory* is deterministic, he himself was not a straightforward determinist, because he did not endorse the claim that his version of QM provides a complete picture of the physical world, and he did not seem to want to endorse a deterministic view of the whole of reality.

Notes

9. One might think that the *conjunction* of (a) and (b) motivates neural determinism, or virtual neural determinism, even if neither (a) nor (b) does so in isolation. But this is false. As Honderich understands these theses, the conjunction essentially says that (i) some sort of mind–brain materialism is true, and (ii) brain events are caused in ordinary ways. But neural indeterminists can endorse this conjunction and then simply claim that some neural events are probabilistically caused.

10. All of the quotes in this paragraph are from private correspondences.

11. One might also try to argue (though I will not do this here) that Tegmark's argument is in fact *not* cogent. Indeed, Hagan, Hameroff, and Tuszyński (2002) have tried to do just this. They attack both of the crucial numbers in Tegmark's argument—i.e., the 10^{-13} figure he comes up with for maximum decoherence time and the 10^{-3} figure he comes up with for the minimum time that the superpositions would have to survive to be relevant to neural processes. In connection with the 10^{-13} figure, they argue that Tegmark ignores a variety of factors at work in the vicinity of microtubules that could increase decoherence time, and taking the various considerations that they cite into account, they recalculate the decoherence time and come up with a range of 10^{-5} to 10^{-4} seconds. In connection with the 10^{-3} figure, on the other hand, they claim that sequences of tubulin-superposition collapses in the range of 10^{-7} to 10^{-6} seconds could result in neural events in the 10^{-2} to 10^{0} range. Thus, in sum, the idea is that the relevant collapses could take about 10^{-7} seconds (faster than the maximum decoherence time of 10^{-4} seconds) and that these could give rise to neural events that fall within the slower-than-10^{-3}-second range. I am not qualified to assess the arguments on either side of this dispute, but I think that most of those who are would side with Tegmark.

12. Haggard and Eimer distinguish the readiness potential (RP) from what they call the lateralized readiness potential (LRP), which appears later than the RP, and they give evidence for thinking that the LRP is more directly correlated with conscious intentions to act than the RP is. They also distinguish between a general intention to perform some action or other and a specific intention to perform an action of a particular kind. The latter intention appears later in the whole volitional process, and Haggard argues that it could be that the formation of this latter intention is consciously controlled, even if the formation of the former is not. (The distinction between these two kinds of intentions, or decisions, is completely irrelevant to Libet's study, because in that study, it was already determined in advance [by the instructions to the participants] what sort of action would be performed; the only question was *when* it would be performed. But, of course, in torn decisions, there is an important distinction between deciding to select an option and deciding which option to select; so for our purposes here, the distinction is important.)

13. It's worth noting that Haggard (see note 12 of the present chapter) describes his view as a sort of amendment to Libet's view: Conscious will can come in after the

readiness potential and either (a) veto the whole process or (b) *modify* it, so that conscious will is relevant not just to *whether* an action is performed but also to *which sort* of action is performed. In discussing Haggard's view, Libet grants that this is consistent with the data, but he says that the view is speculative, i.e., that there's no good evidence for it (see Haggard and Libet 2001, 61). I think that Libet is obviously right about this, but the reverse is true as well: There's no evidence suggesting that Haggard's view is false. And likewise for the issue I'm concerned with here: There's no evidence for thinking that in torn decisions, which tied-for-best option is chosen is causally influenced by prior-to-choice brain processes.

14. In admitting that consciousness lags behind action in cases involving knee-jerk reactions, I do not mean to suggest that people can't be morally responsible in such cases. For I am not claiming, and I wouldn't claim, that the only time people are morally responsible (or, indeed, L-free) is when they make torn decisions. For more on this, see chapter 3, section 3.4, especially note 31.

15. Actually, decisions like this are probably best thought of not as torn decisions, but as *Buridan's-ass decisions*; see sections 3.2.1 and 3.4 for discussions of this distinction.

16. See Fischer and Ravizza 1998 on the topic of free will and reasons responsiveness.

17. For instance, the question of whether there are any such things as abstract objects (i.e., nonspatiotemporal objects) is a so-called metaphysical question, and it's pretty clearly not an empirical or a logical question, but I have argued elsewhere (see Balaguer 1998, especially chapter 8) that there is no fact of the matter about the answer to this question.

References

Albert, D. (1992). *Quantum Mechanics and Experience*. Cambridge, Mass.: Harvard University Press.

Aune, B. (1967). "Hypotheticals and 'Can': Another Look." *Analysis* 27:191–195.

Austin, J. L. (1961). "Ifs and Cans." In *Philosophical Papers*, ed. J. O. Urmson and G. Warnock, 153–180. Oxford: Clarendon Press.

Ayers, M. R. (1968). *The Refutation of Determinism*. London: Methuen.

Balaguer, M. (1998). *Platonism and Anti-Platonism in Mathematics*. New York: Oxford University Press.

Balaguer, M. (1999). "Libertarianism as a Scientifically Reputable View." *Philosophical Studies* 93:189–211.

Balaguer, M. (2004). "A Coherent, Naturalistic, and Plausible Formulation of Libertarian Free Will." *Noûs* 38:379–406.

Balaguer, M. (2009a). "The Metaphysical Irrelevance of the Compatibilism Debate (and, More Generally, of Conceptual Analysis)." *Southern Journal of Philosophy* 47:1–24.

Balaguer, M. (2009b). "Why There Are No Good Arguments for Any Interesting Version of Determinism." *Synthese* 168:1–21.

Bell, J. S. (1964). "On the Einstein-Podolsky-Rosen Paradox." *Physics* 1:195–200.

Bell, J. S. (1982). "On the Impossible Pilot Wave." *Foundations of Physics* 12:989–999.

Bernstein, M. (1995). "Kanean Libertarianism." *Southwest Philosophy Review* 11:151–157.

Berofsky, B. (1987). *Freedom from Necessity*. London: Routledge and Kegan Paul.

Berofsky, B. (2000). "Ultimate Responsibility in a Determined World." *Philosophy and Phenomenological Research* 60:135–140.

Berofsky, B. (2002). "Ifs, Cans, and Free Will: The Issues." In Kane 2002a, 181–201.

Blumenfeld, D. (1971). "The Principle of Alternative Possibilities." *Journal of Philosophy* 68:339–345.

Bohm, D. (1952). "A Suggested Interpretation of Quantum Theory in Terms of 'Hidden Variables.'" *Physical Review* 85:166–193.

Bohm, D., and B. J. Hiley (1993). *The Undivided Universe: An Ontological Interpretation of Quantum Mechanics*. London: Routledge.

Bok, H. (1998). *Freedom and Responsibility*. Princeton: Princeton University Press.

Bramhall, J. (1655). *A Defense of True Liberty*. Reprinted 1977. New York: Garland.

Brasil-Neto, J. P., A. Pascual-Leone, J. Valls-Solé, L. G. Cohen, and M. Hallet (1992). "Focal Transcranial Magnetic Stimulation and Response Bias in a Forced Choice Task." *Journal of Neurology, Neurosurgery, and Psychiatry* 55: 964–966.

Broad, C. D. (1952). "Determinism, Indeterminism, and Libertarianism." In *Ethics and the History of Philosophy*, 195–217. London: Routledge and Kegan Paul.

Campbell, C. A. (1967). *In Defense of Free Will*. London: Allen and Unwin.

Campbell, J. K. (1997). "A Compatibilist Theory of Alternative Possibilities." *Philosophical Studies* 67:339–344.

Chisholm, R. (1964a). "Human Freedom and the Self." Reprinted in Watson 1982, 24–35.

Chisholm, R. (1964b). "J. L. Austin's Philosophical Papers." *Mind* 73:20–25.

Chisholm, R. (1995). "Agents, Causes, and Events: The Problem of Free Will." In O'Connor 1995, 95–100.

Clarke, R. (1993). "Toward a Credible Agent-Causal Account of Free Will." *Noûs* 27:191–203.

Clarke, R. (1994). "Ability and Responsibility for Omissions." *Philosophical Studies* 73:195–208.

Clarke, R. (1995). "Indeterminism and Control." *American Philosophical Quarterly* 32:125–138.

Clarke, R. (1996). "Agent Causation and Event Causation in the Production of Free Action." *Philosophical Topics* 24:19–48.

Clarke, R. (2002). "Libertarian Views: Critical Survey of Noncausal and Event-Causal Accounts of Free Agency." In Kane 2002a, 356–385.

References

Clarke, R. (2003). *Libertarian Accounts of Free Will*. New York: Oxford University Press.

Copp, D. (1997). "Defending the Principle of Alternative Possibilities: Blameworthiness and Moral Responsibility." *Noûs* 31:441–456.

Crisp, T., and T. Warfield (2000). "The Irrelevance of Indeterministic Counterexamples to Principle Beta." *Philosophy and Phenomenological Research* 61:173–184.

Dayan, P., and L. F. Abbott (2001). *Theoretical Neuroscience*. Cambridge, Mass.: MIT Press.

de Broglie, L. (1930). *Rapport au V'ieme Congres de Physique Solvay*. Paris: Gauther-Villars.

Deecke, L., B. Grotzinger, and H. H. Kornhuber (1976). "Voluntary Finger Movement in Man: Cerebral Potentials and Theory." *Biological Cybernetics* 23:99.

Dennett, D. (1978). "On Giving Libertarians What They Say They Want." In *Brainstorms*. Cambridge, Mass.: MIT Press.

Dennett, D. (1984). *Elbow Room*. Cambridge, Mass.: MIT Press.

DeWitt, B. (1970) "Quantum Mechanics and Reality." *Physics Today* 23:30–35.

Donagan, A. (1987). *Choice*. London: Routledge and Kegan Paul.

Double, R. (1991). *The Non-Reality of Free Will*. New York: Oxford University Press.

Dworkin, G. (1988). *The Theory and Practice of Autonomy*. Cambridge: Cambridge University Press.

Earman, J. (1986). *A Primer on Determinism*. Dordrecht: Reidel.

Ekstrom, L. W. (1995). "Causes and Nested Conditionals." *Australasian Journal of Philosophy* 73:574–578.

Ekstrom, L. W. (1998). "Freedom, Causation, and the Consequence Argument." *Synthese* 115:333–354.

Ekstrom, L. W. (2000). *Free Will: A Philosophical Study*. Boulder, Colo.: Westview Press.

Everett, H., III (1957). "'Relative State' Formulation of Quantum Mechanics." *Review of Modern Physics* 29:454–462.

Falk, A. (1981). "Some Modal Confusions in Compatibilism." *American Philosophical Quarterly* 18: 141–148.

Festinger, L. (1957). *A Theory of Cognitive Dissonance*. Palo Alto: Stanford University Press.

Fischer, J. M. (1982). "Responsibility and Control." *Journal of Philosophy* 79:24–40.

Fischer, J. M. (1983). "Incompatibilism." *Philosophical Studies* 43:127–137.

Fischer, J. M. (1994). *The Metaphysics of Free Will: A Study of Control.* Oxford: Blackwell.

Fischer, J. M. (1999). "Recent Work on Moral Responsibility." *Ethics* 110:93–139.

Fischer, J. M. (2002). "Frankfurt-type Examples and Semi-Compatibilism." In Kane 2002a, 281–308.

Fischer, J. M., and M. Ravizza (1998). *Responsibility and Control: A Theory of Moral Responsibility.* Cambridge: Cambridge University Press.

Foley, R. (1979). "Compatibilism and Control Over the Past." *Analysis* 39:70–74.

Frankfurt, H. (1969). "Alternate Possibilities and Moral Responsibility." *Journal of Philosophy* 66: 829–839.

Frankfurt, H. (1971). "Freedom of the Will and the Concept of a Person." *Journal of Philosophy* 68:5–20.

Gallois, A. (1977). "Van Inwagen on Free Will and Determinism." *Philosophical Studies* 32:99–105.

Ginet, C. (1966). "Might We Have No Choice?" In Lehrer 1966b, 87–104.

Ginet, C. (1980). "The Conditional Analysis of Freedom." In *Time and Cause*, ed. P. van Inwagen, 171–186. Dordrecht: Reidel.

Ginet, C. (1990). *On Action.* Cambridge: Cambridge University Press.

Ginet, C. (1996). "In Defense of the Principle of Alternative Possibilities: Why I Don't find Frankfurt's Argument Convincing." *Philosophical Perspectives* 10:403–417.

Ginet, C. (2002). "Reasons Explanations of Action: Causalist versus Noncausalist Accounts." In Kane 2002a, 386–405.

Ginet, C. (2007). "An Action Can Be Both Uncaused and Up to the Agent." In *Intention, Deliberation, and Autonomy*, ed. C. Lumer and S. Nannini, 243–256. Hampshire: Ashgate.

Glannon, W. (1995). "Responsibility and the Principle of Possible Action." *Journal of Philosophy* 92:261–274.

Goetz, S. (1997). "Libertarian Choice." *Faith and Philosophy* 14:195–211.

Greenspan, P. S. (1976). "Wiggins on Historical Inevitability and Incompatibilism." *Philosophical Studies* 29:235–247.

Hagan, S., S. R. Hameroff, and J. A. Tuszyński (2002). "Quantum Computation in Brain Microtubules: Decoherence and Biological Feasibility." *Physical Review E* 65:061901.

References

Haggard, P., and M. Eimer (1999). "On the Relation between Brain Potentials and the Awareness of Voluntary Movements." *Experimental Brain Research* 126: 128–133.

Haggard, P., and B. Libet (2001). "Conscious Intention and Brain Activity." *Journal of Consciousness Studies* 8:47–63.

Haji, I. (1992). "A Riddle Regarding Omissions." *Canadian Journal of Philosophy* 22:485–502.

Haji, I. (1993). "Alternative Possibilities, Moral Obligation, and Moral Responsibility." *Philosophical Papers* 22:41–50.

Haji, I. (1999). "Indeterminism and Frankfurt-style Examples." *Philosophical Explorations* 2:42–58.

Haji, I. (2002). "Compatibilist Views of Freedom and Responsibility." In Kane 2002a, 202–228.

Hameroff, S. R., and R. Penrose (1996). "Conscious Events as Orchestrated Space-Time Selections." *Journal of Consciousness Studies* 3:36–53.

Hausman, D. (1998). *Causal Asymmetries*. Cambridge: Cambridge University Press.

Hobart, R. E. (1934). "Free Will as Involving Determination and Inconceivable Without It." *Mind* 43:1–27.

Hobbes, T. (1651). *Leviathan*. Reprinted 1962, New York: Collier Books.

Hodgson, D. (2002). "Quantum Physics, Consciousness, and Free Will." In Kane 2002a, 85–110.

Honderich, T., ed. (1973). *Essays on Freedom of Action*. London: Routledge and Kegan Paul.

Honderich, T. (1988). *A Theory of Determinism: The Mind, Neuroscience, and Life-Hopes*. Oxford: Oxford University Press.

Honderich, T. (2002). "Determinism as True, Compatibilism, and Incompatibilism as False, and the Real Problem." In Kane 2002a, 461–476.

Horgan, T. (1985). "Compatibilism and the Consequence Argument." *Philosophical Studies* 47:339–356.

Hume, D. (1748). *An Inquiry Concerning Human Understanding*. Reprinted 1955. Indianapolis, Ind.: Bobbs-Merrill.

Hunt, D. (2000). "Moral Responsibility and Avoidable Action." *Philosophical Studies* 97:195–227.

Isen, A., and P. Levin (1972). "Effect of Feeling Good on Helping." *Journal of Personality and Social Psychology* 21:384–388.

James. W. (1884). "The Dilemma of Determinism." Reprinted in *The Will to Believe: Human Immortality*, 145–183, 1956. New York: Dover.

Kane, R. (1985). *Free Will and Values*. Albany, N.Y.: SUNY Press.

Kane, R. (1996). *The Significance of Free Will*. New York: Oxford University Press.

Kane, R. (1999). "Responsibility, Luck, and Chance: Reflections on Free Will and Indeterminism." *Journal of Philosophy* 96: 217–240.

Kane, R., ed. (2002a). *The Oxford Handbook of Free Will*. New York: Oxford University Press.

Kane, R. (2002b). "Free Will: New Directions for an Ancient Problem." In *Free Will*, ed. R. Kane, 222–248. Oxford: Blackwell.

Kant, I. (1788). *The Critique of Practical Reason*. Reprinted 1927 (trans. T. K. Abbott). New York: Longman, Green.

Kapitan, T. (1991). "Ability and Cognition: A Defense of Compatibilism." *Philosophical Studies* 63:231–243.

Kapitan, T. (1996). "Modal Principles in the Metaphysics of Free Will." *Philosophical Perspectives* 10:419–445.

Kapitan, T. (2000). "Autonomy and Manipulated Freedom." *Philosophical Perspectives* 14:81–104.

Kapitan, T. (2002). "A Master Argument for Incompatibilism?" In Kane 2002a, 127–157.

Kochen, S., and E. P. Specker (1967). "The Problem of Hidden Variables in Quantum Mechanics." *Journal of Mathematics and Mechanics* 17:59–87.

Kornhuber, H., and L. Deecke (1965). "Hirnpotentialanderungen bei Willkurbewegungen und passiven Bewegungen des Menschen." *Pfluegers Arch Gesamte Physiologie Menschen Tiere* 284:1–17.

Lamb, J. (1977). "On a Proof of Incompatibilism." *Philosophical Review* 86:20–35.

Lamb, J. (1993). "Evaluative Compatibilism and the Principle of Alternative Possibilities." *Journal of Philosophy* 90: 517–527.

Lehrer, K. (1966a). "An Empirical Disproof of Determinism." In Lehrer 1966b, 175–202.

Lehrer, K., ed. (1966b). *Freedom and Determinism*. New York: Random House.

Lehrer, K. (1968). "'Can's without 'If's." *Analysis* 29:29–32.

Lehrer, K. (1976). "'Can' in Theory and Practice: A Possible Worlds Analysis." In *Action Theory*, ed. M. Brand and D. Walton, 67–97. Dordrecht: Reidel.

References

Lewis, D. (1981). "Are We Free to Break the Laws?" *Theoria* 47:113–121.

Libet, B. (2002). "Do We Have Free Will?" In Kane 2002a, 551–564.

Libet, B., C. Gleason, E. Wright, and D. Pearl (1983). "Time of Conscious Intention to Act in Relation to Cerebral Potential." *Brain* 106:623–642.

Locke, J. (1689). *An Essay Concerning Human Understanding*. Reprinted 1959. New York: Dover.

Malcolm, N. (1968). "The Conceivability of Mechanism." *Philosophical Review* 77:45–72.

McCall, S. (1994). *A Model of the Universe*. Oxford: Oxford University Press.

McCann, H. (1998). *The Works of Agency: On Human Action, Will, and Freedom*. Ithaca, N.Y.: Cornell University Press.

McKay, T., and D. Johnson (1996). "A Reconsideration of an Argument Against Compatibilism." *Philosophical Topics* 24:113–122.

McKenna, M. (1997). "Alternative Possibilities and the Failure of the Counterexample Strategy." *Journal of Social Philosophy* 28:71–85.

Mele, A. (1995). *Autonomous Agents*. New York: Oxford University Press.

Mele, A. (1999a). "Kane, Luck and the Significance of Free Will." *Philosophical Explorations* 2:96–104.

Mele, A. (1999b). "Ultimate Responsibility and Dumb Luck." *Social Philosophy and Policy* 16: 274–293.

Mele, A. (2006). "Free Will and Luck." New York: Oxford University Press.

Mele, A., and D. Robb (1998). "Rescuing Frankfurt-style Cases." *Philosophical Review* 107:97–112.

Milgram, S. (1969). *Obedience to Authority*. New York: Harper and Row.

Nahmias, E., S. Morris, T. Nadelhoffer, and J. Turner (2005). "Surveying Freedom: Folk Intuitions about Free Will and Moral Responsibility." *Philosophical Psychology* 18:561–584.

Narveson, J. (1977). "Compatibilism Defended." *Philosophical Studies* 32:83–88.

Nathan, N. (1992). *Will and World*. Oxford: Oxford University Press.

Nelkin, D. (2005). "Freedom, Responsibility, and the Challenge of Situationism." *Midwest Studies in Philosophy* 29:181–206.

Nichols, S. (2006). "Folk Intuitions on Free Will." *Journal of Cognition and Culture* 6:57–86.

Nozick, R. (1981). *Philosophical Explanations*. Cambridge, Mass.: Harvard University Press.

O'Connor, T. (1993). "Indeterminacy and Free Agency: Three Recent Views." *Philosophy and Phenomenological Research* 53:499–526.

O'Connor, T., ed. (1995). *Agents, Causes, and Events*. New York: Oxford University Press.

O'Connor, T. (2000). *Persons and Causes*. New York: Oxford University Press.

Otsuka, M. (1998). "Incompatibilism and the Avoidability of Blame." *Ethics* 108:685–701.

Parfit, D. (1995). "The Unimportance of Identity." In *Identity*, ed. H. Harris, 13–45. Oxford: Clarendon Press.

Penrose, R., and S. R. Hameroff (1995). "What 'Gaps'? Reply to Grush and Churchland." *Journal of Consciousness Studies* 2:98–111.

Pereboom, D. (2001). *Living without Free Will*. Cambridge: Cambridge University Press.

Prigogine, I. (1996). *The End of Certainty*. New York: Free Press.

Reid, T. (1788). *Essays on the Active Powers of the Human Mind*. Reprinted 1969. Cambridge, Mass.: MIT Press.

Rowe, W. (1987). "Two Concepts of Freedom." *Proceedings of the American Philosophical Association* 62:43–64.

Sanford, D. (1991). "'Could's, 'Might's, 'If's and 'Can's." *Noûs* 25:208–211.

Slote, M. (1982). "Selective Necessity and the Free Will Problem." *Journal of Philosophy* 79:5–24.

Smilansky, S. (2000). *Free Will and Illusion*. Oxford: Clarendon Press.

Stapp, H. (1993). *Mind, Matter, and Quantum Mechanics*. New York: Springer.

Stapp, H. (1998). "Pragmatic Approaches to Consciousness." In *Brain and Values*, ed. K. H. Pribram, 237–248. Thieme: Erlbaum.

Strawson, G. (1986). *Freedom and Belief*. Oxford: Clarendon Press.

Strawson, G. (2000). "The Unhelpfulness of Indeterminism." *Philosophy and Phenomenological Research* 60:149–155.

Strawson, P. F. (1962). "Freedom and Resentment." *Proceedings of the British Academy* 48:1–25.

References

Stump, E. (1990). "Intellect, Will, and the Principle of Alternative Possibilities." In *Christian Theism and the Problems of Philosophy*, ed. M. D. Beaty, 254–285. Notre Dame: University of Notre Dame Press.

Stump, E. (1999). "Dust, Determinism, and Frankfurt: A Reply to Goetz." *Faith and Philosophy* 16:413–422.

Taylor, R. (1966). *Action and Purpose*. Englewood Cliffs, N.J.: Prentice-Hall.

Taylor, R. (1974). *Metaphysics*. Englewood Cliffs, N.J.: Prentice-Hall.

Tegmark, M. (2000). "The Importance of Quantum Decoherence in Brain Processes." *Physical Review E* 61:4194.

Thorp, J. (1980). *Free Will*. London: Routledge and Kegan Paul.

van Inwagen, P. (1975). "The Incompatibility of Free Will and Determinism." Reprinted in Watson 1982, 46–58.

van Inwagen, P. (1978). "Ability and Responsibility." *Philosophical Review* 87:201–224.

van Inwagen, P. (1983). *An Essay on Free Will*. Oxford: Clarendon Press.

van Inwagen, P. (2002). "Free Will Remains a Mystery." In Kane 2002a, 158–177.

Velmans, M. (1991). "Is Human Information Processing Conscious?" *Behavioral and Brain Sciences* 14:651–669.

Vihvelin, K. (1988). "The Modal Argument for Incompatibilism." *Philosophical Studies* 53:227–244.

Vihvelin, K. (1991). "Freedom, Causation, and Counterfactuals." *Philosophical Studies* 64:161–184.

Vihvelin, K. (1995a). "Causes, Effects, and Counterfactual Dependence." *Australasian Journal of Philosophy* 73:560–573.

Vihvelin, K. (1995b). "Reply to 'Causes and Nested Conditionals.'" *Australasian Journal of Philosophy* 73:579–581.

Wallace, R. J. (1994). *Responsibility and the Moral Sentiments*. Cambridge, Mass.: Harvard University Press.

Waller, B. (1988). "Free Will Gone Out of Control: A Review of R. Kane's *Free Will and Values*." *Behaviorism* 16:149–162.

Walter, H. (2001). *Neurophilosophy of Free Will*. Cambridge, Mass.: MIT Press.

Watson, G. (1975). "Free Agency." *Journal of Philosophy* 72:205–220.

Watson, G., ed. (1982). *Free Will*. Oxford: Oxford University Press.

Wegner, D. M. (2002). *The Illusion of Conscious Will*. Cambridge, Mass.: MIT Press.

White, M. (1993). *The Question of Free Will: A Holistic View*. Princeton: Princeton University Press.

Widerker, D. (1987). "On an Argument for Incompatibilism." *Analysis* 47:37–41.

Widerker, D. (1991). "Frankfurt on 'Ought' Implies 'Can' and Alternative Possibilities." *Analysis* 49:222–224.

Widerker, D. (1995a). "Libertarianism and Frankfurt's Attack on the Principle of Alternative Possibilities." *Philosophical Review* 104:247–261.

Widerker, D. (1995b). "Libertarian Freedom and the Avoidability of Decisions." *Faith and Philosophy* 12:113–118.

Wiggins, D. (1973). "Towards a Reasonable Libertarianism." In Honderich 1973, 31–61.

Wolf, S. (1990). *Freedom Within Reason*. New York: Oxford University Press.

Wyma, K. (1997). "Moral Responsibility and the Leeway for Action." *American Philosophical Quarterly* 34:57–70.

Zimmerman, D. (1994). "Acts, Omissions, and Semi-Compatibilism." *Philosophical Studies* 73:209–223.

Index

Abbott, L. F., 153
Ability to do otherwise, 47–48
Abstract objects, 184n17
Active control. *See* Conscious control
Agent causation, 16, 21, 67, 87, 177n16
 event-causal accounts of, 87, 177n16
Agent involvedness. *See* Appropriate nonrandomness
Albert, D., 182n8
Ambiguity. *See* Analyses of free will, and ambiguity
Analyses of free will, 26–45, 50–51, 55–63, 177n18. *See also* Conceptual analysis
 and ambiguity, 55, 59
 and carving nature at the joints, 23, 37 (*see also* Conceptual analysis, and human-being freedom)
 and coherence, 23, 30, 36, 38–39, 41
 and contextualism, 55, 59
 and human-being freedom, 30, 36–38, 48–49
 and imprecision, 55–62
 and incoherence, 59
 and moral responsibility, 30, 36, 39–45
 and ordinary language, 23, 28–35, 41, 45
 and the issue of what's worth wanting, 36, 39–44
 and the which-kinds-of-freedom-do-we-have question, 36–38, 45

Antecedent determining control, 99–100
Antimetaphysicalism, 22–24, 167–169
Appropriate nonrandomness, 7–13, 83, 84–120
A priori argument for determinism, 135–137
A priori argument for libertarianism, 137–141
Attacks on metaphysics. *See* Antimetaphysicalism
Aune, B., 171n1, 173n10
Austin, J. L., 50, 173n10
Authorship, 7–10, 84–106. *See also* Plural authorship
Autonomy, 36, 44, 61
Ayers, M. R., 173n10

Bell, J. S., 182n7, 182n8
Bernstein, M., 92
Berofsky, B., 92, 171n1, 173n10, 173n11
Blips. *See* Neural blips
Blumenfeld, D., 173n14
Bohm, D., 145–146, 182n8
Bok, H., 5, 46, 171n1, 173n11
Bramhall, J., 171n3
Brasil-Neto, J. P., 163–165
Broad, C. D., 171n5
Buridan's ass decisions. *See* Decisions, Buridan's ass

Campbell, C. A., 67, 171n3
Campbell, J. K., 173–174n14
Cartesian dualism. *See* Mind–brain dualism
Carving nature at the joints. *See* Analyses of free will, and carving nature at the joints
Causation. *See* Agent causation; Libertarianism, event-causal; Probabilistic causation
Chance objection to libertarianism. *See* Luck objection to libertarianism
Character, 93, 120, 124
Chisholm, R., 67, 171n3, 173n10, 174n5, 177n16
Clarke, R., 67, 92, 107, 171n3, 173–174n14, 174n5
Coherence. *See* Analyses of free will, and coherence
Coherence question, the. *See* Question, coherence, the
Collapse of the wave function, 144–146, 148, 155–157
Compatibilism, 3, 4–6, 17–20, 25–63, 171n1, 171n2. *See also* Consequence argument, the
Compatibilism question, the. *See* Question, compatibilism, the
Compatibilistic libertarianism. *See* Libertarianism, compatibilistic
Compatibilist intuitions about free will, 57–58
Conceptual analysis, 25–30, 35–37, 41–42, 44, 50–51, 55–63, 88–89, 172n4, 177n18. *See also* Analyses of free will
  and concept articulation, 35
  and correctness conditions, 28–30, 35–37, 41–42
  and experimental philosophy, 29, 172n4
  and intuitions, 29
  and metaphysics (*see* Metaphysics, and conceptual analysis)

Confabulation, 54, 143, 163–164
Conscious control, 101–104
Consciousness, slowness of. *See* Slowness of consciousness
Consequence argument, the, 50–53, 173n12
Contextualism. *See* Analyses of free will, and contextualism
Contrastive explanations, 117–118
Control, 7–10, 84–106
  active (*see* Conscious control)
  antecedent determining (*see* Antecedent determining control)
  conscious (*see* Conscious control)
  lack of, 100, 179n23
  plural (*see* Plural control)
  spontaneous (*see* Spontaneous control)
Copenhagen interpretation of quantum mechanics, 182n7
Copp, D., 173–174n14
Crisp, T., 173n12

Dayan, P., 153–154
de Broglie, L., 182n8
Decisions
  Buridan's ass, 72–73, 79, 120–122
  as conscious, intentional, and purposeful, 85–89
  non-torn, 120–130
  torn, 21–22, 68–70, 71–75, 76–120, 131–135, 141–143, 155–167
Decoherence, 156, 183n11
Deecke, L., 159
Degrees of indeterminacy and L-freedom, 76–83
Deliberation, 113–114, 118–119
Dennett, D., 67, 107, 113–114, 118–119, 171n1, 171n3
Determination by reasons, 95–96, 121–129
Determined-or-Randomism (D-or-R-ism), 8–10

Determinism, 2–3, 6–7, 131–169
  a priori argument for, 135–137
  degrees of, 76–83
  as depressing, 105, 112, 125–126, 179n26
  empirical arguments for, 141–165
  FE-, 12–15, 18–20, 26–27
  for-all-practical-purposes (see Determinism, virtual)
  hard, 3
  macro-level, 142, 147–151
  neural, 142, 151–154
  soft, 3–4, 6, 25
  success-of-science argument for, 149–150
  torn-decision, 142, 155–165
  universal, 142–147
  virtual, 11, 142, 149, 151–165
Deterministic interpretations of quantum mechanics, 145–147, 182n7
DeWitt, B., 182n8
Dignity, 36, 44, 61
Direct referentiality, 49, 173n9
Donagan, A., 67, 171n3
Double, R., 5, 46, 92, 114, 171n1, 171n5, 173n11
Do-we-have-free-will question, the. See Question, do-we-have-free-will, the
Dualism. See Mind–brain dualism
Dworkin, G., 5, 46, 171n1, 173n11

Earman, J., 182n7
Efforts of will, 70, 74, 179n23
Ekstrom, L.W., 67, 171n3, 173n12, 174n5, 177n16
Eliminativist views of decisions, 71, 175n7, 175n8
Empirical arguments for determinism, 141–165
Event-causal libertarianism. See Libertarianism, event-causal
Everett, H., III, 182n8
Experimental philosophy, 29, 172n4

Facts of the matter. See Factual emptiness
Factual emptiness, 23–24, 43, 56, 61–63, 111, 159, 167, 169, 171n4, 179n25, 184n17
Fairness. See Moral responsibility, and fairness
Falk, A., 173n10
FE-determinism. See Determinism, FE-
FE-determinism question, the. See Question, FE-determinism, the
Festinger, L., 163–164
Firing, neural, 153–154, 157
Fischer, J. M., 5, 6, 46, 54, 92, 171n1, 173n11, 173n12, 173n13, 173–174n14, 174n1, 184n16
Foley, R., 173n12
Folk meaning, 19, 23, 27–36, 41–42, 45, 55–57, 59–61, 168, 172n4
For-all-practical-purposes determinism. See Determinism, virtual
Frankfurt, H., 5–6, 19, 22, 27, 46, 50, 53, 54, 65, 171n1, 172n3, 173n11, 173–174n14
Frankfurt-case argument, the, 50–51, 173n14
Frankfurtian freedom. See Freedom, Frankfurtian
Freedom
  Frankfurtian, 5–6, 19, 22, 27, 46, 53–54, 65
  human-being, 48–49 (see also Analyses of free will, and human-being freedom)
  Humean, 4–6, 16, 19, 22, 27, 34, 45–46, 50, 53–55, 65, 174n15
  libertarian (see L-freedom)
  moral responsibility, 42
  ordinary-language, 116–117, 180n29
  varieties worth wanting (see Worth wanting, the issue of)
Freedom-enhancing indeterminism. See Indeterminism, freedom-enhancing

Free will. *See also* Freedom
  and intuitions (*see* Intuitions about free will)
  and the metaphysical component of the problem, 28, 53–54, 168
  and the moral component of the problem, 28, 53
  problem of, 1–15
  and the semantic component of the problem, 28, 53
  varieties worth wanting (*see* Worth wanting, the issue of)

Gallois, A., 173n12
Ginet, C., 12, 67, 68, 171n3, 173n12, 173–174n14, 178n22
Glannon, W., 173–174n14
Goetz, S., 67, 171n3
Greenspan, P. S., 173n12
Grotzinger, B., 159

Habits, 102
Hagan, S., 183n11
Haggard, P., 161, 183n12, 183n13
Haji, I., 92, 171n2, 173n11, 173–174n14
Hameroff, S. R., 135, 143, 155–159, 181n3, 183n11
Hard determinism. *See* Determinism, hard
Hausman, D., 176n13
Hidden variables, 145–146, 148, 151, 154
Hiley, B. J., 146
Hobart, R. E., 6, 9–10, 12, 66, 171n1, 174n2
Hobbes, T., 4, 6, 9–10, 12, 66, 171n1, 174n2
Hobbes-Hume-Hobart argument against libertarianism, 9–10
Hodgson, D., 156
Honderich, T., 143, 147–154, 183n9
Horgan, T., 173n12

Human-being freedom. *See* Freedom, human being; Analyses of free will, and human-being freedom
Hume, D., 4–6, 9–12, 16, 19, 22, 27, 33–34, 41–42, 45–46, 50, 52–55, 65–66, 137, 171n1, 172n3, 173n10, 174n15, 174n2
Humean freedom. *See* Freedom, Humean
Humean responsibility. *See* Moral responsibility, Humean
Hunt, D., 173–174n14

Identity theory. *See* Token–token identity theory; Type–type identity theory
Imprecision. *See* Analyses of free will, and imprecision
Incoherence. *See* Analyses of free will, and incoherence
Incompatibilism, 2, 9, 10–11, 13–14, 51–53, 55–62
Incompatibilist intuitions about free will, 57–58
Indeterminacy, 75–83, 171n4. *See also* Indeterminism
  degrees of (*see* Degrees of indeterminacy and L-freedom)
  freedom-enhancing, 96–106 (*see also* Libertarianism)
  macro-level, 182n5 (*see also* Determinism, macro-level)
  moment-of-choice, 16, 21, 67, 75–76, 107–110, 132, 158–159 (*see also* Libertarianism, non-Valerian)
  prior-to-choice, 16, 67, 75–76, 107–110, 132, 158–159 (*see also* Libertarianism, Valerian)
Indeterminism, 6–7, 131–169. *See also* Indeterminacy
  freedom-enhancing, 96–106 (*see also* Libertarianism)

kind needed for libertarianism (*see*
 Indeterminism, TDW-)
no-freedom-enhancing (*see*
 FE-determinism)
TDW-, 75–83, 131–169
Indeterministic interpretations of
 quantum mechanics, 68, 145–147
Interpretations of quantum mechanics,
 68, 145–147, 182n7
Intuitions, use of, 29, 50–51, 89
Intuitions about free will, 56–60
Ion channels, opening and closing of,
 153–154
Isen, A., 163–164

James, W., 25
Johnson, D., 173n12

Kane, R., 7, 15, 20, 67–70, 73–74, 83,
 92, 99–100, 114, 123–124, 171n3,
 173n12, 173–174n14, 176n14,
 177n16, 178n22, 179n23
Kanean self-forming actions, 73–74
Kant, I., 22, 25, 42–43, 137–141
Kantian argument for libertarianism.
 See Moral-responsibility argument
 for libertarianism
Kapitan, T., 171n1, 173n12
Kind-term analysis of 'free will', 37,
 48–50, 172n6
Kind-term analysis of 'moral responsi-
 bility', 140–141
Kochen, S., 144
Kornhuber, H., 159

Lamb, J., 173n12, 173–174n14
Lateralized readiness potential, 183n12
Lehrer, K., 171n1, 173n10
Levin, P., 163–164
Lewis, D., 171n1, 173n12
L-freedom, 7–8, 10–11, 15–18, 65–130
 as applied to decisions, 121–122
 degrees of (*see* Degrees of indeterminacy and L-freedom)
 derivative, 123–124
 partial, 78–83
 as applied to persons, 121
 and the issue of what's worth
 wanting, 106–113
Libertarian freedom. *See* L-freedom
Libertarianism, 10, 15–18, 65–130
 agent-causal. *See* Agent causation
 compatibilistic, 17–18, 55
 event-causal, 16, 21, 67, 176n13
 incompatibilistic, 18
 metaphysical, 17–18, 55
 moral responsibility argument for (*see*
 Moral responsibility argument for
 libertarianism)
 noncausal, 16, 67, 176n13
 non-Valerian, 16, 21, 67, 75–76,
 107–110, 113–114, 132, 174n5
 semantic, 17–18
 Valerian, 16, 67, 107–110, 113–114,
 132, 174n5
Libertarian responsibility. *See* Moral
 responsibility, libertarian
Libet, B., 143, 155, 159–162, 183n12,
 183n13
Lincoln, A., 181n1
Locke, J., 171n1
Luck objection to libertarianism, 13, 67,
 92–95

Macro-level determinism. *See*
 Determinism, macro-level
Magnetic stimulation to the brain,
 163–165
Malcolm, N., 181n4
Many-worlds interpretation of quantum
 mechanics, 145–146
Materialism. *See* Mind–brain
 materialism
McCall, S., 67, 171n3
McCann, H., 67, 171n3
McKay, T., 173n12
McKenna, M., 173–174n14
Meaning. *See* Folk meaning

Measurement, problem of, 145
Mele, A., 5, 46, 67, 92, 161, 171n1, 171n3, 173n11, 173–174n14
Metaphysical component of the problem of free will. *See* Free will, and the metaphysical component of the problem
Metaphysical interestingness, 30–31
Metaphysical libertarianism. *See* Libertarianism, metaphysical
Metaphysical problems, 23–24, 168–169
Metaphysics
  attacks on (*see* Antimetaphysicalism)
  and conceptual analysis, 25, 30–45
Microtubules, 155, 183n11
Milgram, S., 163–164
Mind–brain dualism, 16, 21, 67, 70, 109, 152
Mind–brain materialism, 3, 67, 70–71, 85, 152, 183n9
Moment-of-choice indeterminacy. *See* Libertarianism, non-Valerian
Moral component of the problem of free will. *See* Free will, and the moral component of the problem
Moral responsibility, 20, 22–23, 28, 36, 39–44, 53–55, 62–63, 107–111, 137–141, 168
  and analyses of free will (*see* Analyses of free will, and moral responsibility)
  and fairness, 41–42
  Humean, 41–42
  libertarian, 41–42
Moral responsibility argument for libertarianism, 22, 42–43, 137–141
Moral responsibility question, the. *See* Question, moral responsibility, the

Nahmias, E., 29
Narveson, J., 173n12
Nathan, N., 173n12
Natural-kind-term analysis of 'free will'. *See* Kind-term analysis of 'free will'
Natural-kind-term analysis of 'moral responsibility'. *See* Kind-term analysis of 'moral responsibility'
Nelkin, D., 163
Neural blips, 106–110
Neural determinism. *See* Determinism, neural
Neural firing, 153–154, 157
Neuroscience, 151–162
Nichols, S., 29
Noncausal libertarianism. *See* Libertarianism, noncausal
Nonrandomness. *See* Appropriate nonrandomness
Nonspecificist views of decisions, 71, 175n7, 175n8
Non-torn decisions. *See* Decisions, non-torn
Non-Valerian libertarianism. *See* Libertarianism, non-Valerian
Nozick, R., 67, 171n3

O'Connor, T., 67, 92, 171n3, 173n12, 178n21
Ordinary language and analyses of free will. *See* Analyses of free will, and ordinary language
Ordinary-language freedom. *See* Freedom, ordinary-language
Ordinary-language meaning. *See* Folk meaning
Otsuka, M., 173–174n14

Paradigm-case-term analysis of 'moral responsibility'. *See* Kind-term analysis of 'moral responsibility'
Parfit, D., 172n5
Partial L-freedom. *See* L-freedom, partial
Penrose, R., 135, 143, 155–159, 181n3
Pereboom, D., 171n5, 173–174n14
Personal identity, 172n5
Phenomenology
  argument from, 89–91
  and torn decisions, 73, 75
Plural authorship, 7, 83, 119

Plural control, 7, 83, 119
Plural rationality, 7, 83, 119
Pretheoretic beliefs, 139–141
Prigogine, I., 182n5
Prior-to-choice indeterminacy. *See* Libertarianism, Valerian
Probabilistic causation, 11, 16, 67, 80, 104, 129, 176n13
Probabilistic laws, 68, 144–145, 150, 153, 182n6
Problem of free will (defined), 1–15
Problem of measurement. *See* Measurement, problem of
Psychology, arguments from, 163–165

Quantum-computer view of the brain, 135, 155–159
Quantum gravity, 155–156
Quantum mechanics, 1, 6, 68, 135, 143–147, 151, 154, 157
Question
  coherence, the, 36–39
  compatibilism, the, 18–19, 25–28, 45–62
  do-we-have-free-will, the, 18–19, 23, 26–28, 30–45, 53
  FE-determinism, the, 18–19, 26–27, 53
  libertarian, the, 20–22, 24, 27, 49–50, 54, 65–130, 166–168
  moral responsibility, the, 20, 22–23, 28, 36, 39–44, 53–55, 62–63, 137–141, 168
  what-is-free-will, the, 18–19, 22–23, 26–61, 168
  which-kinds-of-freedom-are-compatible-with-determinism, the, 45–50
  which-kinds-of-freedom-do-we-have, the, 19, 22, 27–28, 34–44, 53–54, 65, 165–167
  worth-wanting, the, 43–44

Randomism. *See* Determined-or-Randomism

Randomness, non-. *See* Appropriate nonrandomness
Rationality, 7, 83, 113–119. *See also* Plural rationality
  strong, 114–115
  teleological, 114–117
  weak, 114–117
Ravizza, M., 5, 6, 46, 54, 171n1, 173n11, 173–174n14, 174n1, 184n16
Readiness potential, 159–162. *See also* Lateralized readiness potential
Reasons, determination by. *See* Determination by reasons
Reasons responsiveness, 6, 54, 65, 166–167
Regress objection to libertarianism, 13, 67, 120
Reid, T., 67, 171n3
Responsibility. *See* Moral responsibility
Rigidity, 49, 173n9
Robb, D., 173–174n14
Rowe, W., 67, 171n3

Sameness, 56–57
Sanford, D., 173n10
Self-forming actions. *See* Kanean self-forming actions
Semantic component of the problem of free will. *See* Free will, and the semantic component of the problem
Semantic libertarianism. *See* Libertarianism, semantic
Ship of Theseus, 56–57
Situationism, 54, 143, 163–164
Slote, M., 173n12
Slowness of consciousness, 163
Smilansky, S., 171n5
Soft determinism. *See* Determinism, soft
Sources, people as, 92, 102, 107, 111
Specker, E. P., 144
Spin, 144–146
Spontaneous control, 98

Stapp, H., 135, 181n3
Statistical laws, 150, 153. *See also* Probabilistic laws
Strawson, G., 92, 120, 171n5
Strawson, P. F., 5, 46, 171n1, 173n11
Strong rationality. *See* Rationality, strong
Stump, E., 173–174n14
Subconscious mental states and events, 71, 81, 86, 93, 101–104, 114–116
Success-of-science argument for determinism, 149–150
Superpositions, 144, 155–157
Synaptic transmission, 153–154, 157

Taylor, R., 67, 171n3
TDW-indeterminism. *See* Indeterminism, TDW-
Tegmark, M., 143–144, 151–152, 155–159, 183n11
Teleological rationality. *See* Rationality, teleological
Thorp, J., 67, 171n3
Token–token identity theory, 70–71, 85–89, 109, 152
Torn-decision determinism. *See* Determinism, torn-decision
Torn decisions. *See* Decisions, torn
Tuszyński, J. A., 183n11
Twain, M., 131, 181n1
Type–type identity theory, 70, 152

Universal determinism. *See* Determinism, universal

Valerian libertarianism. *See* Libertarianism, Valerian
van Inwagen, P., 20, 50–53, 92, 137–141, 171n3, 173n7, 173n12, 173n14, 174n5, 178n21
Velmans, M., 160, 163
Vihvelin, K., 171n1, 173n12
Virtual determinism. *See* Determinism, virtual

Wallace, R. J., 5, 46, 171n1, 173n11
Waller, B., 92
Walter, H., 160
Warfield, T., 173n12
Watson, G., 5, 46, 171n1, 173n11
Wave-function collapse, 144–146, 148, 155–157
Weak rationality. *See* Rationality, weak
Wegner, D. M., 163
What-is-free-will question, the. *See* Question, what-is-free-will, the
Which-kinds-of-freedom-do-we-have question, the. *See* Question, which-kinds-of-freedom-do-we-have, the
White, M., 173n10
Widerker, D., 173n12, 173–174n14
Wiggins, D., 67, 171n3
Wolf, S., 5, 46, 171n1, 173n11
Worth wanting, the issue of, 36, 39–44, 84, 105, 106–113, 119
and analyses of free will (*see* Analyses of free will, and the issue of what's worth wanting)
Worth-wanting question, the. *See* Question, worth-wanting, the
Wyma, K., 173–174n14

Zimmerman, D., 173–174n14